INCREDIBLE TASTE OF INDIAN VEGETARIAN CUISINE

UMA AGGARWAL

Map of India

INCREDIBLE TASTE OF
INDIAN VEGETARIAN CUISINE

UMA AGGARWAL

ALLIED PUBLISHERS PRIVATE LIMITED
NEW DELHI BANGALORE HYDERABAD AHMEDABAD
NAGPUR MUMBAI LUCKNOW CHENNAI KOLKATA

ALLIED PUBLISHERS PRIVATE LIMITED

1/13-14 Asaf Ali Road, **New Delhi**–110002
Ph.: 011-23239001 • E-mail: delhi.books@alliedpublishers.com

87/4, Chander Nagar, Alambagh, **Lucknow** - 226005
Ph.: 0522-4012850 • E-mail: appltdlko9@gmail.com

17 Chittaranjan Avenue, **Kolkata**–700072
Ph.: 033-22129618 • E-mail: cal.books@alliedpublishers.com

15 J.N. Heredia Marg, Ballard Estate, **Mumbai**–400001
Ph.: 022-42126969 • E-mail: mumbai.books@alliedpublishers.com

60 Shiv Sunder Apartments (Ground Floor), Central Bazar Road
Bajaj Nagar, **Nagpur**–440010
Ph.: 0712-2234210 • E-mail: ngp.books@alliedpublishers.com

F-1 Sun House (First Floor), C.G. Road, Navrangpura
Ellisbridge P.O., **Ahmedabad**–380006
Ph.: 079-26465916 • E-mail: ahmbd.books@alliedpublishers.com

751 Anna Salai, **Chennai**–600002
Ph.: 044-28523938 • E-mail: chennai.books@alliedpublishers.com

The Hebbar Sreevaishnava Sabha, Sudarshan Complex - 2
No. 22, Seshadri Road, **Bangalore** - 560009
Ph.: 080-22262081 • E-Mail: bngl.books@alliedpublishers.com

3-2-844/6 & 7 Kachiguda Station Road, **Hyderabad**–500027
Ph.: 040-24619079 • E-mail: hyd.books@alliedpublishers.com

Website: www.alliedpublishers.com

© 2016, Allied Publishers Pvt. Ltd.

No part of the material protected by this copyright notice may be reproduced or utilized in any form or by any means, electronic or mechanical including photocopying, recording or by any information storage and retrieval system, without prior written permission from the copyright owners.

ISBN : 978-93-85926-02-0

Published by Sunil Sachdev and printed by Ravi Sachdev at Allied Publishers Private Limited, Printing Division, A-104 Mayapuri Phase II, New Delhi - 110064

CONTENTS

Appetizers and Snacks

Samosa 3
Pastry with Spicy Filling

Vegetable Pakora 5
Vegetable Fritters

Palak Pakora 7
Spinach Fritters

Makki ke Vade 8
Corn Fritters

Channa Dal Vada 9
Chick Pea Fritters

Urad Dal Vada 11
Urad Dal Fritters

Aloo ki Tikki 12
Potato Cutlets

Dal ki Tikki 14
Black Bean Patties/Burgers

Bonda 15
Potato Croquettes

Arbi Tikka Masala 17
Grilled Yams in Peanut Sauce

Paneer Cocktail 18
Fried Cheese Cubes

Tori Vadas 20
Zucchini Bites

Dahi Vada and Pakori 21
Lentils Fritters Soaked in Spicy Yogurt

Uppama 23
Cream of Wheat Flavoured with Nuts and Spices

Poha (or Aval) Khatta Meetha 25
Spicy Rice Flakes

Dhokla 26
Rice and Lentil Cakes Flavoured with Cilantro

Khaman Dhokla 27
Cream of Wheat Cakes Flavoured with Cilantro

Papad 29
Spiced Lentils Wafers

Namkeen Kaju 30
Cocktail Cashew Nuts

Mathri 31
Crunchy Spicy Crackers

Chakli 32
Spicy Saltine Crisps

Golgappa-Paanipuri 34
Flour Puffs Filled with Tamarind Water

Chaat Papri 36
Tortilla Chips with Tamarind Sauce

Bhelpoori 37
Crunchy Rice Puffs and Salad in Sweet and Sour Sauce

Phalon ki Chaat 38
Fruit Chaat

Shakarkandi ki Chaat 40
Spicy Sweet Potato Salad

Bharwan Khumb 41
Stuffed Mushrooms

Rice, Pulav and Breads

Zeera Chawal 45
Plain Cumin Rice

Matar Chawal 46
Peas Pulav

Matar-Paneer Pulav 47
Fried Cheese and Peas Pulav

Nariyalwale Chawal 49
Coconut Rice

Gobhi Pulav 50
Cauliflower Pulav

Nimbuwale Chawal 52
Lemon Rice

Imliwale Chawal 53
Tamarind Rice

Navratan Pulav 54
Multicoloured Rice Pulav

Khumbwale Chawal 56
Mushroom Pulav

Khichdi 57
Rice and Lentils with Vegetables

Chappati 59
Whole Wheat Griddle Bread

Plain Parantha 61
Un-Stuffed Griddle Fried Bread

Lachhedar Parantha 62
Onion Stuffed Griddle Fried Bread

Gobhi ke Paranthe 63
Cauliflower Stuffed Griddle Fried Bread

Methi Paranthe 65
Fenugreek Leaves Flavoured Griddle Fried Bread

Aloo ke Paranthe 66
Stuffed Potato Griddle Fried Bread

Mooli ka Paranthe 68
Daikon Stuffed Griddle Fried Bread

Paneer aur Dal ke Paranthe 70
Cheese and Lentils Stuffed Griddle Fried Bread

Nan 72
All Purpose Flour Tandoori (Clay Oven) Bread

Bhatura 74
Deep Fried All Purpose Flour Bread

Puri 75
Deep Fried Whole Wheat Bread Puffs

Makki ki Roti 76
Griddle Corn Flour Bread

Rava Dosa 77
Cream of Wheat Crepes

Idli 78
Steamed Rice Cakes

Aadai 80
Spicy Rice and Lentils Pancakes

Khasta Kachauri 81
Crisp Pastries Fried

Exotic Vegetables

Navrattan Curry 85
Mixed Vegetable Curry

Undiya 87
Grilled Mixed Vegetable Curry from Gujarat

Bread Kofta Curry 89
Bread Croquettes Curried in Gourd Sauce

Ghia Kofta Curry 91
Bottle Gourd Croquettes Curry

Malai Kofta Curry 93
Creamy Cheese Croquettes in Curry Sauce

Mixed Vegetable Kofta Curry 95
Vegetable Croquettes Curry

Arbi ki Curry 97
Yam Curry

Aloo ki Subzi 98
Potato Curry

Bhindi ki Subzi 99
Okra Curry

Bharwan Baingan 100
Stuffed Eggplants

Bharwan Bhindi 101
Whole Stuffed Okra

Bharwan Shimla Mirch 102
Stuffed Green Bell Peppers

Shimla Mirch, Aloo Tamatar ki Subzi 104
Bell Pepper, Potatoes and Tomatoes Stir-Fry

Bharwan Tamatar 105
Stuffed Whole Tomatoes

Bharwan Tinda 107
Stuffed Round Gourd

Bharwan Karela 109
Stuffed Bitter Gourd

Bhuni hui Bhindi 111
Okra Stir-Fried

Bhune hue Karele 112
Bitter Gourd Stir-Fried

Oven mein Bhuni hue Gobhi 113
Baked Cauliflower

Bhune hue Baingan ki Subzi 114
Grilled Egg Plant Curried

Gobhi aur Aloo ki Subzi 116
Cauliflower and Potatoes Stir-Fry

Gobhi aur Anjeer ki Subzi 117
Cauliflower with Figs Stir-Fry

Baingan, Aloo aur Tamatar ki Subzi 118
Eggplants, Potatoes and Tomatoes Stir-Fry

Aloo aur Pyaz ki Subzi 119
Potatoes and Sliced Onions Stir-Fried

Aloo aur Beans ki Subzi 120
Green Beans and Potatoes Stir-Fried

Makki aur Palak ki Subzi 121
Corn Curry with Spinach

Kele ki Subzi 122
Raw Bananas Curry

Shakarkandi ki Subzi 123
Sweet Potato Curry

Kamal Kakadi, Khumb, Paneer aur Matar ki Subzi 124
Lotus Roots, Cheese Cubes, Mushrooms and Peas Curry

Soya ki Subzi 126
Tofu Curry

Parwal aur Aloo ki Subzi 127
Pointed Gourd Curry

Kaddu ki Subzi 128
Pumpkin Stir-Fried

Musli ki Subzi 130
Asparagus Stir-Fry

Patta Gobhi aur Matar ki Subzi 131
Cabbage and Peas Stir-Fried

Shalgam ki Subzi 132
Turnips Stir-Fried

Chukandar ki Subzi 133
Beetroots Stir-Fry

Tori ki Subzi 134
Flavourful Zucchini

Aloo Dum 135
Fried Potato in Creamy Sauce of Yogurt

Methi Aloo ki Subzi 137
Fenugreek Leaves and Potatoes Stir-Fry

Sarson ka Saag 139
Mustard Greens Curried

Gajar aur Aloo ki Subzi 141
Carrots and Potatoes Stir-Fried

Palak aur Aloo ki Subzi 142
Spinach with Potatoes Curried

Palak Paneer 143
Spinach and Cheese Cubes Curried

Matar Paneer 145
Peas and Cheese Cubes Curried

Sukhi Arbi 147
Yam Stir-Fried

Palak aur Khumb ki Curry 148
Mushrooms in Spinach Sauce

Kathael ki Subzi 149
Jackfruit Stir-Fried

Khatte Meethey Baingan 151
Eggplant in Sweet and Sour Sauce

Baingan Dum 153
Fried Eggplant Curried

Beans Nariyal ke Saath 154
Beans Stir-Fried with Coconut

Legumes

Channa Dal 157
Gram Dal

Dal Makhani 159
Whole Black Beans with Cream

Dal Panchratan 161
Five Lentils Curried

Palak aur Mung ki Chilkewali Dal 163
Spinach and Split Green Lentils

Sukhi Dal 165
Dry Lentils Curried

Sabut Mung ki Dal 166
Whole Mung Beans

Rajmah 168
Curried Red Kidney Beans

Sambhar 170
Lentils Curried with Vegetables in Tamarind Sauce

Chole Curry 172
Garbanzo (Chickpeas) Curried

Khatte Chole 174
Chickpeas in Tamarind Sauce

Karhi 176
Gram Flour Curry

Accompaniments and Soups

Gobhi ka Shorba 183
Cauliflower Soup

Makki ka Shorba 184
Cream of Corn Soup

Kaddu ka Shorba 185
Cream of Pumpkin Soup

Milijuli Sabjion ka Shorba 186
Mixed Vegetable Soup

Bhune hue Aloo aur Leek ka Shorba 187
Roasted Potato and Leek Soup

Tamatar ka Shorba 188
Tomato Soup

Nariyal ka Shorba 189
Coconut Soup

SALADS

Kosambari Salad/Mung ki Dal ka Salad 193
Carrots, Radishes and Beans Salad

Channa aur Rajmah ka Salad 194
Cooked Beans Salad

Pyaz, Chukandar aur Tamatar ka Salad 195
Onion, Beetroot and Tomato Salad

Milijuli Sabjion ka Salad 196
Mixed Vegetable Salad

Mooli ya Gajar ka Salad 197
Radish or Carrot Salad

RAITAS, CHUTNEYS AND ACHAARS

Boondi Raita 203
Fried Gram Flour Balls in Yogurt

Kheere ka Raita 204
Cucumber Raita

Pudina ke Raita 205
Mint Condiment

Subjion ka Raita 206
Fresh Vegetable Raita

Aam ka Raita 207
Mango Raita

Kela aur Kishmash ka Raita 208
Bananas and Raisins Raita

Seb ki Chutney 209
Apple Dip

Channa Dal Chutney 210
Gram Legume Dip

Nariyal ki Chutney 211
Coconut Dip

Dhaniye ki Chutney 213
Coriander Dip

Pudina ki Chutney	214
Mint Dip	
Mungphali ki Chutney	215
Peanut Dip	
Lal Mirchi ki Chutney	216
Red Pepper Dip	
Aam ki Meethi Chutney	217
Sweet Mango Dip	
Imli ki Chutney	218
Tamarind Dip	
Tamatar ki Chutney	220
Tomato Dip	
Milijuli Sabjion ka Khatta Meetha Achaar	221
Classic Sweet and Sour Pickle of Mixed Vegetables	
Aam ka Achaar	222
Mango Pickle	
Hari Mirch ka Achaar	223
Green Chilies Pickle	
Nimbu ka Achaar	224
Lemon Pickle	

Desserts

Burfi	227
Milk Fudge	
Besan ki Burfi	228
Gram Flour Fudge	
Jalebi	230
Fried Spiral Sweet Rings	
Rasgulla	232
Cheese Balls in a Sweet Syrup	
Rasmalai	233
Sweet Cheese Patties in Cream	
Gulab Jamun	235
Golden Cream Cheese Balls in Syrup	
Suji Halwa	237
Cream of Wheat Pudding	

Kulfi Faluda 239
Indian Ice Cream with Starchy Noodles

Phirni 240
Ground Rice Pudding

Kheer 241
Rice Pudding

Sevian Kheer 242
Sweet Vermicelli Pudding

Meethey Chawal 243
Sweet Rice Pulav

Shahi Tukra 244
Rich Bread Pudding with Dry Fruits

Mango Pie 246

Nan Khataii 247
Eggless Crisp Biscuits

Unniappam 249

Drinks

Masala Chai 253
Spiced Tea

Kashmiri Kahva 254
Kashmiri Tea

South Indian Coffee 255

Dahi ki Lassi 256
Yogurt Shake

Gajar ka Doodh 257
Sweetened Carrot Milk

Sambharam 258
Spicy Yogurt Drink

Thandai 259
Milk and Almond Drink

Panna 260
Mango Drink

Kanji 261
Fermented Carrots Drink

Zeera Paani 262
Cumin Flavoured Drink

Kokum Water 263
Kokum Drink

Kala Khatta 264
Spiced Indian Blackberry Drink

Falooda Drink 265
Sweetened Milk Flavoured with Ice-Cream and Starchy Noodles

Coconut Water 267

Author in a Food and Wine Festival Las Vegas, U.S.A.

Lord Ganesha, Remover of all Obstacles

Preface

I have lived In United States now for almost 50 years. I was raised in a very traditional family with a great respect and pride in Indian culture, history and human values. Food was prepared at home with great emphasis on cleanliness and It was well balanced with fresh herbs and spices keeping in mind six different tastes mentioned in Ayurvedas. Indian cuisine originated from ayurvedas. These ancient treatise were written thousands of years ago. It clearly says that food prepared with herbs and spices will certainly prolong your life because their use not only makes the food delicious but there is hidden bonus of them promoting digestion and acting as antooxidants. As the food is digested properly minimum amount of harmful oxidants or carcinogen remain in your body to weaken your immune system. You stay healthy, alert, sharp and have greater capability to fight germs and diseases. Indian cuisine is unique in its emphasis on making sure that each food should achieve maximum digestibity by spicing it correctly, cooking it right and by using the most fresh ingredients possible. History also tells us that for thousands of years many cultures from all over the world have sailed to India in search of these spices so that they could also follow this same concept of indian cuisine.

Recent reseach is also proving it beyond doubt that spices have tremendous health benefits and Indians have had this knowledge for thousands of years. You will notice that these days you can find capsules of different spices like Turmeric, Cinnamon, Bitter melon extract and more on the shelves of pharmacies and grocery stores.

I have emphasized this in this book and my next book the "Incredible taste of Non Vegetarian Cuisine". Non Vegetarian food is more of a challenge for the human body as meats are carcinogenic and produce more toxins if they are not digested well and therefore proper spicing and proper cooking here is more important than anywhere else.

Remember when you eat well, you sleep well there by you perform well and that becomes your destiny.

Best wishes,

Uma Aggarwal

Acknowledgements

Let me take this opportunity of thanking the ones who have helped me in the publication of this incredible book. First and foremost I want to mention Late Mr Surjojit Banerjee editor Allied publishers. While tirelessly working on this book he passed away very recently. It was a very tragic and sudden death. My tributes to him for his honest efforts and dedication. Thanks Mr. Banerjee from the bottom of my heart. I am really going to miss his editorial comments. I also want to thank my husband Dr Surinder K Aggarwal who stood behind me always supporting me to finish this project, my sister Dr Nirmala Gupta who hosted me in Delhi during my proof reading of this book. My daughters Drs Aanshu Shah and Tushina Reddy and my son Arun Aggarwal for their understanding and love. I would also like to thank my friends Madhu Raizada, Nita Khurana who shared couple of their recipes with me. My friend Mrs. Girija Vijay and her husband Dr. Kamla Kant Vijay, Subhash and Maria Annette Janveja for their encouragment and their helpful hints. I must ackowledge here the bright smiles of my beautiful grandkids who always thought what a great cook I am and always showed their trust in me.

Last but not the least I would also like to offer my sincere thanks to the team of printing division of Allied publishers, the designer Mr Joshi, and Mr Ashok Seal who constantly kept working hard to put this book together and did everything possible to make it happen.

Uma Aggarwal

Bouquet of Flowers

Natraj (a Form of Lord Shiva)

An ancient holy city of Varanasi

Author in a Radio Interview

Introduction

Indian cuisine is famous around the world and enjoys the enviable reputation of being very unique and healthy. With a charm of its own, it has such a great variety of tastes, colours and aroma that those who experience it once, sometimes find other foods somewhat tasteless.

India is an ancient country and was once called the 'golden sparrow'. Several invaders like Alexander the Great, the mighty Gengis Khan and Taimur the Lame came here to seek its riches, jewels and spices. In fact, the lure of the spices that are used in Indian cuisine is what brought the British, the French, the Dutch and the Portuguese to the Indian coast. India has seen the rise and fall of many empires and dynasties. Subsequently, it has absorbed some of their cultures and cuisines. Because of the assimilation of these cultures and their influence, there has emerged a cuisine of unparalleled variety and taste.

For thousands of years Indians have used spices to decorate and enhance the enticing aroma of their cuisine. They use them like an artist trying to paint a beautiful picture. This painting of colour and flavour in Indian food is not out of somebody's imagination but originates from the basic philosophy and thought enshrined in the ancient *Vedas*. It clearly emphasizes that in order to stay healthy and happy one should eat food which has a mix of herbs and spices. When this is followed, the results can be beyond our imagination — a colourful, fragrant, exotic and romantic fare that is not only exquisite and delicious but by far the most healthy cuisine in the world. The art of Indian cooking lies not in heavy spicing, but how delicately one uses these herbs and spices. It is an art to use the selected spices, and if you use them correctly and precisely, it brings about the dormant flavours of a dish or it can drown the undesirable taste of another. Besides, these spices have innumerable health benefits which I have tried to emphasize wherever possible.

Sampling of Indian food is an unforgettable experience. The delicious curries and beautiful *pulavs* (often spelt *pilafs*) will haunt one's memory forever and the mere mention of *gulabjamans, samosas,* and *kebabs* will make the mouth water. Along with the pleasures comes the hidden dividend of health benefits. Its *dals* (lentil preparations) are full of digestible proteins. Its various delicious vegetable curries contain many vitamins and have lots of fibre. Indian breads are commonly made with whole-wheat flour rich in essential nutrients and minerals. The food is ideally prepared with all fresh ingredients. Yogurt, very good for our digestive system, is also an essential part of an Indian meal.

This book offers innumerable number of proteinaceous vegetarian dishes. My love of Indian cooking, its artful, deliberate use of spices, the health benefits, and the joy I have seen in sharing this cuisine, are some of the reasons which have inspired me to write this book. To help you understand the origin and foundations of Indian cooking, I have also included bits of information on the history of the Indian subcontinent and its influence on Indian cooking. The recipes are written with a global appeal in mind and most of them include its Indian name and an English description as well as step-by-step instructions on how to create a quick, easy, delicious and healthy Indian dish. I have also described the health benefits of each spice used and its Indian name. The recipes are authentically Indian but often I have fused readily available ingredients in America, so as to appeal to the western palate. Helpful *'Hints'* and *'Notes'* are given in some recipes to help you in preparation of that recipe.

India is one of the most diverse countries with many religions and races living together for centuries. It has 28 States and 7 Union Territories each with their own official languages and cuisines. I have tried to give you a glimpse into most of these cuisines. The book has recipes for every occasion – from an easy and simple quick preparation to a classic weekend dinner you might have had at an upmarket restaurant. Photographs of recipes, Indian landscape and historical monuments intersperse the text and provide much visual relief.

I welcome you now into my Indian subcontinent kitchen and take you on a journey to explore the exquisite world of Indian cuisine in all its glory.

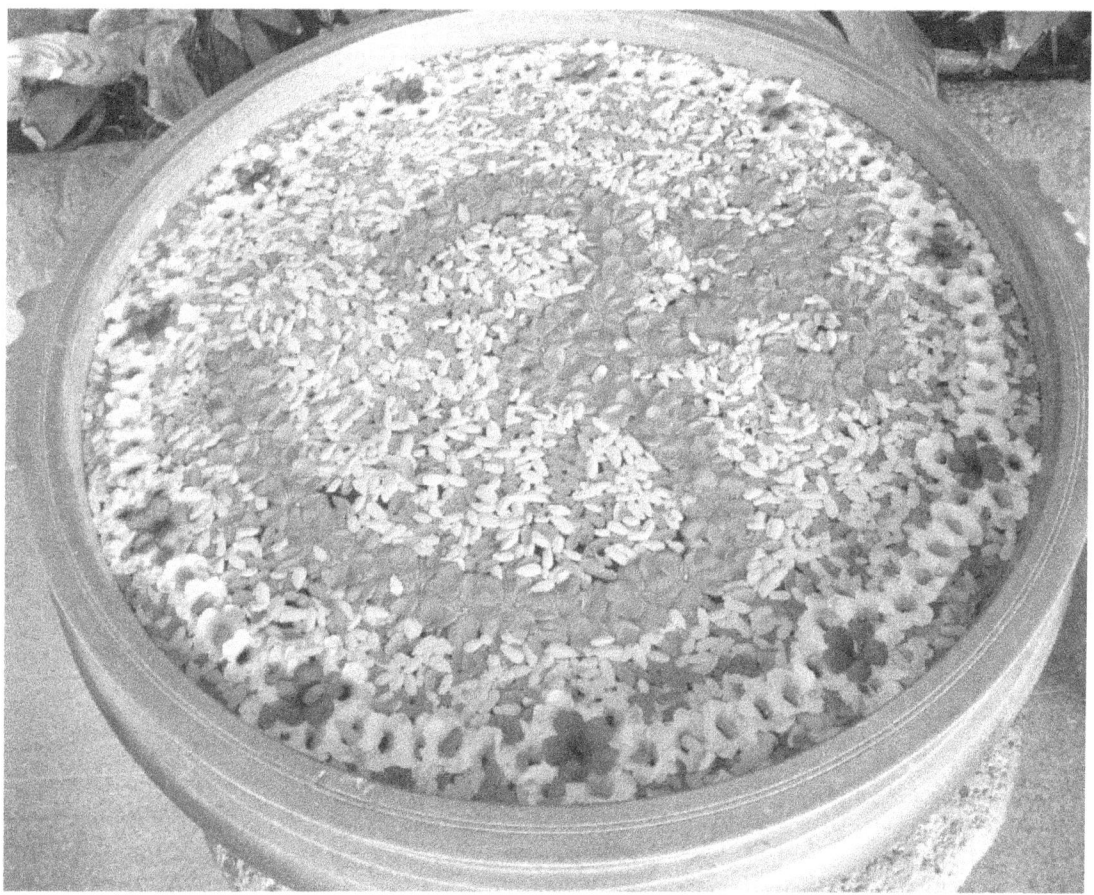

For thousands of years Indians have used spices to decorate and enhance the enticing aroma of their cuisine. They use them like an artist trying to paint a beautiful picture

History and origin of Indian cuisine

The strongest influence on Indian cuisine, or at least among 80 percent of Indians is of *Ayurveda*, a treatise on health. Its origins are in the *Atharva Veda*, the contents of which date back to around 1,000 BC. It is not only the science of health but covers the whole subject of life in its various ramifications. According to *Ayurveda* a person can stay healthy only if one regulates one's diet, exercises, recreates and controls sensual pleasures, and is generous, just, truthful, forgiving, and has a happy family life. In other words if you are unhappy and have bottled up emotions, diseases emanate. There are three primary forces in your body called *vata, pitta,* and *kapha*, translated as air, fire and water. Air means that which moves, like breathing and beating of the heart. Fire is bile which digests things including mental digestion or the ability to comprehend, *Kapha* is phlegm which holds things together. *Ayurveda* believes that when these three are thrown out of balance and aggravated, they manifest themselves in the body and one contracts all sorts of diseases. According to *Ayurveda* diseases should first be treated with food, and medication should only be given later, if needed. Hippocrates also said, "Let your food be your medicine… and let your medicine be your food." Treatments using foods are based on the six tastes of foods which are sweet, salty, sour, pungent, bitter and astringent. Each taste has its specific therapeutic value. The tastes increase or decrease the three forces of our body as the case may be. Everyone needs a certain amount of each of these six tastes depending on the individual's physique. Too much of any one taste can be harmful.

The sweet taste gives strength to the tissue elements and harmonizes the mind. The sour taste stimulates the digestive fire and sour foods like lime and tamarind are easy on digestion and good for the heart. The salty taste stimulates digestion and clears the channels in the body by causing sweating. Pungent tastes as in onion, pepper and garlic help digestion, improve metabolism and dilate channels of the body. Bitter foods like bitter gourd, fenugreek seeds and lemon rind eliminate bacterial and viral elements, purify the blood and enhance metabolism. Potatoes, apples, betel nut leaves, and most green vegetables and drinks like tea have an astringent taste and heal ulcers and wounds. They also act as water absorbent in the body and help in the assimilation of moisture and fat. A lack of any of these tastes in the food will aggravate the body forces and cause all sorts of health problems. There are several great schools of *Ayurvedic* medicine in India, the US, and Europe, based on these very ideas and theories.

In a traditional Indian meal you will be able to observe and appreciate the distribution of various dishes according to the above–mentioned six different tastes. A typical meal has a dash of hot and bitter sweet pickle, has plenty of rice and bread rich in sugar, spicy-salty and sour tasting vegetable, and meat curries rich in astringent and pungent taste because of the ingredients used in these dishes. A yogurt based item is added to coat the stomach of excessive burning due to spices and replenishing the essential stomach bacteria which are naturally found in the yogurt. Lentils provide the much needed proteins for the majority of the vegetarian population. Vegetable curries give the fibre as well as the astringent taste with vitamins. *Ayurveda* strongly believes that 'you are what you eat'. It does specify the preparation of different meats but it also specifies that consumption of flesh induce the factor of violence and give rise to emotions like fear and hatred. So in order for you to get spiritually enlightened and to keep your mental well-being meats are not recommended.

Influences from the 'Outsiders'

Indian cuisine truly offers a mind–boggling variety of foods today because of the influences from the past cultures of the Mughals, the Persians, the Zoroastrians and the Greeks that came and merged into the local culture. The most significant influence in the north including Punjab, Haryana, Kashmir, Uttar Pradesh and Delhi is from the Mughals who were the Central Asian invaders and ruled India for about 400 years. They were connoisseurs of food and brought with them the taste for lamb, chicken, nuts and dried fruits, and thus came about the wonderful *tandoori* dishes, *kormas*, *kebabs*, *biryani*, *pulavs* and desserts like Baklava. Prior to their arrival, the foods in the north and south were prepared with the belief that eating meat is not good for mental and spiritual well-being and was consumed only by a select group of people.

In the south there was a major influence on local foods left by the great spice traders who were Phoenicians, Romans, Portuguese and the Arabs. Marco Polo came to India in 1294, and Vasco da Gama in 1498; the Dutch and the British came in the 17th century – these seafarers brought with them new foods that worked their way into south Indian cuisine. Saffron from the Arabs, fenugreek from the Mediterranean, chili peppers, the new world tomatoes, potatoes and the cashew came with the Portuguese.

Regional and climatic influences

Each state evolved its very own cuisine influenced by the climate of the region and the availability of certain raw foods. The people of Rajasthan, the desert state, make up for the lack of colour in their landscape by flaunting vivid colours in their dresses as well as in their cuisine. They use plenty of red chili and turmeric in all the dishes. Similarly in Kashmir since saffron and dry fruits grow in abundance, they lend a lot of colour, distinction and delicacy to the foods of this region. Cinnamon, mace, nutmeg, cardamom and black pepper are used here in food to ward off the long winter chill and the cold weather. In contrast, in the naturally warm and humid southern climates, tamarind, coconut and curds take over to impart a cooling effect to the cuisine while the fragrant curry leaves and mustard seeds provide a peppy counterpoint. The food in the south is generally light and digestible but chili-hot to induce perspiration which is what is needed in a hot climate to cool you off and also help clean the body channels. Karnataka produces perhaps the best coffee, cardamoms and cashew nuts. The seacoast of Kerala is abundant in fish, shellfish and coconut especially in the summer and monsoon months. Mustard seeds and fragrant curry leaves grow in abundance here. Along their extensive waterways, you can see green rice paddies that are the staple food of Kerala. Talking of seafood also takes you to another region of India – Bengal. The Bengalis boast that no one can cook or savour fish like they can. They are quite convinced that no oil has a better flavour as the mustard oil has and no blend of spices is as flavourful as *panchphoran* and certainly no dessert as delectable as the *rasgulla* or *rasmalai*. The Bay of Bengal offers a rich haul of fish, shellfish and its hot and humid climate is perfect for growing rice, mustard and coconut.

If you still have not had your fill of hot and spicy food you could move on to Goa. Here, you can look forward to more seafood and other fiery specialties flavoured with coconut and the locally grown cashew. If you decide to cook Goan food, keep a bottle of vinegar or preferably cashew vinegar called Feni, because it creeps into many preparations giving them a distinctive flavour.

Still talking of exquisite blending, one comes to Hyderabad, where Muslim and Hindu influences blend so very harmoniously in the exotic, aromatic way. In the cuisine of this famous state dishes like *Bagara Baingan*, *Shikampuri Kebab*, various curries, fragrant *Pulavs* and desserts give you a good example of this harmonious blend.

Indian cuisine truly offers a mind-boggling variety of food. The Mughal, the Persian, the Zoroastrian and the Greek influence strongly reflects in numerous dishes popular even today. It can be seen significantly in Punjab, Haryana, Kashmir, Uttar Pradesh and Delhi which bears the hallmark of the Mughals who were the Central Asian invaders and ruled India for about 400 years.

The north Indian state of Punjab is an agricultural state with a very dry and hot summer, perfect weather for growing wheat and corn. It is referred to as the bread basket of India – its people have a good appetite and like to fix quick hearty meals. Their mustard greens preparation called *Sarson ka Saag* which is quite hot and delicious for the palate, is usually topped with lots of home made butter and suitable for the climate of this state. A Punjabi will consider the meal of *Sarson ka Saag* and *Makki ki Roti* (mustard greens and cornmeal bread) quite wholesome and delicious enough to be irreplaceable.

The foods of Gujarat are hot, spicy and sweet because Gujaratis like to add a dash of sugar to all their dishes. Their *papads* (paper thin tortillas made with the lentil flours) are the glory of each of their meals. They make this very delicious snack called *dhokla* (steamed rice cakes) with amazing finesse. Their sweet and sour *chidva* is being relished all over India and is a famous teatime snack.

From the state of Maharashtra comes the delectable pomfret fish. The food here has a perfect blend of sweet, sour and fiery tastes which will make your tongue tingle for days. To satiate your sweet tooth do not forget that from this state also comes the king of mangoes, *Alphanso*.

Each spice has dozens of different flavours depending on whether they are cooked in oil or dry roasted or ground. When they are cooked in oil it is called *tadka* (tempering). This technique is quite unique to Indian cooking. Spices when cooked in hot oil, transfer their flavour to that oil and anything cooked in it carry the flavour of these spices. Some spices used in a ground form are for taste and those used whole are for aroma. The spices used as whole are discarded during eating. Once in a while some spices are roasted and ground to enhance the taste and to decorate the main course dish. The genius of Indian cooking lies in mixing and matching different spices for each dish. The spices should be used as fresh as possible – they stay fresh if they are whole and can be ground as needed. There are regional variations on use of these spices and in this book my focus will be more on the regional specialties. The choice of spices makes the sum total of the taste and flavour of a dish. Thickening agents used for the curries are mainly onions, coconut milk, groundnuts or seeds, heavy cream and sometimes yogurt.

Beneficial uses of all the spices are recorded in the ancient treatises and I have mentioned their uses and health benefits. For example cinnamon helps lower high cholesterol levels and regulates blood–sugar whereas cumin, fennel and cardamom help in the digestion of the food. Ginger is called the universal healer and turmeric acts as antiinflammatory, an anti cancer agent, and helps in the prevention of Alzheimer's disease. It has in fact been called the 'solid gold' of India.

As I rave enthusiastically over the exquisite Indian cuisine, let me assure you that there is nothing complicated about preparing these dishes. What is essential is a thorough knowledge of all the fresh herbs and spices, their unique flavouring and combinations. Some basic experimentation can prepare you for this unique journey.

Spices that are used in Indian cooking – their origin and health benefits with their Botanical names

The Spice Box: Traditionally, in earlier times, when a girl got married she used to get a spice box as a part of her dowry which had spices that the bride would take with her to start her new household. These boxes could be beautifully, ornamented or simple wooden boxes. Nowadays, they may not be an item of dowry but the spice box is still an essential item of a Indian lady's kitchen. Listed below are some of the gems from my Spice Box.

Carom Seeds / *Ajwain* : Carom seed or Bishop's weed or Lovage (*Ajwain*) / (*Carum Capticum*) – resembles parsley seeds. They are used in lemon pickles and in batter for frying fritters (*pakoras*). They are also used in the flavoring of vegetable dishes like carrots, cabbage and some breads. They are also used to relieve stomach pain due to gas or indigestion. *Ajwain* contains thymol which is germicidal and antiseptic, and is valued in *Ayurvedic* medicine for diarrhoea, colic, flatulence, asthma and indigestion. It helps expel gas and mucus.

Asafoetida / *Heeng* : A gum derived from the root of a plant (*Ferulla alliacea*). Used in the preparation of pickles, *sambhar, rasam*, and some lentil preparations. Native to Iran. It is also called the devil's dung. It should be stored in an air tight container because of its smell. This smell goes away once it is cooked. It even eliminates offending smell of any food it is used for like meats and fish. It is mainly antiflatulent and digestive, is helpful in cases of asthma, and bronchitis. It is a folk tale remedy to treat cold in children. It has been reported that in humans it acts both as a contraceptive as well as abortifacient. Therefore, it is used in very minute quantities.

Bay leaves / *Tej patta* : Bay leaves come from the Bay laurel tree (*Laurus nobilis*) native to the Mediterranean and Asia Minor. They are admired for their beauty, smell and medicinal uses. In Indian cooking bay leaves are used mainly for flavouring curries and *pulavs*. This tree is considered sacred in Greece and Rome and is popular for its healing power. Untimely withering of a laurel tree manifested disaster for the ancient Romans and Greeks. Oil of bay leaves is used as a rub to relieve joint pains and it also prevents tooth decay. Its use in food promotes appetite and helps in secretion of upper digestive track juices. It has a strong aroma and makes an effective anti dandruff rinse. Greeks welcomed their Olympic champions with wreathes of bay leaves.

Black pepper / *Kali mirch* : It is called the *king of spices* and is used as a condiment and also well-known for its medicinal values. A native of Malabar Hills of western India it is a fruit of the *Piper Nigum L.* It has been a highly prized spice as far back as 2nd century A.D. Christopher Columbus set out to discover India in search of cloves and black pepper. A culinary spice, which is used all over the world by almost every race and in all cuisines. It is bitter, carminative, diuretic, digestive and a stimulant. It is useful to treat arthritis, fever, cough, dysentery, dyspepsia and flatulence. It is a marvel of nature and is used in *Ayurvedic, Unani* and Persian medicine.

In India it grows mainly in Kerala. Boiled in tea with basil leaves, it is used to cure common colds and asthma and is used extensively in Indian cooking – ground as well as whole to flavour dishes.

Brown Cardamoms / *Ilaichi* : Large Brown Cardamoms (*Amomum sublatum*) are valued as the *queen of spices* in the annals of herbs and spices. There are two varieties of cardamoms, large brown and smaller green. Large brown is mostly used in Indian entrée dishes and is used as a whole spice to flavour the curries and *pulavs*. It is grown only in north-east India and Sikkim and is extensively used in Chinese and Vietnamese cooking. It has a strong aroma and when its seeds are ground it forms a part of *garam masala* recipe. Green cardamoms (*Amomum elettaria*), besides flavouring some meat curries and other main dishes, are used in powder form to flavour most Indian desserts. It is native to India, Guatemala and Sri Lanka. The sugared and silver coated pods are offered as a mouth freshener after a feast in weddings and other celebrations in India. Tea made with cardamoms cures any digestive disorders and cures depressions. Daily gargles of cardamom tea prevents flu, relieves cough and throat problems. It is a calcium supplier to the body if taken regularly, and also prevents dizziness.

Cayenne pepper / *Lal mirch* : It is also called dried fruit of capsicum (*Capsicum fourtescens*). The small variety is very hot. Chilies are a great source of Vitamin C and help in digestion. The correct use of red chili is of great importance, if you want to make a gourmet style curry with a perfect red color. India is the largest producer of chili. It is grown throughout India but chilies from Kashmir are best to give the red colour to curries and at the same time it is mild in taste. It is very effective when added to liniments for arthritis, muscle aches and benefits the heart, blood circulation and wheezing.

Cinnamon / *Dalchini* : It has been known since remote antiquity. Native to the hills of south India (*Cinnamon verum*) it is the dried inner bark of a type of laurel tree. It is mostly used whole to give flavour to the dishes and is also used as a powder to make *garam masala*. In the west it is mostly used to garnish and to add flavour to desserts. Recent research has indicated it to have great effect in making insulin more sensitive. It was highly prized among ancient nations and was regarded as a gift for monarchs and nobles.

Clove / *Laung* : (*Eugenia caryophyllates*) It is the dried unopened flower bud of an evergreen tree native to India. It has a sweet penetrating smell. In powder form it is part of the recipe of *garam masala*. As a whole-spice it is used to flavour rice and curries. Its health benefits are numerous. Clove oil will stop a toothache and is useful for the common cold. It promotes sweating in patients with fevers, colds and flu. Its hot and sweet taste has made it a breath freshener since antiquity. It is a powerful phyto chemical that numbs pain and kills bacteria and fungi.

Coconut / *Nariyal* : It is also known as *Cocos nucifera*. In south India the abundant coconut palm is called the **'the tree of life'**. The fruit yields a rich meat, milk and oil, ingredients that are used in South Indian cooking. It requires a lot of skill to extract meat and milk from a fresh coconut. Dried grated unsweetened coconut is available in Indian grocery stores and health food stores and it works very well as a substitute. Imagine how boring the beaches would be without tall, elegant swaying palm trees and how boring would the world be without its flavour in tropical drinks.

Coriander seeds / *Dhania* seeds : It is one of the oldest known spices and is also known as *Coriandrum satiram*. It is one of the most widely used seasoning in India and it has a lemony aroma. It is mostly used in all vegetable, meat and lentil preparations in its unroasted ground form. It should be cooked in hot oil over low heat for a minute for its full flavour to be released. To enhance the flavour of some dishes the seeds are roasted on a hot griddle (*tawa*) without oil for 3 minutes or so and ground just before use. Coriander has diuretic properties and is used for the treatments of upper abdominal problems like flatulence or mild cramp like gastrointestinal upsets. Coriander is grown all over India. The state of Rajasthan and parts of central India produce most of the coriander needed in India but the variety from Rajasthan has the best flavour and aroma.

Cumin seeds / *Zeera* powder : Cumin seeds (*Cuminum cyminuml*) are one of the most universally used spices with a pleasant, unassertive flavour. The seeds are pale green in colour and resemble fennel seeds. In Indian cusine, cumin seeds are used to flavour almost all meats, vegetable, and lentil preparations. They are cooked very briefly in hot oil over low heat until they start popping to release their full flavour and are used for tempering (*tadka*) invariably. They can be dry roasted on a hot griddle and ground into a powder to flavour prepared dishes like *raita* (a yogurt preparation), *pulav* (a rice dish) and *chaat*.

Cumin has many health benefits. In south India it is used in its unroasted ground form. It is used as a remedy for colic, dyspepsia and headache and is also antispasmodic and carminative. It is sometimes compounded with other drugs to form a stimulating liniment.

Stone flower / *Dagadphool* : Only used in Indian cuisine, it is a combination of fungus and algae and is a lichen. It is used in the *Goda masala* mix. Its health benefits and medicinal values are not known.

Fennel seeds / *Saunf* : These seeds (*Foeniculum vulgare*) look a bit like cumin seeds but are much plumper and greener. Fennel powder is a part of *Kashmiri* cuisine and is used extensively in meat preparations. Fennel seeds are also a part of *panchphoran,* a five-spice mixture from Bengal, and is used in almost all Bengali cooking. In north India, Fennel seeds are seldom used in cooking but they form a major part of pickles, *chutneys* and several snack preparations. Fennel seeds are also used all over the country as an after meal mouth freshener — sometimes dry roasted or sweetened — they are presented as a mint when you are leaving the restaurant after a hearty Indian meal. They are known for their digestive quality and are very therapeutic when boiled in the tea for the cure of common cough and cold. Fennel seeds also help cancer patients in providing them a good mouth freshner after radiation and chemotherapy treatments and are used in different cuisines of the world.

Fenugreek seeds / *Methi seeds* : These angular yellowish seeds (*Trigonella foneum*) are a very healthy spice to use. In north India, these are first fried in hot oil for a few seconds before the other ingredients are added. They are used in pickles, *chutneys* and several vegetable dishes. In western, eastern and southern India these seeds are used in meat and fish dishes. In Bengal these are a part of *panchphora*n. In south India, fenugreek seeds are used in *dosa, sambhar* and *idli* preparations. These seeds have antiseptic properties and are very digestive in nature. In India, traditionally, it is given to new mothers to relax their uterus post delivery. Use of Fenugreek seeds also regulates blood sugar and is very helpful for diabetic patients. They are also effective as an antioxidant and is rarely found in western cuisine.

Mixture of Spices / *Garam masala* : This Spice Mixture has the most exotic aroma and flavour and is used towards the end of cooking to garnish the dish and to retain its full flavour. *Garam* literally means hot in Hindi and *Masala* means spices. So *garam masala* is a mixture of those spices, which according to the ancient *Ayurveda*, produce heat in the body. Typical *garam masala* would be a mixture of powdered large cardamoms, black pepper, cinnamon, cloves, cumin, nutmeg and mace. Almost all Indian grocery stores sell it. It is used to garnish meat, poultry, fish and vegetable curries before serving. It is also used to garnish yogurt preparations like *raita, dahi vada* and *chaat* among the north Indian dishes. It is gaining popularity in American cuisine also.

Nigella / *Kalonji* : This tear shaped tiny black seed (*Nigella saliva*) is mostly used in oven breads but in Bengali food it is part of *panchphoran* five spice mixture. Some vegetable dishes like eggplants, cabbage etc. team very well with Nigella. It is also used in sweet mango *chutney*, mango pickles and other pickles. This black seed has unique medicinal properties, containing eight of the essential amino acids found in the body proteins. Nigella seeds have anticancer, antibacterial, anti inflammatory and non allergenic properties and strengthen the body's immune system besides helping in bronchial asthma and arthritis.

Black Mustard seeds / *Rai* : Ancient *Vedic* writings dating back 5,000 years mention mustard seeds (*Brassica atba nigra*). Mustard seeds have been used for thousands of years in Greece and Egypt for flavour and as medicine. Even the *New Testament* compares our faith in God with mustard seeds. When we keep using our faith like mustard seeds it grows into a large plant with leaves and flowers. Both mustard seeds and greens are edible. Used most extensively in South Indian cuisine, mustard seed acts as a laxative when taken whole. It has Omega 3 fatty acid, is diuretic and reduces migraine attacks. It also helps to cure rheumatoid arthritis, helps reduce blood pressure and inhibits growth of cancer cells. Its leaves are rich in minerals like selenium, phosphorus, manganese, iron, calcium, and zinc; Vitamin B and C, dietary fiber, proteins and phytonutrients. There are three varieties of Mustard seeds. The round little balls are either yellowish, reddish brown (*sarson*) or black (*rai*). The reddish brown variety is mostly grown and used all over India. In south India most dishes are flavoured by these seeds. They are first heated in oil and once they start popping the rest of the ingredients are added. Whether it is a non-vegetarian dish, rice, *sambhar, idli* or the famous *dosa* or any of their *chutney*s. Even in Bengal, Gujarat and Maharashtra, mustard seeds are used in almost every dish. In Punjab, mustard greens are a favourite winter vegetable and mustard oil is also used as a preservative in pickles and for cooking. I think it is the most used spice in the whole of India. It is also used as a powder in a marinade to coat the fish or to make a sauce in Bengal giving a rather pungent spicy taste. When the seeds are used whole they give a sort of sour nutty flavour as well as a nice speckled look to the dish and they are supposed to be antiseptic in nature. In western cuisine, mustard seeds are used as a ground paste on hamburgers and marinades.

Cobra's Saffron / *Naagkeshar* : The dry flowers of *Naagkeshar* (*Mesua ferrea*) tree are used in the *goda masala* mix. The *Naagkeshar* tree is one of the highly regarded and sacred trees. Native to India, its other name is *Naagchampa*. This is a tree of healing, pleasing and attractive qualities. The flowers of this tree are offered to Lord Buddha in temples. These flowers are fragrant and their oil has significant anti fungal, antibacterial, antiinflammatory, antihemorrhagic as well as antihelminitic properties. Extract from its leaves is used in *Ayurvedic* medicine and is useful for alleviating asthma and bronchial spasms.

Nutmeg and Mace / *Jaiphal* and *Javitri* : Nutmeg (*Myristica fragrans*) is the seed of a pear shaped fruit and its outer covering, when dried, is called mace. These two spices are used very delicately to flavor meats and few vegetable dishes. In India, it is used as a medicinal herb by women who have just delivered babies. It is said that these herbs helps clean the blood and give strength to the body. In the north of India nutmeg and mace are a part of the spice mixture, *garam masala*. India is the most eminent supplier of nutmeg and mace to the world.

Five spice mixture / *Panchphoran* : *Panch* means five and *phoran* means seeds. It originated in Bengal. The mixture has fennel seeds, brown mustard seeds, nigella seeds, fenugreek and cumin seeds in equal amounts. It is used as tempering (*tadka*) to flavour vegetables or lentils, as whole seeds mixture or as a ground powder. Grind them all well in a coffee grinder and store in an airtight container in a cool place. The flavour will be retained longer in the seeds (2 months) but powder should not be stored for more than 3 or 4 weeks.

South Indian spice mixture / *Podi powder* : Roast and grind coarsely a mixture of ½ cup *urad dal*, ½ cup *channa dal*, 2 Tbs red hot chili powder, 1 Tbs sesame seeds and add to it ½ tsp salt with ¼ tsp asafoetida. Store it in an airtight container and season your vegetables, lentils and curries as you please.

Turmeric / *Haldi* : Called the solid gold of India or the saffron of India. This root of a plant (*Curcuma Longa*) is boiled, dried and powdered before use. This is the spice which gives yellow colour to the curries. Fresh turmeric is available in the spring months in India and it actually gives a better yellow colour to the dish. It is found in almost every Indian household. It has antiinflammatory properties and prevents certain cancers and even Alzheimer's disease. It also acts as an antiseptic. Its paste applied over a wound or a swelling greatly reduces pain and swelling. It takes a little frying in hot oil to release its flavour and then it gives a beautiful yellow colour to every dish you prepare. It is also used as a dye and also in the preparation of cosmetics and medicines for skin problems. It is grown mainly in the southern states of India. It is important that Turmeric is of good quality and therefore should be bought from a proper grocery store.

Star anise / *Badalphool* : Native to China and Vietnam, Star anise (*Pimpinella anisum*) is not too common in North Indian cuisine. People in China used to chew star anise as a mouth freshener thousands of years ago and even to this day it is a major ingredient of Chinese five spice mix. Shanghai style of Chinese cuisine makes the most of this spice. However, Beijing, Cantonese and Sichuan styles also make wide use of this spice in their spice powder. It is an ingredient of *podi powder* of south of India and is used in *goda masala* mix of Maharashtra and is called *Badalphool*. It was also used in the summer palace kitchens of the Mughals in

Kashmir to flavour different non-vegetarian preparations. Japanese plant star anise trees in their temple gardens and use the bark of its tree as incense. Extract of star anise called shikimic acid is a key ingredient in bird flu medicine. In the west the extract is used to flavour wines and baked goods, fruit compotes and jams. It was perhaps introduced in the Indian continent by Chinese travellers or vice versa.

Author speaking about the Health Benefits of Indian Cuisine in Las Vegas, U.S.A.

The significant health benefits of spices in daily use

Herbs and spices can tranfrom dull, bland food into delicions dishes, but many also come with unexpected health benefits. Beyond adding complex flavour to a variety of ingredients, many herbs and spices pack a plethora of health perks. Here is a list of a few main spices in everyday use, highlighting many benefits including possible protection against some of the deadliest chronic conditions, like cancer, diabetes and heart disease. They can also be used in place of other flavour boosting substances.

It has been proven that herbs and spices act as potent antibiotics, blood thinners, anticancer agents, antiinflammatory, insulin regulators and antioxidants. When taken in small doses in regular foods they act as unique health boosters. Inflammation is a suspect in heart disease, stroke, cancer, Alzheimer's disease and arthritis.

Chewing a piece of **ginger** with lemon juice and salt is an excellent way to prevent digestive troubles. Ginger tea works excellent for coughs, cold, bronchitis, asthma, whooping cough and tuberculosis of lungs. Scienfifically it is shown that the use of **Ginger** compounds reduces pain and acts as a Cox-2 inhibitor, similar to the anti-arthritic drug celebrex. There is strong evidence that ginger is antiinflammatory. When patients with osteoarthritis of the knee were treated with 255 mg of ginger extract twice a day they showed far less pain than those with placebo. It is also a potent antitumor agent.

Both Ayurveda and traditional Chinese medicine have utilized this health promoting spice to treat colds, diabetes, indigestion and high cholesterol. As a blood thinner, cinnamon prevents heart attacks. Additionally, cinnamon may be used in the treatment of respiratory and sinus congestion, bronchitis, colds and 'flu. It is both an expectorant and a decongestant. A whiff of **Cinnamon** can enhance motivation, alertness, blood flow, which in turn would stimulate the brain. Modern science has proven that cinnamon's most active ingredient MHCP increased the processing of blood sugar 2000% in test-tube studies. So for diabetic patients, cinnamon when sprinkled in tiny amounts in desserts or by flavouring their tea, will make their insulin intake more efficient.

In Ayurvedic practices, **Turmeric**, the golden spice, is considered to have many medicinal properties including strengthening the overall energy of the body, relieving gas, dispelling worms, improving digestion, regulating menstruation, dissolving gallstones and relieving arthritis. Modern in vitro studies reveal that turmeric is a potential antioxidant, anti-inflammatory, antimutagenic, antimicrobial, and anticancer. Turmeric, used in cooking and in some remedies has significant antioxidant abilities at different levels of action. Studies indicate that sufficient levels of turmeric may be consumed from curries in vivo to ensure adequate antioxidant protection.

Turmeric contains high concentrations of the potent antioxidant curcumin. In test tubes, 80% of malignant prostrate cells self-destructed when exposed to curcumin. Its antiinflammatory activity reduces arthritic swelling and progressive brain damage in animals. It also fights heart burn, indigestion and Alzheimer's disease. Mice that were fed ½ tsp of curcumin daily developed 50% less brain plaques (main cause of Alzheimer's disease) than those that did not and it is a far safer antiinflammatory agent with the minimum side effects than any other found at the drug store.

Red pepper has seven times more vitamin C and is rich in minerals like molybdenum, folate, potassium, thiamin, and copper, and therefore reduces the risk of colon cancer. It dilates airways to hungs and reduces inflamation of lungs and emphysema. It can fight congestion faster than drugstore decongestants. It makes your nose run, so you can breathe easier. Mice injected with cancer cells and red pepper extract had smaller tumors than the mice without any. It helps combat wheezing.

The most effective killers of bacterial species in current research are in order, **onion, garlic, allspice, oregano, thyme, tarragon, cumin, cloves, bay leaf, and cayenne pepper**. According to modern research the strongest antioxidants are **oregano, thyme, sage, cumin, rosemary, saffron, turmeric, nutmeg, ginger, cardamom, coriander, basil, and tarragon**. Oregano oil has been found as effective as the common antibiotic drug vanomycin in treating staph infections in mice.

So the use of spices not only contributes to flavour, aroma, colour, taste and pungency to the food but has unparalleled pharmaceutical and medicinal benefits as well.

Spice container

Significant health benefits of fresh herbs and seasonings

Almost all curries have these green herbs in one form or another. They give a refreshing look to the dish and are also very ealthy. In India some vendors only sell these green herbs and spices.

Onions / *Pyaz*: One of the oldest vegetables known to mankind. They are eaten chopped, sliced, used in cooking food, fresh salads and as a spicy garnish. It is one of the most widely used vegetable in cuisines all over the world. Onions are fundamental to Indian cooking. Almost all main course dishes first get a garnish of onions. The Egyptians worshipped them and buried their pharaohs with slices of onions. Greek athletes ate them in large quantity to get muscle strength and the Roman gladiators rubbed their bodies to get muscle strength. In the Middle Ages they were used as money. They were introduced to North America in 1492 by Columbus during his expeditions. Onions are a powerhouse of health benefits ranging from being antiinflammatory, anticholesterol, anticancer and a powerful antioxidant.

Ginger / *Adrak*: Originated in India, this plant has been traditionally used in *Ayurvedic* medicine for its health benefits for nearly 5,000 years. It is one of the wet trios used in the beginning of each curry. Along with black pepper, it was one of the main trading spices as far back as 2,000 years in the Roman Empire and mid-eastern countries. Its health benefits are innumerable. It breaks down fatty foods for easy digestion and is excellent for reducing gas. It is a natural antihistamine and antiinflammatory. Relieves nausea and morning sickness and lowers cholesterol. It is more effective when used with garlic. Ginger tea is my favourite on a wintry day to relieve minor cold and flu symptoms.

Garlic / *Lahsan*: Garlic is also an essential part of the Indian curry *masala*. Since time immemorial garlic has been used to ward off evil spirits, build stamina, enhance immunity and ward off infections. It has been proven by research that garlic used on a regular basis reduces blood pressure and plays a role preventing cancer. It lowers cholesterol and relieves asthmatic conditions.

Green chilies / *Hari mirch*: Green chili pepper is also one of the wet trio used in the *curry masala*. Its benefits are numerous. It is rich in Vitamin A and C. They enhance and stimulate digestion. Capsicum stimulates the mucous membranes of the nose, therefore increasing blood flow to these membranes and help us clear the nose. Chilies lower blood sugar as they stimulate the pancreas to produce more insulin. They also kill cancer cells and are highly effective in killing bacteria and viruses in the body.

Cilantro or coriander leaves / *Dhania*: Besides acting as a beautiful garnish for all the curries, this herb has numerous health benefits. It protects you against Salmonella, aids in digestion and helps alleviate the symptoms of arthritis. It is antiflatulent, antiinflammatory and lowers blood sugar. It protects against the urinary tract infection. It is a good source of iron, magnesium, rich source of phytonutrients and flavonoids. Cilantro is mostly used for garnishing and you may think that you can do without it but it is probably the most important of all the ingredients.

Curry leaves / *Kadi patta*: Used in *Ayurvedic* medicines because of their many health benefits. Curry leaves have a special place in Indian cuisine. They are native to India and Sri Lanka and are rich in Vitamin C, Calcium, Phosphate, Iron and Nicotinic acid. They have been used in south India for thousand of years to flavour curries and *sambhar* and are now used extensively all over India. Curry leaves paste is used to cure minor cuts and abrasions. The extract of curry leaves prevents diarrhoea and vomiting and it strengthens the stomach functions.

Dill / *Sooa*: It was used in ancient Rome. In Greece, Hippocrates used it on the burn wounds of his soldiers. They are stomach soothers and help overcome insomnia and have very high calcium content. Except among the Persian community, it is not used much in Indian cooking.

Fenugreek leaves / *Methi*: If you are looking to stop those crunky mid-day crashes and stave off diabetes at the same time, fenugreek may be ideal for you. Fenugreek is a herb that has long been used in cooking and in traditional Asian medicine to stabilize blood sugar and fight diabetes. Native to India and southern Europe, the Mediterranean and North Africa, fenugreek is used in the herbal medicinal tradition of the Middle East, India, Egypt, and later in China and Europe. Known as *methi* in India. It was used by ancient Egyptians to combat fever and chronic cough. It is very easy to grow from seeds and has a very unique flavour but a slightly bitter taste. It is used in practically all cuisines in every part of India and has great therapeutic benefits. It lowers blood sugar and acts as a great digestive aid. It relieves congestion, reduces inflammation and fights infection. Stimulates the production of mucosal fluids to remove allergens and oxidants from the respiratory tract. It is mixed in the flour to make breads like *parantha* and *poori*. When chopped fine it can be mixed in fritter batter to make appetizers like *pakoras*. It is used to make vegetable stir-fries. It is sold dried in stores also and can be used after soaking in the water for a while. Its seeds give the same type of benefits as its leaves. Fenugreek is available fresh as well as dry.

Holy Basil / *Tulsi*: Queen of herbs, Tulsi is the most revered plant in India for more than 5,000 years. It still adorns the courtyard of many Indian households. It has its great medicinal significance and is called the '*elixir of life*' as it promotes longevity. *Tulsi* leaves, when boiled with tea leaves, make a perfect cup of tea, that has tremendous calming effect on the human mind and body. The extract prevents and cures common colds, headaches, stomach disorders, heart diseases and is a universal healer of malarial fever. It is known to regulate blood sugar and blood pressure.

Neem (*Azadirachta indica*): In India, the Neem tree is known as a '*divine tree*', '*heal all*', '*nature's drug store*', '*village pharmacy*' and a '*wonder tree*'. Its tender shoots and flowers are used as a vegetable. Neem is used to make a soup-like dish in south India called *Ugadi pachdi* on *Ugadi* day and is also used to make a soup *Veerampoo Rasam*. In Maharashtra, on *Gudi Padva,* the new year festival, there is an ancient practice of drinking Neem juice before starting the festivities. It is used in *Ayurvedic* medicine as an antiseptic to fight viruses and bacteria. It is also used for urinary disorders, diarrhoea, fever, skin disorders, burns and inflammatory diseases. Its leaves are sprinkled fresh near the beds of patients of flu and fever to disinfect the air of viruses and bacteria.

Mint / *Pudina*: Originating in India and the Mediterranean regions, Mint symbolized hospitality and welcome in ancient Rome and Greece. In earlier times Mint was used as an air freshener and as a perfume in bathing soaps. It has always been an aid to digestion, heartburn and acts as a powdered antioxidant and relieves the symptoms of cold and flu. Mint is used as base for an ancient drink *zeerapaani*. It contains Vitamin A, C and B2, and a wide range of minerals like manganese, copper, iron, potassium and calcium. A cup of Mint tea soothes and calms the body and mind. Besides cooking, it is used universally in toothpastes, gums, soaps and medicines. It is used to adorn drinks, desserts, curries, meats and almost any dish.

Henna / *Mehndi*: (*Lawsonia Inermis*): It is a very active disinfectant and the extract of *mehndi* leaves helps when taken in jaundice. It also acts as an antiseptic, bactericide, fungicide and as an insect repellent. Its paste when applied reduces body temperature, fever, burning feet and even hysteria. The paste made of ground seeds of henna and anise with water or vinegar is used as a remedy for headache.

Henna has been in use in India for over 5000 years. This herb has tremendous importance as a dye with numerous healing properties. Its cosmetic use in an Indian wedding is of great importance as no wedding is complete without it. The night before the wedding is called *Mehndi Raat* (night). The bride and all the women of the family adorn and deck their hands and feet with fine designs using *mehndi* paste. It gives a beautiful reddish brown colour to the skin and the patterns stay on the skin for at least 7-10 days. *Mehndi* is also widely used in Egypt, Iran, Pakistan, Yemen and African countries. Cleopatra used to dye her hair with henna. Henna promotes hair growth and gives the hair beautiful dark brown colour with a shiny lustre. The uses are numerous and in western countries men and women are using it for tattoos and as a hair dye.

Special ingredients to highlight the flavour and aroma of curries and other main courses

Nuts and seeds: Almonds, cashew nuts, pistachios are used to decorate and flavour rice *pulav* to give it a rich and nutritious look along with ground mixture of seeds of watermelon, cantaloupe, pumpkin and squash called *Char magaz* are also used as a thickening agent in the curries. The same mixture of these nuts when mixed with milk, water and sugar is made into a cooling drink called *Thandai (see the recipe in the drinks section)*. This drink is very popular in the hot summer months in the state of Punjab. Sesame seeds are widely used to make *ladoos* or sweet round balls when mixed with sugar and dry milk powder. Poppy seeds are used to flavour breads like *Nan* and when ground they are used in various non-vegetarian curries. Almonds, pistachio and cashews also ground and mixed with dry milk powder and sugar to make *Burfi*. Sure enough, nuts do highlight the flavour and aroma of various dishes.

Screw pine flower essence / *Kewra* : The flower is grown in Orissa and Kerala and belongs to the screw pine family of plants. In Sanskrit, the plant is called *Ketaki*. It has a very strong aroma. The extract of the male flowers is made into *kewra* essence and a drop of this when mixed with water, is sold as *kewra* water. This water is used to flavour *kormas, kebabs, and biryanis*. It is used mainly in Hyderabad and Lucknow, the two cities famous for Mughal cuisine. *Kewra* essence is also used in flavouring several desserts. The *Kewra* flowers are dislillated into sandalwood oil. *Kewra attar* has about 3% to 5% *Kewra* oil, and the remainder is sandalwood oil. In Ayurveda, this oil is used as a stimulant and to treat rheumatoid arthritis.

Powdered rose flower petals and its essence / *Gulab patti - Gulab jal* : Rose petals are sun-dried and ground for use in cooking, and are part of the marinate of meats in Mughlai cuisine in India. They have very astringent and antiinflammatory properties. These are used to flavour *sherbets* and to sprinkle over *biryani, pulav* and some sweets. Rose (attar) has been is use since Lord Krishna's times. Rose was his favourite flower. Hindus wash the altars of their deities with rose water.

Rose essence is one of the safest substances for healing. It has been primarily used for anti-stress therapy. If someone is depressed, suffering from anxiety or feeling mentally exhausted, smelling Rose essence helps immediately because the mind feels fresh. The nervous system gets relief and a calm soothing stage of mind is attained. It has a cleansing effect on the liver, kidneys and spleen. In case of skin care it decreases the aging process, enhances smoothness of the skin, reduces wrinkles on the face, and helps the skin of the body acquire a healthy glow and charm. It is also good for respiratory disorders. It has been used to mask the taste of many obnoxious food dishes as well as to make them tastier to eat, on account of its rich and smooth flavour. It is useful in reducing extra fat from the body.

From the time of Cleopatra, most of the Persian, European and Indian queens loved the rose for its wonderful healing qualities due to its soothing and cooling effects. After a whole day's hard work, in the early evening, some Ayurvedic doctors recommend the rose drink as a refreshner. This drink is referred to often as "Gulab Lassi".

Fresh rose petals have been cooked with granular sugar without water under hot sunlight through a specific process, producing semi-solid thick paste like jam, known as *Gulkand*. It is good for memory, eyesight and is a good blood purifier. It reduces extra heat from the body, and calms the body and mind. Indian Ayurvedic doctors use it for cancer patients.

Saffron / *Kesar* : It is widely used in Indian cooking and was a favorite of the Mughlai courts. It is the stigma of the flower of the crocus family and grows mainly in the Kashmir valley in India. It is also imported from Spain and Mediterranean countries. It is used to flavour *biryani, pulavs, kormas, kebabs* and many desserts. The strands are soaked first in a little warm water or milk and then transferred to the dish. It should be stored in a refrigerator, otherwise it loses its flavour very quickly.

Raisins / *Kishmish* : Raisins are used to flavour desserts like *halwa* (a cream of wheat pudding) and *kheer* (the rice pudding). These are very popular desserts in north India. Raisins are also used to flavour *pulavs, raita* as well as *tamarind chutney.*

Lentils / *dal* : In dishes like the Persian *dhansak* lentils are used as a thickening agent. Sometimes meats are also cooked with lentils. In south India some vegetables and almost all rice dishes get flavoured with not only the wet trio but also a teaspoonful of *urad dal* and sometimes *channa dal*. They are fried in hot oil and then rest of the ingredients are added. Some lentils are ground roasted and then mixed with *khoa* (dried milk) sugar and *ghee* to make *pinni* – a popular dessert also flavoured with almonds, pistachio and raisins.

Very thin silver and gold leaves to decorate desserts / *Varq* : These are prepared by beating real gold and silver metal into ultra thin leaves to decorate Indian desserts. A trace of these is no health hazard.

Barfi, a popular Dessert

Thickening agents used in Indian curries

Onions / *Pyaz* : Onions are invariably used in most Indian dishes for gravy. They are finely chopped or puréed and first fried in hot oil in a thick bottom pan so they do not stick to the bottom. Regular stirring is required during this process of frying. They are cooked until they start turning brown. Sometimes a little water can be added to prevent sticking to the pan. Onions are usually fried with chopped ginger, garlic and green pepper to give bulk to the gravy and also make it healthy and flavorful. All the other ingredients are then added to this gravy. Garlic tends to cook faster and therefore it is added at the end.

Heavy cream : It was imbibed into Indian cooking from the Mughlai cuisine. The cream gives nice rich taste to a dish. It is used mainly in meat curries and some vegetable curries like *palak paneer*, *kofta* curry or a mixed vegetable curry. It is mostly added at the end of the cooking. As soon as the curry is done lower the heat, add the cream and simmer for few minutes and serve.

Nuts and seeds / *Mewa or beej* : Groundnuts, poppy seeds and sesame seeds are used widely as thickening agents in curries around the country. They were introduced by the Mughals. When groundnuts are used in *curry masala* as a thickening agent, it is important that you keep stirring to prevent it from sticking to the bottom of the pan, otherwise the curry will lose its entire flavor. Nuts not only give texture to the curry but also provide a very good flavor if cooked with care.

Mustard seeds / *Rai* : Mustard seeds are used for gravy only in some parts of India like Bengal and Goa. Ground seeds are used as a paste to coat the fish or chicken before cooking. This paste gives them flavor as well as some gravy. In Bengal, mustard seeds are used as thickening agent in meats and vegetable dishes too.

Peanuts / *Moongphali* : Peanuts are native to Gujarat, many parts of southern India, and are widely used as a thickening agent in curries of these regions.

Lentils : Lentils are used as thickening agents in dishes like *Dhansak* and *Khichdi*. They are either ground first or cooked and then ground and mixed with the basic onion, ginger and garlic mixture and fried in hot oil before being added to the rest of the ingredients.

Yogurt / *Dahi* : It can be used at the end of cooking of the curry *masala*. It adds little sourness and a creamy texture to the curry. Lower the heat and then add the well-beaten and smooth yogurt. Gently stir it in and simmer the curry until done and serve. Plain yogurt can be purchased at your local grocery store but nothing beats homemade yogurt which can be made at home.

Souring agents for the curries and other stir-fries

Tomatoes : Tomatoes are grown throughout the country and are an essential part of a curry for giving it a beautiful red colour, and a little sourness. They are usually added and cooked with onions, ginger, garlic and green chilies in the beginning in hot oil, with the *curry masala*.

Yogurt / *Dahi* : It is often used as souring agent and sometimes as a fermenting agent to make some breads like *nan* and *bhatura*. Meats are often marinated, prior to cooking, in spiced smoothly beaten yogurt. Sometimes, it is added to the gravy of the curry of dishes like lamb, chicken and fish and in some vegetable curries too. Yogurt gives a creamy as well as a slightly sour taste to the curry. It is also used as a base to make a typical *besan* (gram flour) curry that is one of the very well liked and popular curries of India.

Vinegar / *Sirka* : Vinegar is used to make *paneer* from milk. As a souring agent it is used in areas where there is Portuguese influence like Kerala, Mangalore and Goa. It is used in Parsi cooking also.

Tamarind / *Imli* : Tamarind grows all over India but it is native to South India. Tamarind which is used widely in South Indian cooking, has numerous medicinal applications. To use in cooking, the flesh of its ripe fruit is first soaked in water and then the pulp is extracted by filtering and squeezing the pulp through cheesecloth. The pulp is what is used in recipes like *sambhar*, *chutneys* and other meat and vegetable dishes. Keep the pulp refrigerated after opening the bottle.

Lemon or Lime / *Nimbu* : Lime is used as a souring agent in the preparation of mint *chutney* and in marinades for chicken and other meats. It is rarely used as a souring agent while cooking. It is always used at the end of cooking. It is a main salad dressing of the tossed green Indian salad and is used in lots of snacks like *chaat* and *bhelpuri*. It is used to make fresh lemonade drink which is also very popular all over India in the summer months. According to Ayurveda, the lemon is considered to be the destroyer of all the three faults, i.e. phlegm, wind and bile. Lemon is very beneficial in numerous diseases like flatulation, vomit, excessive bile like formation, control of dysentery, worms in the stomach, cleaning out the effects of poison from the body, cough and phlegmatic disorders. It is also an excellent appetizer, and strengthens the bone.

Cocum *(Garcinia indica)* **:** It grows mostly in coastal regions of southern India. The fruit has deep purplish flesh and that is what is used in cooking. It is used in *Sindhi Besan Curry* and in Goan fish curries as a souring agent. It has anti-allergic properties and is also used to make a refreshing drink like lemonade called Kokum water. It gives a very pale purplish colour to a dish. It is used in Gujarat, Maharashtra and in Konkani cooking as a souring agent.

Raw mango powder / *Amchoor* : Raw mango slices are dried and then powdered to make *amchoor*. It is used as souring agent in *samosas* filling and some vegetables like okra, bitter gourd, and yams in north Indian cooking. It is also used in marinating fish in some parts of the country. It is also used as a souring agent in snacks and *chaat* and grilled meats.

Dry pomegranate seeds crushed / *Anaardana* : Dried seeds of pomegranate are roasted and powdered to be used as souring agent in chick-peas curry and *samosas*. It is mostly used only in north Indian cooking and its use is limited to the dishes specified. In Indian culture, the pomegranate fruits has been prized as a balancing tridoshic healthy fruit since times immemorial. Pomegranate tastes astringent, is mild to drink and increases the power of the intellect and strength.

Author in a Book Fair, Las Vegas, NV, U.S.A.

Special spice mixes

to enhance the flavour of various lentils, rice, meats and vegetable preparations

North Indian spice powder mix / *Garam masala*
It is used to garnish and flavour numerous dishes and is one of the most used spice mixes in Indian cooking.

Cinnamon powder	1 Tbs	Cloves powder	1 tsp
Cumin seeds powder	1 tsp	Black pepper powder	1 Tbs
Cardamom powder	1½ tsp	Coriander powder	1 Tbs
Nutmeg powder	½ tsp	Mace powder	½ tsp

Mix all the spice powders in a bowl and store in an airtight container. The shelf life is about 2 weeks. You can use it longer but it will not be as fresh and fragrant. No roasting of spices is required prior to making the *masala*.

Five spice mix from Bengal / *Panchphoran*
The spices mix is used whole for *tadka* or tempering in Bengal to flavour vegetables, lentils and other main course dishes. It is used in powder form also in some recipes.

Fennel seeds	1 Tbs	Nigella seeds	1 Tbs
Fenugreek seeds	1 Tbs	Cumin seeds	1 Tbs
Brown mustard seeds	1 Tbs		

Mix them in equal amounts. Use them whole or grind them as needed. No roasting of spices is needed.

Sambhar spice powder from south India
Used to flavour *sambhar* (a lentil curry from south India). It is a delicious, very fragrant lentil curry prepared with almost every meal in south India. It is served with *dosas, Idlis*, plain rice and all appetizers like *vadas*, corn fritters and *uttapam* etc.

Coriander seeds	1½ cup	Red chili peppers broken	1 cup
Fenugreek seeds	2 Tbs	Black mustard seeds	1½ tsp
Cumin seeds	1 Tbs	Cinnamon stick	½ inch
Coconut powder	½ cup	Asafoetida powder	1½ tsp
Turmeric	1 tsp	Bay leaves firmly packed	¼ cup

Roast together chili peppers, fenugreek seeds, mustard seeds, coriander seeds and cumin seeds until fragrant. Set them aside. In the same pan roast coconut powder until light brown. Transfer the roasted coconut powder into the rest of the spices. Dry roast the curry leaves until fragrant and add them also to the rest of the spices. Cool and add the asafoetida powder and turmeric. Store in an airtight container. It will stay fresh for at least 3–4 months in a refrigerator. Grind to use when needed.

South and east Indian spice mixture / *Podi powder* The spice mix is used to flavour vegetable dishes and some lentils primarily in south India.

Mung dal	4 Tbs	*Channa dal*	2 Tbs
Urad dal	2 Tbs	Coriander seeds	2 Tbs
Cumin seeds	1 Tbs	Sesame seeds	4 Tbs
Curry leaves	8–10	Coconut powder	2 Tbs
Garlic pods	8–10	Salt	to taste
Turmeric powder	1 tsp	Asafoetida powder	½ tsp
Red chili dry crushed (use according to taste)	2 Tbs		

Roast and grind together the *urad dal, channa dal, mung dal,* red dry chilies, sesame seeds, coriander seeds, cumin seeds and curry leaves. Cool the spices and grind them in a coffee grinder. Add the salt, turmeric powder and asafoetida powder and store in an airtight container.

North Indian pickled spice powder / *Achari masala* Used for flavouring certain meat and vegetables dishes like okra, eggplant and potatoes.

Chili peppers	2 tsp	Cumin seeds	2 tsp
Mustard seeds	2 tsp	Nigella seeds	2 tsp
Fenugreek seeds	2 tsp	Fennel seeds	2 tsp
Turmeric	1 tsp	Coriander powder	1 Tbs
Salt	to taste	Paprika	1 tsp

Pan-fry the chili peppers, cumin seeds, mustard seeds, nigella seeds, fenugreek seeds and fennel seeds in 3 Tbs of oil. Cool the spices and grind them in a coffee grinder. Add salt, turmeric, coriander powder and paprika to the ground mixture. The *masala* is ready to be used for stuffing okra or eggplants or to marinate or for adding it to the curry of any meat you desire. It is used in *Achari Chicken* in this book. It can be stored for a couple of weeks in an airtight container.

Ceylonese spice powder mix
Spice powder from Sri Lanka, it is used mostly in Ceylonese cooking to flavor vegetable dishes and lentil curries. The spice mix has great similarity with the *podi powder* of south India.

Raw rice	2 Tbs	Cinnamon 2 pieces	2 inch
Cloves	½ tsp	Coriander seeds	4 Tbs
Curry leaves	8–10	Black peppers	1 Tbs
Green cardamom seeds	1 tsp	Cumin seeds	2 Tbs
Mustard seeds	1 Tbs	Coconut powder (grated unsweetened)	2 Tbs

Roast the rice on a hot iron griddle on medium low heat until light red in color and set it aside in a bowl. Roast the coconut powder separately and set it aside. Transfer the rest of the spices into the hot skillet and roast them until just fragrant. Remove them from heat and add the roasted rice and roasted coconut. Cool the roasted spices and store them in an airtight container. Grind them before use as needed to flavour.

Tandoori (Grilling) masala
It is used mostly in grilling *Seekh Kebabs,* Chicken *Tikka*, fish and other meats and vegetables cooked on the grill.

Paprika	1 tsp	Coriander powder	1 Tbs
Cumin powder	1 tsp	Red pepper	1 tsp
Amchoor	1 Tbs	*Garam masala*	1 tsp
Salt	1 tsp	Mustard seeds or ground (crushed)	1 tsp

Mix the powders and add to the marinade or as directed in the recipe. No roasting of spices is needed.

Chaat masala
It is used to flavour the fruit snacks and other snacks as directed in the recipes.

Red pepper	1 tsp	*Garam masala*	1 tsp
Salt	1 tsp	*Amchoor*	1 Tbs
Kala namak (Black salt)	1 tsp	Cumin powder (roasted ground)	1 Tbs

Mix together the powders and use the mixture for flavouring your favourite snacks.

Rasam masala mix
Rasam masala is used in a soup known in south India as *Rasam*. It is usually served before the dinner. It is a *toor dal* soup flavoured with tamarind pulp, tomatoes, coriander leaves, lemon, crushed garlic, ginger, a dash of *garam masala*, and *rasam masala* mix.

Dry red chilies crushed	¼ cup	Coriander seeds	½ cup
Cumin seeds	1 Tbs	Curry leaves	8–10
Black pepper corns	1 tsp	Mustard seeds	¾ tsp

Dry roast the spices on a hot iron griddle on medium-low heat until they become fragrant and lightly roasted. Cool them and store them in an airtight container. Keep the container at a cool place. If refrigerated the mix can stay fresh for months. Grind the spices before use.

Tea masala
This *masala* is used to flavour the Indian tea or *chai*.

Cardamom powder	½ tsp	Cinnamon powder	½ tsp
Cloves powder	½ tsp	Ginger powder	½ tsp
Black pepper powder	¼ tsp		

Mix the powders together and use when needed to flavour your tea. It can stay fresh for 6–8 weeks on the kitchen shelf.

Goda masala

Mix from Maharashtra. It is used in many vegetarian and meat dishes and lentils. The cuisine of Maharashtra includes hot and aromatic dishes which are flavoured with hot and tangy *Goda masala*. It can be added before or after to vary the taste from mild to strong.

Cloves	1 tsp	Cinnamon	2 tsp
Black cardamom seeds	2 tsp	Bay leaves	5–6
Dagadphool	1 tsp	*Naagkeshar*	1 tsp
Badalphool	1 tsp	Red chilies	2½ Tbs
Sesame seeds	2½ Tbs	Coconut powder	1 cup
Asafoetida	2 tsp	Turmeric powder	1 tsp
Oil	½ cup	Salt	1 Tbs

Heat ¼ cup of oil and fry the cloves, cinnamon, cardamom, *Dagadphool* (a lichen), *Naagkeshar* (*Nagchampa* flower), *Badalphool* (star anise), bay leaves and lastly cumin seeds. Remove the fried spices onto a plate lined with paper towel and drain the oil. Fry the red chilies and coriander seeds one after another and transfer them to the same plate. Roast the coconut powder over low heat and set it aside. Fry the sesame seeds and mix them with coconut powder. Grind the spices very fine in a coffee grinder and set them aside. Grind the coconut and sesame seeds together and mix them with rest of the *masala*. Add salt, turmeric powder and asafoetida to the mixture. Stir and mix the spices well. Store in an air tight container. It will stay fresh for a long time. It is hard to find *naagkeshar* and *dagadphool* outside India but some Indian grocery stores may carry them. If not available this *masala* can be made without these two ingredients also and it will still be as good.

Malwani masala

(From the Malabar coastal region of Karnataka and Kerala): Is used in gravies for chicken, meats, vegetables and rice dishes.

Dry red chilies	5 cups	Coriander seeds	2 cups
Cloves	¾ tsp	Peppercorns	1 Tbs
Fennel seeds	2 Tbs	Cumin seeds	1 tsp
Shahi zeera	1 tsp	Cinnamon (two)	1 inch
Stone flower	1 Tbs	*Naagkeshar*	1 tsp
Mustard seeds	1 tsp	Turmeric powder	1 tsp
Asafoetida	1 tsp	Nutmeg	2
Badalphool	½ tsp	Black cardamom seeds	½ tsp

Dry roast the ingredients, cool and grind them to use.

Bombay *masala* mix / *Pathare Prabhu masala*

It is used by the *Pathare Prabhu* community of Bombay. This community has a great history of nobility and integrity. They have preserved their traditions and culture. They use it to flavour their vegetable curries, meat curries and rice dishes.

Coriander seeds	1 cup	Cumin seeds	3 Tbs
Mustard seeds	3 Tbs	Whole wheat	¼ cup
Channa dal	¼ cup	Dry red chilies	1 cup
Turmeric powder	1 Tbs	Fenugreek seeds	1 tsp
Asafoetida	⅛ tsp	Peppercorns	1 Tbs

Dry roast all on an iron griddle (except turmeric powder and asafoetida) individually and cool. Grind them for use.

Golden Temple, Amritsar, India

Special flours, lentils, cereals and other ingredients used in Indian cooking

Ayurveda recommends having grains at each meal if you are a vegetarian, to provide adequate energy for the body. According to the traditional wisdom of Ayurveda, grains help to build bone tissue and muscle and give bodily strength and endurance. According to modern methods of nutrition analysis, grains provide carbohydrates, protein, iron, calcuim, potassium and vitamins necessary for a balanced diet. Ayurvedic treatment emphasizes more on fasting and diet restrant rather than on consuning medicines to fight dieseases.

Whole wheat flour / *Atta* flour or *chappati* flour : For making the typical Indian *chappati* or *roti* (staple diet of north Indians) nothing is better than the whole-wheat flour. It can be substituted by fine ground whole-wheat flour for tortillas.

Gram flour / *Besan ka Atta* : It is prepared by grinding black grams and is very high in protein content. It is used extensively in Indian cooking to make vegetable fritters or *pakoras* and it is also mixed, half-and-half, with wheat flour to make breads for diabetics. It is also used to make some desserts like *burfi* and *laddoos*. It also acts as a binding agent.

With its nutritional value, proteins and vitamins, besan is also a leading skin care remedy. Besan flour, when mixed with yogurt, turmeric and lemon, removes the tan formed due to exposure to the sun. It is also gluten free.

Rice flour / *Chawal ka Atta* : It is used to make dessert called *phirni* in north India, but in south India, rice flour is used as a staple food. It is used most extensively in making many main course dishes like *dosas, idlis* and *appam.*

Its inclusion and importance in the diet is because of its gluten free characteristic. Rice flour is low in sodium, saturated fat and cholesterol.

Cream of wheat / *Suji* : Semolina or farina is the granular cereal derived from the proteinaceous germ of wheat. Cream of wheat comes packed with iron and also offers a generous amount of calcium. It is used in India for making desserts like *halwa, gulabjaman* and *laddoo* etc. It is a highly prized cereal of India and is used in several savoury dishes like *rava dosa, idli, uppama* etc. Partially cooked cream of wheat is used as a breakfast cereal and is commonly available at any local grocery store in the western countries.

All purpose flour / *Maida* : Fine ground wheat flour is used in making only few breads like *nans* and some desserts in India but in western countries it is more or less a staple flour in making all breads, cakes and some sauces and has many more uses. It can be purchased at grocery stores anywhere in the world.

Millet flour / *Bajre ka Atta* : Obtained from the plant called *Panicum Milaceum*. Millet flour is used the most in Gujarat, Rajasthan and Punjab states of India in making griddle breads. It is the oldest and highly nutritive grain of India.

Millet provides a host of nutrients, has a sweet nutty flavour, and is considered to be one of the most digestible and non-allergenic grains available.

Sorghum flour / *Jawar ka Atta* : Related to millet, Sorgham is used to make breads in India. It is highly proteinaceous and has no gluten. , It is mostly mixed with wheat flour to make breads. Some of its varieties produce sugar. It is the third most produced grain in America but is not used for human consumption.

Sorghum flour is a powerhouse of nutrition and adds superb flavour to gluten free baking. It is high in protein, iron and dietary fiber, making sorghum flour welcome in pantries around the world. Evidence confirms that sorghum is completely gluten-free and the gram provides health benefits that make it a worthy addition in any diet.

Corn flour / *Makki ka Atta* : The flour is made into delicious breads in all parts of India especially in Punjab but it is not a staple food as it is in Mexico and western countries. Corn is consumed fresh as a whole stalk grilled and smeared with lemon juice, salt and pepper called *bhutta* and it is sold by vendors at street corners all over India. It is not used as extensively as a cooked vegetable as in the western countries. It can be purchased from Indian as well as Western grocery stores.

Known to many ancient cultures, corn's health benefits are so immense that people all over the world continue to use this grain widely in their daily cooking. According to Ayurveda, corn is diuretic and very good for people with high blood pressure.

Cream of rice / Suji: Used in making *rava idli or dosa* in South Indian cooking and making the *kheer* or pudding in North India.

Fine vermicelli / *Sevian* : It is a type of vermicelli. Cooked especially on *Eid* (a Muslim festival) by the Muslim community as *sevian* which is a very well liked dessert all over India. These are also cooked as spicy noodles and used for snacks. Available in Indian and Pakistani grocery stores in western countries.

***Basmati* Rice:** It is long grain very fragrant rice grown in the foothills of the Himalayas. This rice is also now grown in America and is available in local supermarkets but does not match the fine quality and fragrance of Indian grown *basmati* rice.

Spiced and roasted wafers / *Papads or Papadums* : These delightful thin wafers made from lentil flour are always made commercially as their preparation needs special skill and experience. They are made of *urad* or *mung dal* flour, oil and spices kneaded well with water into a very smooth and tight dough. Then they are rolled very thin like tortilla and air-dried. These are served with a regular meal toasted or deep fried in hot oil. These can be served as a snack and can be bought as mild or highly spiced, from your local Indian grocery store. Papadums are the ornaments of a Gujarati meal.

Indian dehydrated milk / *Khoa* : This is another preparation from homogenized milk. The milk is cooked on low heat until it dries up to a stiff dough. Continuous stirring is important because milk tends to stick to the bottom of the pan and burns very easily. This is a key ingredient which is used to make desserts like *burfi, gulabjaman, pinnis,* carrot *halwa* etc. Nowadays *khoa* is substituted by using 'Half and Half' dry milk powder or heavy cream and cooked on low heat stirring continuously, until it is dry. Now it is ready to be used as needed.

Indian style Ricotta cheese / *Paneer* : It can be purchased as a slab from an Indian grocery store. Refrigerate until ready to use. Ricotta cheese is very wet, and when it is used as *paneer*, the water has to be squeezed out by putting a lot of weight over it for at least 4–6 hours. Remove Ricotta from the plastic container onto a double layer of paper towel and cover it with more paper towel. Wrap it in a small cloth towel and put some heavy object over it to squeeze out all the moisture (3–4 hours). When it is a firm slab, cut into cubes and use as directed. You can prepare *paneer* at home too.

Author in a Book Fair, Phoenix, Arizona, U.S.A.

Dal / Legumes used in Indian cooking

For vegetarians, beans, dals and lentils constitute an important source of nutrition—they provide protein, complex carbohydrates, fibre and vitamins. Versatile and tasty, dals and lentils lend themselves to being used to make salads, appetizers, soups, main dishes, sides and even dessert. They work well with other foods such as grains, vegetables, herbs and spices. Lentils have been consumed since prehistoric times and they have been believed to have originated in central Asia. Traces of the earliest use of lentil seeds can be traced back to 8000 years at the archeological sites in the Middle East.

Black beans / *Urad* : It is used extensively in Indian cooking. These are black beans just like *mung* beans but lot more proteinaceous. They are cooked whole, split or washed. In south India its flour is used in making *dosa* and *idli* (staple food of southern India besides rice). Sometimes it is browned in oil and is used to flavor rice and other vegetable dishes to give them a little crunchy taste.

Split hulled black grams / *Channa dal* : Used in making *dal* in north and south and are also used in tempering to garnish rice and vegetable dishes. In ground form its uses are mentioned under 'gram flour'. They are highly recommended for people with celiac dieseases as the gram has no gluten. Daily use of black grams can cure you of diabetes, sexual dysfunction, nervous disorders, hair disorders, digestive system disorders and reheumatic afflictions.

Yellow beans /*Toor* : These small pale yellow beans cook rather quickly and are used mostly in south India to make *sambhar* and also cooked sometimes as *dal* all over India. They also make a very good base for some soups in Indian cooking. This dal is praised in Ayurvedic texts for its nutritional value and ease of digestion.

Very small red beans / *Masoor* : The whole beans are beige in color and when hulled and washed, they have pale reddish color. They do not take very long to cook. Masoor dal contain high levels of protein, including essential amino acids, isoleucine and lysine, and are an essential source of inexpensive protein diet.

Green beans / *Mung* : *Mung* beans are extensively used for bean sprouts as salads in various parts of the world. In Indian cooking they are used as whole, split or washed for making *dals*. They are dark green on the outside and light yellow on the inside. They are easily digestible and therefore given to very young children when they start their solids. They cook pretty fast and are also used for making *khichdi*. Mung beans, split, with skins removed (also known as mung dal) are held to be excellent for all three *doshas*. Easier to digest than most other beans and dals, mung dal can be taken everyday. When cooked, mung dal takes on the consistency of porridge.

Chick-peas (*Garbanzos*) / *Kabuli channa* : Chick-peas (highly proteinaceous among all the beans) are commonly used in cuisines all over the world. They are never sold split or hulled and are cooked always as whole beans. In mid-eastern cooking these are a source of many main dishes like Humus and some of their sauces and soups. In Indian cooking they are usually curried (Chick-pea Curry or *Khatta Channa*) or added to salads or *chaats* (snack).

Chick Peas

They used to take a long time to cook but pressure cooking has made it very easy to cook them. They are always preferred over other beans as a good meal for their rich protein content.

Red kidney beans / *Rajmah* : They are also quite proteinaceous and used all over the world. In western countries they are served as re-fried beans and also used in soups. In Mexican cooking, these beans play a major role in preparation of almost every dish. Kidney beans are always sold whole – and cooked as whole beans. In India they are very popular in Punjab and are called *Rajmah*. Here, they are served curried as well as in salads and some snacks. These beans can be bought in any grocery store anywhere in the world.

Whole black grams / *Channa* : Whole grams are cooked in their dry as well as green form and their curry is very popular in North of india. Dry roasted grams are sold by the vendors as "Channa Jor Garam"a delicious spicy proteinaceous snack every body likes.

Peas / *Matar dal* : Dry peas are often used to make dal and the beans are either green or yellow. Both make a very delicious preparation.

Split peas are high in protein and low in fat, The split pea is known to be a natural food source that contains some of the highest amounts of fibre. Fibre is known to help the digestive system and to make people feel full and satiated.Most of the calories come from protein and complex carbohydrates. Yellow split pea is the main ingredient of the Iranian food "khoresh gheymeh", which is served on the side of white rice in Iranian cuisine. It is also an important ingredient in the famous Kufteh Tabrizi, a kofta speciality from Northern Iran,and Yellow split peas are used to make a sweet snack in Beijing cuisine.

Black eye beans / *Lobia* : These dry beans are cooked all over India. Sometimes tender green black beans or *lobia* is also available with the vegetable vendors and their curry is more delicious than the dry beans. Its flour is used to make fritters in some parts of India.

An excellent source of calcium, folate and vitamin A. beans are the 'musical fruit' because they contain saponins to protect themselves against insects. Saponins form the sudsy foam on the surface of a cooking pot of beans. They prevent protein digestion resulting in stagnation and gas of the bowels.

Lima beans and soya beans : are usually cooked as a vegetable while they are still green and fresh. But dry beans are also curried like all other lentils. Several by-products are equally popular now, like soy sauce, tofu, soybeans etc. Lima Beans are equally nutritious and a rich source of folate, phosphorus, protein, potassium, vitamin B1, iron, magnesium, and vitamin B6. They have a high fibre content and lower the blood sugar levels while providing steady, slow-burning energy.

High in protein and used as a vegetarian and lactose alternative for many foods, soya has transcended its Asian origins to become the most widely cultivated legume across the globe. The soya bean plant is native to China, where it has been cultivated for well over 13,000 years. It was an essential crop for the ancient Chinese who regarded it a necessity for life. Soy bean is the single most beneficial food promising the health maintenance of the heart, bone, prostrate and immune system.

Lord Budha, Thailand

Appetizers and Snacks

There are many appetizers in Indian food, as Indians love to snack and munch. Afternoons are tea times and Indians love to socialize. There is always time for a small sweet and spicy snack for the guests. As is the custom, it is common practice to serve the guest with a cup of tea and some snack. The smell of spices and *chutneys* served with various appetizers activate your taste buds.

Popular snacks like *pakoras, samosas, corn puffs, cheese puffs, tapioca potato puffs, cutlets* are fritters and finger foods. You can make them by dipping the raw or cooked vegetables into spicy gram flour batter. They are then deep fried. Each of these snacks are served with a certain *chutney* like coconut, mint, tamarind or red pepper *chutney*. From the north of India comes various fruit *chaats, golgappas* (thin wafers filled with boiled chopped potatoes, chick-peas, *Tamarind chutney*, and *Zeera paani*), *dahivadas*, and the regular *chaat*. From Maharashtra and Gujarat come the *bhelpuri, poha* or *aval, dhokla, khandvi,* and *muthia*. Appetizers like *vadas, bondas, uppama,* come from the south and are proteinaceous and rich in carbohydrates as lentils and grains play a major part in their preparation. Though south Indian yet they are popular all over the country. They are served with *sambhar* and *chutney*. There are several baked and grilled snacks and in this category come the vegetarian *kebabs, cocktail paneer,* various cutlets and *tikkis*. These snacks have their origin during the Mughal times. All these snacks are served as appetizers or hors d'oeuvres and they go beautifully as a first course with any dinner of your choice.

APPETIZERS AND SNACKS

Samosa

Pastry with Spicy Filling

Serves: 24
Cooking Time: 20 Minutes

Ingredients

Pastry shells:

Vegetable oil	½ cup
All purpose flour	4 cups
Salt	as needed
Water	as needed
Carom seeds	1 tsp

Stuffing:

Vegetable oil	¼ cup
Ginger	1 Tbs
Garlic	1 Tbs
Green chilies chopped (optional)	1 tsp
Onion chopped	1 cup
Peas frozen	1½ cup
Cumin seeds	1 tsp
Salt	1½ tsp
Red pepper	1 tsp
Coriander powder	2 Tbs
Water	4 Tbs
Potatoes chopped	3 cups
Coriander leaves chopped	2 Tbs
Garam masala	½ tsp
Mango powder or *amchoor* Or	1 Tbs
Lemon juice	2 Tbs
Vegetable oil (for frying)	4 cups

Deep fried pastries filled with spiced potatoes are among the most famous snacks in Indian cuisine. Sometimes ground meat and chicken fillings are also used. These are served in restaurants all over the world. Samosa is a signature snack of India. It is famous all over the world today. It is enjoyed in a cocktail or a casual party where a small and cute version becomes a food statement. The other dumplings of this category are Italian Ravioli, Chinese potstickers, Japanese gyoza, Polish pieorgi, Turkish manti, Russian pelmeni, Ethiopian tihlo, Ghanian fufu.

Method

1. Rub the oil into the flour, add carom seeds, salt and water and knead into smooth dough (uncooked tortilla dough) and leave it covered with a wet cloth.

   (Step 1 can be avoided if uncooked tortillas are used.)

2. Heat the oil and add the chopped ginger, garlic, chilies, and chopped onions and fry for few minutes until the onions turn slightly brown and add the peas. Stir for a while and add the cumin seeds and when they stop popping add the salt, red pepper and coriander powder and stir well.

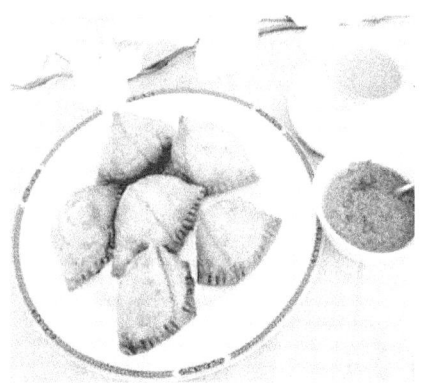

3. Mix 4 Tbs of water and cook on slow heat and then add the chopped cooked potatoes and add the coriander leaves, *garam masala*, *amchoor* or the lemon juice, stir 4–5 min and cool.

4. Divide the dough (prepared as in Step 1) into 24 equal pieces. Shape them into balls, dredge them with the dry flour and roll them into rounds 4–6 inch in diameter as thin as possible. Cut each into 2 halves. Moisten the edges of each half. Hold one of these from its two extremes, keeping the arc of the circle downward and fold it over, so that they meet each other and form a cone opposite the centre of the arc. Coat the edges with the little paste made from flour and water.

5. Fill the cone thus formed with a tablespoon of the stuffing. Seal by pinching the edges all around and decorate with very small scallops. Set them aside in a large deep dish lined with wax paper to be fried. Cover them with a slightly wet paper towel.

6. Heat the oil to 150°C or 300°F in a deep frying pan and fry the *samosas* till crisp and golden in colour. If the *samosas* are turning brown too fast, lower the heat and cook them till they brown slowly. Serve with mint *chutney*, tamarind *chutney* or ketchup. They make a superb appetizer.

Vegetable Pakora

Vegetable Fritters

Serves: 8-10
Cooking Time: 15 Minutes

Ingredients

Gram or split-pea flour	4 cups
Salt	1½ tsp
Red pepper	1½ tsp
Coriander powder	1½ Tbs
Cumin powder	1 tsp
Garam masala	1 tsp
Onions chopped	1 cup
Ginger chopped	2 Tbs
Garlic chopped	2 Tbs
Green chillies chopped	2 Tbs
Water	as needed
Carom seed or *Ajwain*	1 ½ tsp
Pomegranate seeds powder	2 Tbs
Or	
Lemon Juice	2–3 Tbs
Coriander leaves chopped	2 Tbs
Baking powder	¼ tsp
Oil for frying	4 cups
Cauliflower florets 2" long	1 cup
Slices of eggplant	1 cup
Sliced Zucchini 2" long and 1/8" thick	1 cup
Slices of peeled potatoes	1 cup
Ricotta cheese slices (well drained and firm cut into slices) or *paneer* rubbed with salt, red pepper, *garam masala* and *amchoor*	20
Spinach chopped	1 cup

These spicy vegetable fritters made in a gram flour batter are among the most favourite and common appetizers of Indian cuisine. They are crispy, crunchy and are traditionally served with tamarind or mint *chutney*. Ketchup can be substituted for the *chutney*. It is a delightful appetizer for every occasion. Similar versions of these fritters (tempuras) are common in Japanese and other Pacific cuisines.

Method

1. Transfer gram flour to a medium size bowl.
2. Add salt, red pepper, coriander powder, cumin powder, *garam masala*, and ½ cup of chopped onions, ginger, garlic and green chilies. Add enough water to make a thick batter. Beat a little and add *ajwain* (carom seeds), ground pomegranate seeds powder, or lemon juice, green coriander leaves and baking powder.
3. Stir the mixture well. Heat the oil to about 300°F in a deep frying pan or a fryer. Do not overheat the oil. Coat the cauliflower florets, eggplant slices, zucchini slices and the potato slices with the batter by dipping them in the batter one by one and deep-fry them in the heated oil until light brown. Similarly coat the cheese slices with batter and fry them. Take them out with a slotted cooking spoon onto a platter lined with paper towels.
4. As soon as the slices of vegetables and cheese slices are all fried add the remaining onions and chopped spinach into the remaining batter and stir the mixture. Drop tablespoons

full of this mixture into the hot oil. A number of them can be cooked at the same time. Fry them on medium heat until golden brown. Take the *pakoras* out of the oil with a slotted spoon onto a platter lined with a few layers of paper towel.

5. Serve them hot with mint *chutney*, tamarind *chutney* or ketchup.

Note: Slow frying of the *pakoras* makes them crisp. If you feel that your pakoras need to be fluffier add a pinch of enos fruit salt.

Samosas - Page 3

Pakoras - Page 5

Dal ki Tikki - Page 14

Tori Vadas - Page 20

Dahi Vada and Pakori - Page 21

Dhokla - Page 26

Bhelpoori - Page 37

Bharwan Khumb - Page 41

Palak Pakora

Spinach Fritters

Serves: 8-10
Cooking Time: 15 Minutes

Ingredients

Gram flour	2 cups
Water	enough to make a thick batter
Salt	to taste
Red pepper	1 tsp
Garam masala	1 tsp
Pomegranate seeds powder	1 Tbs
Baking powder/Fruit salt	a pinch
Cabbage chopped	1 cup
Fenugreek leaves chopped	1 cup
Spinach chopped	2 cups
Ginger chopped	1 Tbs
Garlic chopped	1 Tbs
Green chilies chopped	1 Tbs
Onions chopped	1 cup
Carom seeds (*ajwain*)	1 tsp
Coriander leaves chopped	2 Tbs
Oil	2 Tbs
Lemon juice	2 Tbs
Coriander seeds crushed	1 Tbs
Oil for frying	4 cups
Vegetable oil or *ghee*	2 Tbs

These fritters are made by mixing chopped cabbage, spinach and fenugreek leaves into spicy gram flour batter and deep-fried. They are so crunchy and delicious that they are often favoured over even the vegetable fritters.

Method

1. Mix together gram flour, salt, red pepper, *garam masala*, pomegranate seeds powder, and baking powder.

2. Add the clean and well drained chopped cabbage, chopped fenugreek leaves, chopped spinach, chopped ginger, garlic, green chilies, onions, carom seeds, chopped coriander leaves, oil or *ghee*, crushed coriander seeds and lemon juice. Mix everything and add water to make a thick batter and beat the batter gently to make it smooth. If the batter gets thin, add more gram flour as needed.

3. Heat the oil to 180°C or 350°F in a heavy-bottom wok or a fryer. Add the batter a large spoonful at a time into the hot oil. A number of *pakoras* can be cooked at a time. Do not overheat the oil and keep the same temperature. Fry the *pakoras* until light golden brown. Remove them with a slotted spoon on a paper towel and drain the oil.

4. They go great as appetizers or as a teatime snack and are served with mint *chutney* or tamarind *chutney*. This is one of the most

Note: If crisper *pakoras* are desired, add 2 Tbs of rice flour to the batter. Pakoras in the shape of round balls can also be made by making a very thick batter.

Makki ke Vade

Corn Fritters

Serves: 6-8
Cooking Time: 10-15 Minutes

These crunchy corn fritters are a very popular appetizer from the state of Maharashtra and have been adopted by almost everyone around the country, because of their light, fluffy and creamy taste. Corn is added to a dough of all-purpose flour flavoured with roasted cumin, green onions, chopped bell pepper and fenugreek leaves and a few more spices. Corn fritters are also popular in European and American cuisines.

Ingredients

Ingredient	Amount
All purpose flour	1½ cups
Rice flour	½ cup
Baking powder	2 tsp
Salt	1 tsp
Milk	1½ cup
Egg beaten	1
Vegetable oil or *ghee* (melted)	2 Tbs
Cumin seeds or powder roasted	1 tsp
Garam masala	1 tsp
Red bell pepper finely chopped	½ cup
Fenugreek leaves	1 Tbs
Green chilies chopped	1 tsp
Frozen thawed corn	1 cup
Green onions chopped	½ cup
Cilantro leaves chopped	½ cup
Ginger fresh chopped	1 tsp
Vegetable oil (for frying)	4 cups

Note: It might sound surprising to some people who think corn as a plain, staple food, or a snack food, or a summertime party food, that corn is actually a unique phytonutrient-rich food that provides us with well-documented antioxidant benefits. These anti-oxidant phyto-nutrients are provided by all varieties of corn. Corn is a good source of panto-thenic acid, phosphorus, niacin, dietary fibre, manganese, and vitamin B6. Its ability to provide many B-complex vitamins including vitamins B1, B5 and folic acid, and its notable protein content (about 5-6 grams per cup), corn is a food that would be expected to provide blood sugar benefits. Corn fritters are very popular all over America, Europe and Asia.

Method

1. Mix together the all-purpose flour, rice flour, baking powder, and salt. Beat together milk, egg, and *ghee* or oil in a separate bowl. Pour the milk and egg mixture into the flour mixture and beat it smooth with a fork or with hand and remove any lumps the batter may have.

2. Add the cumin seeds, *garam masala*, chopped bell pepper, fenugreek leaves, green chilies, thawed corn, green onions, cilantro leaves, and ginger and stir them well into the batter.

3. Heat the oil in a frying pan to 350°F and drop the batter in spoonfuls into the oil, few at a time. Fry them on medium-low heat until they are golden brown (about 2–3 minutes).

4. Take them out with a slotted spoon onto a paper towel and drain the excess oil.

5. Serve them with a mint *chutney* or tamarind *chutney* as an appetizer or with a meal.

Channa Dal Vada

Chick Pea Fritters

Serves: 4
Cooking Time: 5-7 Minutes

Ingredients

Channa dal/chick peas/ Fava beans	1 cup
Piece Ginger	1 Inch
Cloves Garlic	5-6
Green chilies	5
Fennel seeds	1 tsp
Onion	1
Coriander and mint leaves chopped/ each	2 Tbs
Cumin powder	1 tsp
Salt as needed	
Lemon Juice	1 Tbs
Rice flour/ semolina or cream of wheat	1 Tbs
Garammasala	½ tsp
Red pepper	½ tsp
Curry leaves or a sprig	2-4
Oil for frying	4 cups

For the dipping Sauce

Greek yogurt	2 Tbs
Green chili	½ tsp
Cilantro	1 Tbs
Salt to taste	
Pinch of black salt	
Pinch of sugar	

These fritters are often prepared as snack or appetizer and can be easily made at home. In the eastern part of India like in the State of Odisa they are available on a roadside eatery and are called "piaji" and they are sold dipped in yellow peas curry (ghuguni) with chopped onions sprinkled with limejuice and chopped coriander leaves. In the south of India they are served with Sambhar and chutney. Mere mention of them almost transports you to the rainy, stormy evenings that would turn fragrant with these fresh out of the oil, crisp, spicy and completely wholesome fritters accompanied with puffed rice and onions marinated with lemon juice and green chilies. Channa dal fritters or "Piaji" has almost the same crispy goodness that you will find in Falafel (the Middle-eastern seasoned fritters made with chick peas and/ or Fava beans) a great favourite of vegetarians in America .

Method

1. Soak channa dal for 3-4 hours. Drain the water completely and grind the dal coarsely.
2. Grind ginger, garlic, chilies and fennel seeds coarsely and mix in it finely chopped onion, coriander, mint, leaves, Cumin powder, salt, Lemon juice, rice flour garam masala, red pepper and curry leaves and set it aside.
3. Keep a bowl with water and wet both hands. Make equal sized balls from the mixture.
4. In the meantime heat oil in a wok or fryer. Shape each ball to flat patties of medium thickness.
5. Deep fry in hot oil until golden brown in colour while turning in between. Also lower the heat to cook to ensure even cooking inside and out. Drain on paper towel.

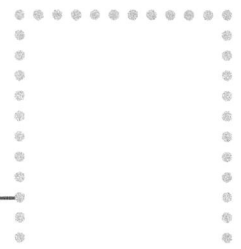

6. Serve with the dipping sauce (Recipe below).

Method

The Dipping Sauce

1. Beat the yogurt smooth and mix in chopped chili, cilantro, salt black salt and sugar. Stir well and serve with the Vadas.

Note: You can also add 1 or 2 spoons of green peas along with channa dal while soaking besides adding spinach, corn, cabbage, beetroot, carrot or mixed vegetable.

Red chori or Red beans are also used to make similar vadas or Fritters. They can also be served with dipping sauce.

APPETIZERS AND SNACKS

Urad Dal Vada

Urad Dal Fritters

Serves: 4-6
Cooking Time: 10 Minutes

Ingredients

Black eyed split and hulled beans soaked	1 cup
Rice flour as needed	
Ginger fresh chopped	1 Tbs
Green chilies fresh (medium hot) finely chopped	2–3
Curry leaves chopped	2 Tbs
Onions chopped	2 Tbs
Baking soda	a pinch
Garlic chopped	1 Tbs
Black pepper corns	½ tsp
Salt	1 tsp
Asafoetida powder	½ tsp
Water as needed	
Oil for Frying	4 cups

A very popular south Indian appetizer made with a base of split hulled black lentil (*urad dal*) batter. No festive occasion in south India is complete without them. They are usually served with *sambhar* and *chutney* to make a complete meal.

Method

1. Soak the *urad dal* in water (enough to cover 1 inch above the beans) for at least 2–3 hours or overnight. Drain the water and grind them with help of water and transfer the batter to a deep salad bowl. Keep the batter rather thick. Add rice flour to make batter thick to make patties. Mix well. Beat the batter with a hard beater to make if fluffy.

2. Add the chopped ginger, chopped green chilies, curry leaves, squeezed onions, a pinch of baking soda, garlic chopped, pepper corns, salt and asafoetida and whip it well to mix it (about 2–3 minutes). Heat the oil in a wok at 350°F.

3. Shape a patty 2" in diameter and ½ inch thick on the palm of your greased hand and stick a finger in the middle to make a hole (it looks like a small doughnut). Drop it in the hot oil with the help of an oiled spatula. Cook slowly on medium heat (2–3 minutes). Several of them can be cooked at the same time. Take care that they do not stick with each other.

4. Fry until golden brown. Remove them from the oil with a slotted large spoon and place onto a platter lined with paper towel to drain excess oil.

5. Serve hot with coconut *chutney*, *channa dal chutney*, or any *chutney* of your choice.

Note: These *vadas* are often stringed into a garland and offered to the lord Hanuman in temples and shrines in south India.

Aloo ki Tikki

Potato Cutlets

Serves: 6-8
Cooking Time: 10 Minutes

Ingredients	
Potatoes	2 lbs
Arrow-root flour	2 Tbs
All purpose flour	2 Tbs
Salt	1 tsp
Ginger	1 Tbs
Onions chopped	1 cup
Garlic	1 Tbs
Green chilies (optional) chopped	2
Vegetable oil	4 Tbs
Cumin seeds	1 tsp
Channa dal soaked overnight	½ cup
Green peas	½ cup
Dry fenugreek leaves	1 Tbs
Red pepper	½–1 tsp
Coriander powder	1 Tbs
Salt as needed	
Garam masala	½ tsp
Water as needed	
Green coriander leaves chopped	1 Tbs
Oil for Frying	4 cups

One of the most popular snack of India. Freshly prepared widely by vendors on hot skillets on street corners. They are very popular among the North Indians. These potato patties stuffed with curried lentils, peas, onions and spices are very delicious. This north Indian snack is mostly favoured as a light teatime snack. They also serve as an appetizer and are served with mint or tamarind *chutney*.

Method

1. Boil the potatoes and peel them. Mix 2 Tbs of arrow-root flour, salt. Stir and mash smooth.

2. Cook the chopped onion, ginger, garlic and green chilies in a skillet in 2 Tbs of oil until light brown and add the cumin seeds. Wait till they pop. Now add the soaked and washed *channa dal* and stir-fry until light brown. Add the peas, dry fenugreek leaves, red pepper, coriander powder, salt, *garam masala* and water, and cook until the *channa dal* is tender. Add the chopped coriander leaves and set aside.

3. Shape the mashed potatoes into balls and stuff them with 1 tsp full of peas and spiced *dal* mixture and flatten them into round or oval patties. Making sure that none of the

stuffing is showing outside the mashed potatoes covering. Set aside.
4. Make a paste with allpurpose flour and a little water and roll the cutlets in this paste and then roll them in bread crumbs. Set them aside. Deep fry them. But if you prefer not to deep fry then follow step 5.
5. Heat a large iron skillet or a pancake maker and cover the surface with a layer of oil. Heat for a minute. Place the patties on the hot oiled skillet and pan-fry them until dark golden brown. Serve them with mint or tamarind *chutney*.

Arrow-root Plant

Note: Arrow-root plant has been in use since times unknown. It is called the obedience plant (*Maranta arundinacea*). It is found in America and some of its species are found in India as well. The plants have tuberous roots containing large amounts of starch. The main use of the arrow-root is as a thickening agent. The rhizomes are peeled, grated and soaked in water. The water turns milky-white and the residue of this milky water is dried and used as an arrow-root starch. It is a white powder similar in texture as corn starch but has lot more potential as a thickening agent. It thickens at a lower temperature and it is clear without any flavour. It also grows in the West Indies. The natives use the paste from its powder to remove poison from those wounded by poisoned arrows, hence the name arrow-root. Its starch is easily digestible and is used to make cookies for infants. It is made into noodles by the Korean people and they also use it in puddings, cakes, hot sauces and jellies. Arrow-root flour is also a great replacement for people who are allergic to gluten found in wheat flour. This starchy powder besides being used in cooking is also used as a baby powder and has been used for making paper.

Dal ki Tikki

Black Bean Patties/Burgers

Serves: 4-6
Cooking Time: 15 Minutes

You will never want to eat frozen veggie burgers again. These are so easy, and you'll be proud to have created such a vegetarian delight. Spiced up with chili sauce, cumin, garlic and chili powder, these quick and easy black bean burgers will make you forget all about frozen, packaged ones.

Ingredients

Can Black beans, drained and rinsed	1 (16Oz.)
Green bell pepper, cut into 2 inch pieces	½
Onion, cut into wedges	½
Cloves garlic, peeled	3
Ginger chopped	1 Tbs
Chopped cilantro	3 Tbs
Egg	1
Chili powder	1 Tbs
Cumin powder	1 Tbs
Thai chili sauce or hot tomato sauce	1-tsp
Bread crumbs	½ cup
Sesame seed buns	6

Garnishes

Mayonaise, Avacado slices, cheese slices onion and tomato slices

For the Spicy Chipotle Mayo

Light mayonnaise	3½ Tbs
Canned chipotle in adobo sauce	1 Tbs

Method

1. Mix the mayonnaise and canned chipotle in adobo sauce and serve with the Burgers.

Method

1. In a medium bowl, mash black beans with a fork until thick and pasty.
2. In a food processor, finely chop bell pepper, onion, and garlic, ginger. Then stir into mashed beans.
3. In a small bowl, stir together egg, chili powder, cumin, and chili sauce.
4. Stir the egg mixture into the mashed beans. Mix in bread crumbs until the mixture is sticky and holds together. Divide mixture into four patties.
5. Freeze at least 2 hours before cooking or keep frozen until ready to cook.

   Heat a lightly sprayed skillet to medium heat and cook frozen burgers about 7 minutes on each side.
6. If grilling, preheat grill over medium heat, and lightly oil a sheet of aluminum foil. Grill 7-8 minutes on each side or you can bake in the oven at 375°F on a lightly oiled baking sheet.
7. Serve the burgers on a sesame seed bun or any bun of your choice with a slice of cheese, slice of onion and tomato or avocado topped with mayonnaise, relish or other garnishes of your choice. Hamburger can now be served with french fries or onion rings or cole slaw.

   Burgers can also be served with the spicy Chipotle sauce or mint chutney. Makes about 4-6 patties.

APPETIZERS AND SNACKS

Bonda

Potato Croquettes

Serves: 8-10
Cooking Time: 15 Minutes

Ingredient	
For the filling:	
Potatoes (medium) boiled and mashed	6
Onions chopped	1 cup
Ginger chopped	1 Tbs
Garlic	1 Tbs
Green chilies chopped (optional)	1 tsp
Vegetable oil	3 Tbs
Cumin seeds*	1 tsp
Salt	1 tsp
Red pepper (optional)	1 tsp
Lemon juice	1 Tbs
Or	
Amchoor	1 Tbs
Raisins*	2 Tbs
Green coriander leaves chopped	¼ cup
Asafoetida (optional)	¼ tsp
Cashew nuts (crushed)	2 Tbs
Coriander powder	1½ Tbs

*You can substitute the cumin seeds and raisins with *urad dal* and mustard seeds in the filling to give it a South Indian flavour.

These well spiced potato balls are dipped into a batter of gram flour, deep-fried and served with *chutney* of your choice. It is a great snack for any time. They are made with variations in different parts of the country. Made crunchy in the south by adding *urad dal* and mustard seeds, in Gujarat made sweet and sour with raisins and lemon juice, but in the north they like to add to this sweet and sour potato mixture, green coriander and cumin seeds that make it quite refreshing. Nevertheless they are light and delicious for any occasion.

The potato is a nutritional powerhouse in terms of the four major micronutrients, but more importantly, it is probably the most universally-loved food; people are passionate about potatoes. When a cook looks for a vegetable side dish with that magic mix of value, versatility and nutritional appeal, they see potatoes. They're the perfect, universally loved canvas for tapping into today's hottest culinary trend. Potato is a source of subsistence for millions and millions of people around the world. Potato is the "second bread" and has saved many populations from starvations especially in Europe.

Method

For Filling:

1. Boil and mash the potatoes and set aside.
2. Cook the onions, ginger, garlic, green chilies in 3 Tbs of oil for 2 minutes and add the cumin seeds* until they crackle and add the

For the batter:

Gram flour sifted	2 cups
Salt	½ tsp
Red pepper	½ tsp
Rice flour	½ cup
Oil for frying	4 cups
Water to make the batter	2 cups

salt, red pepper, lemon juice, raisins, chopped green coriander leaves, cashew nuts (crushed), coriander powder and the mashed potatoes. Stir and cook the mixture for 2 minutes. Cool and make them into balls the size of walnuts and set them aside in a deep flat pan in a single layer and cover them with a plastic wrap.

Batter preparation:

3. Make a batter by mixing the gram flour, rice flour, salt, pepper, and the asafoetida powder and water. If the batter is too thick add a little more water.

4. Heat the oil in a deep wok at 325–350°F. Dip the mashed potato balls in the batter and fry them in the heated oil, few at a time. Keep the temperature down so that they take about 3–5 minutes to turn golden brown.

5. Take them out with a slotted spoon and drain them out on a paper towel. Serve them with tomato *chutney*, tamarind *chutney*, mint *chutney* or any other *chutney* of your choice. Makes excellent teatime snack or an appetizer.

Arbi Tikka Masala

Grilled Yams in Peanut Sauce

Serves: 4-6
Cooking Time: 10 Minutes

Ingredients

Boiled yam (medium size) peeled	12

Marinade:

Yogurt	½ cup
Peanuts	¼ cup
Tamarind	½ tsp
Ginger chopped	1 tsp
Olive oil or *ghee*	1 Tbs
Garlic chopped	1 tsp
Salt	1½ tsp
Turmeric powder	1 tsp
Red pepper	1 tsp
Coriander powder	1 Tbs

Tempering (*Tadka*):

Vegetable oil	2 Tbs
Mustard seeds	1 tsp
Cumin seeds	½ tsp
Red pepper (dry) crushed	1 tsp
Curry leaves chopped	6–8
Amchoor	1 tsp
Garam masala	½ tsp
Coriander leaves chopped	2 Tbs

Boiled and peeled yam marinated in spicy peanut sauce and grilled or baked in the oven with a southern flavour of curry leaves and mustard seeds. It make a very nice addition to any dinner as an appetizer or an accompaniment. Yam leaves wrapped in a filling of spiced rice and pan-fried are a delicacy in the south.

Method

1. Boil the yam and peel them. Flatten them between your palms and set them aside. If the yam size is too large, cut them in ½ inch pieces and then flatten them between your palms. Blend yogurt, peanuts, tamarind, ginger, oil, garlic, salt, turmeric powder, red pepper, coriander powder, in a blender and grind smooth.

2. Add the yam to the above marinade and coat them well. Transfer them to the oven in a baking pan with a grilling rack and bake at 400°F for about 15–20 minutes, until they are light brown.

3. Remove from the oven and set them aside. Heat the oil in a non stick small frying pan and add the mustard seeds, cumin seeds and wait till they start popping. Then add the dry red pepper, curry leaves, and stir well. Add the *amchoor* and *garam masala*, and mix well. Add the cooked yam and stir to coat the yam *tikka* on both sides. Sprinkle with chopped coriander leaves. Serve as appetizer or a vegetable accompaniment.

Paneer Cocktail

Fried Cheese Cubes

Serves: 8-10
Cooking Time: 15 Minutes

Ingredients

Cumin seeds	2 tsp
Sesame seeds ground, roasted	1 Tbs
Oil for frying	3 cups
Ricotta cheese drained of all water or *paneer* slab cut into one inch long and ½ inch thick pieces	2 lb
Mustard seeds	½ tsp
Vegetable oil or *ghee* (for cooking)	2–3 Tbs
Ginger chopped	1 Tbs
Garlic chopped	1 Tbs
Turmeric powder	¾ tsp
Coriander powder ground	1 Tbs
Salt	1 tsp
Red pepper	1 tsp
White onion sliced vertically in strings	1 cup
Bell pepper sliced in thin strips	½ cup
Water	1 cup
Garam masala	½ tsp
Cilantro leaves finely chopped	2 Tbs
Amchoor (use if serving as an appetizer)	1 Tbs
Green onions chopped	2 Tbs
Lemon juice	1 Tbs

Note: Drain the water from the Ricottacheese by wrapping it in a clean fine clothand leaving it under a heavy weight for couple of hours.

Deep fried *paneer pieces* or ricotta cheese cubes when cooked with chopped green bell pepper strips, ginger, garlic, lemon juice and spices are delicious and healthy. These are quite easy to fix too. Serve them with any wet curry and bread or best as an appetizer.

Method

1. Roast 1 tsp cumin seeds and sesame seeds on a hot skillet (*tawa*) and grind them with a mortar and pestle. Set them aside. Heat the oil for frying in a deep saucepan or a fryer. Cut the cheese (*paneer*) slab into one inch cubes. Deep fry the cubes until slightly brown and take them out of the oil onto a platter lined with a paper towel. Drain the oil and set them aside.

2. Heat the oil for cooking in a deep large thick-bottom saucepan. Add the remaining cumin and mustard seeds, and when they start popping, add the ginger and green chilies. Fry for 2 minutes and then add the garlic. Stir and fry for 2 more minutes.

3. Lower the heat and add the turmeric, coriander powder, salt and red pepper. Mix well. Add the deep fried cheese (*paneer*) cubes, onions and bell pepper. Stir to mix and coat the cubes well.

4. Add the water and cover the pan with a lid. Let it simmer for at least 5 minutes or until the cheese (*paneer*) cubes become soft but still holding their shape.

5. Add the *garam masala*, ground roasted cumin, sesame seeds, cilantro leaves, *amchoor*, chopped green onions and the lemon juice.
6. Stir gently to coat the cubes with spices and serve as an appetizer.

Note: You can also string the uncooked cubes of paneer, bellpeppers, baby tomatoes and mushrooms after coating them in a moxtures of spices (salt, red lepper, coriander powder, amachoor, and lemon juice and grill them as Kabobs as shown in the picture. Serve them sprinkled with garam masala, ground roasted cumin powder, cilatnro leaves chopped green onions, and lemon juice. They make a great appetizer that way too. Serve with mint chutney, ketchup or tamarindchutney. They will make a great snackbefore dinner..

Tori Vadas

Zucchini Bites

Serves: 4-6
Cooking Time: 10 Minutes

Ingredients

Olive oil	1 Tbs
Onion chopped fine	1
Chopped ginger	1 tsp
Finely chopped garlic and Green chili each	1 tsp
Cumin seeds	½ tsp
Carrot chopped fine	1 Large
Zucchini chopped fine	1 Large
Salt	1 Tsp
Red pepper	½ tsp
Garammasala	½ tsp
Cilantro chopped	1 Tbs
Eggs	3 Large
Cream	¼ cup
Cheese grated (Cheddar or parmesan)	1 cup
Self-rising flour	½ cup

These savoury zucchini and cheese mini muffins are nice to serve with pasta, chili, or soup, or as appetizer. Whip up these delicious zucchini bites in a jiffy. They can be served warm or at room temperature. Even children who do not like zucchini will love them and they would disappear quickly from the serving plate. When you have an abundance of zucchini in your garden make these spicy muffins and they are sure to please everyone. Much healthier than fried zucchini, these crispy little bites make a yummy snack or side dish!

Method

1. Preheat the oven at 350°F and grease a mini muffins pan.
2. Heat the oil in a small cooking pan of fry pan and sauté the onions, ginger, garlic and green chilies. Wait till these are slightly brown and add the cumin seeds and let them crackle.
3. Add the grated carrot and zucchini. Stir and fry for about 2 minute. Add the salt, red pepper, garam masala and cilantro. Stir and set the mixture aside to cool.
4. Beat eggs, cream and cheese in a medium size bowl. Stir in the zucchini mixture and the flour. Mix it well to evenly distribute the ingredients.
5. Grease a muffin pan and spoon mixture into the muffin holes and bake 15-20 minutes.
6. Serve with ketchup or any chutney or dip of your choice.

Dahi Vada and Pakori

Lentils Fritters Soaked in Spicy Yogurt

Serves: 8-10
Cooking Time: 15-20 Minutes

Ingredients

Urad dal and *mung dal* (each) soaked overnight	1 lb
Baking soda	$1/8$ tsp
Cashew nuts or raisins	2 Tbs
Vegetable oil (for frying)	4 cups
Yogurt well beaten and sweetened	4 cups
Cumin seeds ground, roasted	1 Tbs
Salt	1 tsp
Red pepper	1 tsp
G*aram masala*	1 tsp
Tamarind chutney	1 cup
Coriander leaves chopped	2 Tbs
Chaat masala	4 Tbs
Pomegranate seeds for decorating	1 cup

Urad dal that is used in making these dumpling is used extensively in Indian cooking. It is very proteinaceous and is an integral part of our food everyday. It is cooked whole, split or washed amd is made into dal. In south India its flour is used in making dosa and idli (staple food of southern India besides rice). Sometimes it is browned in oil and is used as tempering to flavor rice and other vegetable dishes. Similarly Mung beans that are used are alsoan important part of our meal on a daily basis Sometimes as dal sometimes as Khichadi orsometimes fried as a snack.

Dahi vada refers to a very popular Indian snack which is believed to have originated in south India. It is mostly consumed as an appetizer but it can also serve as a side dish in a meal if consumed in large quantities.

Method

Dahi Vada:

1. Wash and grind the *urad dal* and add a pinch of baking soda to the batter.
2. Beat the batter well and set it aside. Keep the batter thick so that the *urad dal vadas* can be shaped into half circles with a cashew nut or a raisin placed inside before shaping. Beating the batter is very important.
3. Heat the oil to about 150°C or 300°F and fry on low heat until light golden brown.
4. Take them out of the oil with a slotted spoon and drain them on a paper towel.

Mung Pakori:

5. When making *mung dal pakoris*, grind the *dal* and prepare the batter as for *urad dal*, shape them round by dropping tablespoonfuls of dough into the hot oil and frying them until light brown. Make sure that the oil does not

get too hot. Soak the *urad dal vadas* as well as *mung dal pakoris* for 5–7 minutes in warm salted water. Squeeze them gently to remove the water and excess fat.

6. Arrange them in a serving dish. Just before serving pour the whisked yogurt on top so as to almost cover them with yogurt. Sprinkle them with salt, red pepper, *garam masala* and ground roasted cumin powder. Before serving top it all with tamarind *chutney*, chopped coriander leaves and fresh pomegranate seeds. They are a stunning presentation for any party or festive occasion. Serve *chaat masala* on the side.

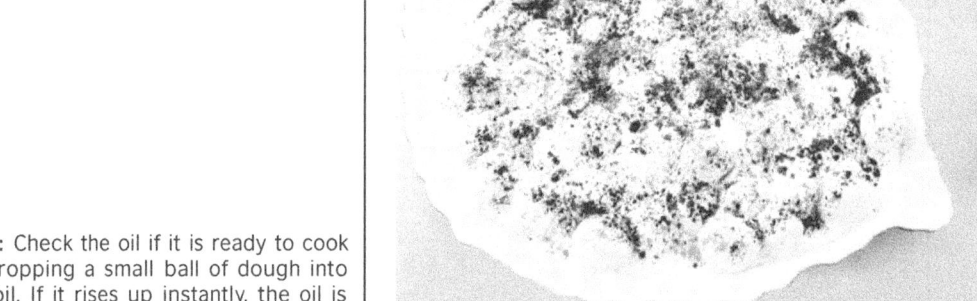

Note: Check the oil if it is ready to cook by dropping a small ball of dough into the oil. If it rises up instantly, the oil is ready to fry.

Uppama

Cream of Wheat Flavoured with Nuts and Spices

Serves: 4-6
Cooking Time: 15 Minutes

Ingredients

Ingredient	Amount
Vegetable oil or *ghee*	¼ cup
Mustard seeds	1 tsp
Cumin seeds	1 tsp
Urad dal	1 Tbs
Yellow spilt peas	1 Tbs
Cashew nuts or peanuts (crushed)	2 Tbs
Uncooked cream of wheat (*Suji*)	1 cup
Onion chopped	½ cup
Ginger chopped	1 tsp
Garlic chopped	1 tsp
Green chilies chopped (optional)	1 Tbs
Fresh cubed potatoes chopped	½ cup
Green peas frozen	¼ cup
Curry leaves chopped	6–8
Red pepper dry (broken in half)	1
Coriander powder	1 tsp
Red pepper	½-1 tsp
Salt to taste or	1–2 tsp
Coconut powder	1 Tbs

One of the most popular south Indian snacks made out of cream of wheat flavoured with mustard seeds and cashew nuts. A wonderful way to turn plain cream of wheat into a wholesome meal. It is quite nutritious. It can be served as a light lunch with yogurt or *raita*.

Method

1. Heat one Tbs of *ghee* or oil in a large frying pan and add the mustard seeds. When they stop popping, add the *urad dal*, yellow split peas and the cashew nuts or peanuts and cook till they start turning brown. Remove with slotted spoon in a bowl and set them aside.

2. Transfer the cream of wheat (*suji*) into the frying pan and fry till light brown (about 10 minutes) on medium-low heat and set it aside.

3. Cook the onions, ginger, garlic, and green chilies in the remaining oil on medium-low heat in a wok and fry till the onions are soft. Add the chopped potatoes and peas. Fry 2–3 minutes and add the curry leaves, cumin seeds, broken whole red peppers, coriander powder, red pepper, salt and keep stirring to mix it well. Add the coconut powder and stir till it starts to turn slightly brown.

4. Add the fried *suji* and fried nuts mixture. Mix everything well. Add the boiling water slowly and keep stirring to mix until all the water is gone. Add more water if necessary. Stir in between to make sure that the cream of wheat is not sticking. Cook till it does not look grainy and all grains are soft and cooked.

Water preferably boiled	3½ cup
Coriander leaves chopped	1 Tbs
Lemon juice to taste	1 Tbs
Garam masala	½–¾ tsp

5. Keep stirring until the mixture separates from the pan.
6. Remove from heat and serve topped with coriander leaves and lemon juice as a breakfast or teatime snack if you wish. It is usually served with *sambhar,* coconut, or *channa dal chutney.*

Note: You can also add ½ cup of shredded carrots with ½ cup of chopped tomatoes at the same time you are frying the potatoes. Cashew nuts can be substituted with fried unsalted peanuts or a tablespoon of raisins. Instant cooked cream of wheat from a local grocery store can be substituted for the *suji.* Less frying time will be needed to fry the cooked cream of wheat. Follow same steps as mentioned above.

Poha (or Aval) Khatta Meetha

Spicy Rice Flakes

Serves: 4-6
Cooking Time: 10 Minutes

Ingredients

Rice flakes or *poha*	2 cups
Water (to soak the *poha*)	
Ghee or clarified butter	3 Tbs
Cumin seeds	1 tsp
Mustard seeds	½ tsp
Shallots finely chopped	½ cup
Garlic chopped	1 tsp
Ginger chopped	1 tsp
Green chilies chopped	1 tsp
Potatoes (medium) finely chopped	1
Cashew nuts roasted, chopped	2 Tbs
Asafoetida	½ tsp
Turmeric powder	½ tsp
Coriander powder	1 tsp
Red pepper	½ tsp
Curry leaves	4–6
Salt	to taste
Fresh lemon juice	2 Tbs
Raisins	2 Tbs
Coconut freshly grated (optional)	½ cup
Or	
Coconut dry powder	2 Tbs
Coriander leaves freshly chopped (optional)	1 Tbs

Before cooking, the *poha* is soaked briefly and handled delicately to make a very delicious teatime snack. It is combined with cashew nuts or peanuts and shallots and is flavoured with garlic, ginger, grated fresh coconut, green chilies, lemon juice, salt and other spices like asafoetida. The aroma of the preparation fills the environment. It can be served with a *raita*, *chutney* or a simple vegetable stir-fry. Try this specialty from the state of Maharashtra.

Method

1. Transfer the *poha* to a bowl and cover it with water for 5 minutes.
2. Drain the water and set the *poha* aside (do not squeeze).
3. Heat the *ghee* in a non-stick large saucepan and when hot add the cumin seeds, mustard seeds and wait till they start popping and then add the shallots, ginger, garlic and green chilies. Add fine chopped potato.
4. Fry until they are light brown and add the cashew nuts, asafoetida, turmeric powder, coriander powder, red pepper, and curry leaves.
5. Stir-fry for ½ minute and add the drained *poha*. Mix gently to coat them with spices and add the salt and lemon juice, raisins and stir the mixture.
6. Cook until the flakes become drier, cooking on low heat stirring gently for about 3–5 minutes. Moisten the *poha* with a couple of tsp of water, if needed.
7. Fold in the grated coconut and coriander leaves and fry for a minute longer. Remove from heat. Serve warm.

Dhokla

Rice and Lentil Cakes Flavoured with Cilantro

Serves: 8-10
Cooking Time: 25 Minutes

Ingredients	
Toor dal	1 cup
Green chilies	6
Yogurt	2 cups
Water as needed	
Asafoetida	¼ tsp
Lemon juice	2 tsp
Sugar	1 Tbs
Salt	1 tsp
Soya oil or any other vegetable oil	4 tsp
Fresh green methi leaves chopped	1 cup
Enos salt	1 tsp
Mustard seeds	1 tsp
Sesame seeds	1 tsp
Red whole chilies (broken)	3
Coriander leaves chopped	1 Tbs

Note: There are many types of dhokla. They can be made from rice and urad dal or pea flour, besan or only suji. Dhokla is served in several decorative ways. You can serve them as sandwiches by coating one piece with mint or tamarind *chutney* and place the other piece over it. Sprinkle with coconut powder or grated fresh coconut and serve. A sprinkle of red pepper or paprika gives it a very colourful look too.

From the state of Gujarat, comes this very fluffy and delightful snack light in texture and with an appetizing look. Made by steaming the spiced and fermented ground *Toor dal* into small cakes. *Dhokla* is enjoyed all over India. This snack is very low in calories but rich in protein. You can serve *dhokla* at mealtime or teatime or with lunch.

Method

1. Soak the *dal* overnight and grind it in an electric blender the next morning with the green chilies and yogurt and little water to a thick batter consistency. Ferment overnight.

2. Add asafoetida, lemon juice, sugar, salt, and 2 tsp of oil. Add the fenugreek leaves, Eno's fruit salt and blend to a thick pouring batter.

3. Pour immediately the batter into greased small moulds for the desired shape or into a 1–2" deep stainless steel plate, with a 4–6 inch diameter that will fit into a large saucepan. Pour water about 2 inches deep in the saucepan and place a wire rack over it. Adjust the plate with the batter or a plate with the batter filled moulds on top of the rack inside the saucepan for steaming. Boil the water. Cover the saucepan with the lid and steam until *dhokla* is done (about 15–20 minutes).

4. Heat remaining 2 tsp of oil in a skillet. Add a tsp of mustard seeds, sesame seeds and the whole red chilies to the oil, wait till the seeds start to pop. Add 2 Tbsp of water. Pour the tempering over the *dhokla*. Cut it in desired shapes. Sprinkle with coriander leaves and serve the pieces with coconut, mint or any *chutney* of your choice. It makes a very light and appealing appetizer.

Khaman Dhokla

Cream of Wheat Cakes Flavoured with Cilantro

Serves: 4-6
Cooking Time: 10 Minutes

Ingredients

Fine *suji* or cream of wheat	¼ cup
Gram flour	2 cups
Lemon juice	2 Tbs
Ginger finely chopped	1 Tbs
Green chilies finely chopped	1 Tbs
Salt	1 tsp
Sugar	1 Tbs
Asafoetida powder	¼ tsp
Yogurt	2 cups
Water as needed	
Enos fruit salt	3 tsp
Tamarind *chutney*	½ cup
Ricotta cheese beaten smooth	½ cup
Vegetable oil	2 Tbs
Mustard seeds	1 tsp
Sesame seeds	1 tsp
Green chilies (small) chopped	2
Red pepper	½ tsp
Curry leaves chopped	1 tsp
Water	2 tbs
Green coriander leaves chopped	½ cup
Grated coconut	2 tbs

Similar to Dhokla, it is a traditional Gujarati snack that cooks fast in the microwave too. It is so soft that it melts in your mouth. Makes a great appetizer. *Khaman dhokla* is different from regular *dhokla* because it is made with Besan and made fluffier by adding more baking agent.

Method

1. Mix together fine cream of wheat, gram flour, lemon juice, ginger, green chilies, salt, sugar, asafoetida powder and yogurt in a deep bowl. Mix and set aside for ½ hour. Add 3 tsp of fruit salt and stir quickly and vigrously.

2. Stir it well and pour immediately one inch layer of it into a greased 2 inch thick aluminium pan or a stainless *thali*, 6–7 in diameter. Boil 2 cups of water in a large wide cooking pan. Place a small rack in it and place the greased pan with batter over it. Cover the cooking pan and let batter steam cook for 15–20 minutes or until the *dhokla* is done. (Insert a toothpick into the centre and if it comes out clean then it is done). If using microwave oven then cook for 2 minutes in a small 5–6 inch diameter and 2 inch deep microwavable plate. Take it out of the oven. Leave it to cool for 2 minutes.

3. Transfer it onto a serving tray. Smear it with a thin layer of tamarind *chutney* and ricotta cheese. Bake another layer of *dhokla* in the same manner and put it on top of the first one. Heat the oil in a small frying pan and add a tsp of mustard seeds and when they start to crackle then add the sesame seeds. Add the asafoetida powder, green chilies 2 Tbsp of water. Remove this tempering from the fire and pour over the top of the *dhokla*. Sprinkle the top with chopped green coriander leaves grated coconut. Cut them into 2 inch squares and serve them with drinks or as a snack with your evening tea.

Gujarati Folk Dance

Papad

Spiced Lentils Wafers

Serves: 6-8
Cooking Time: 5 Minutes

Ingredients

Papad (if large then broken in halves)	10
Vegetable oil (for frying)	4 cups

You will need tongs to fry the *papdums*.

Crunchy wafers made out of washed split *urad* and *mung dal* are always made commercially as their preparation requires great amounts of skill and experience. Purchase them from an Indian grocery store and serve them either deep-fried or directly roasted on the fire. They are usually highly spiced with black pepper and red pepper though mild varieties are also available. They are usually served as an appetizer with some mild *chutney* or as a crunchy accompaniment to a full meal. A specialty of Gujarat where it is always served with a meal.

Method

1. Heat the oil to 300°F–340°F in a deep wide saucepan and make sure that the oil is ready by dropping a little piece of *papad* into the hot oil to see if the piece rises to the top.
2. Once the oil is ready, drop the broken halves into the hot oil one by one.
3. They will expand in the hot oil and turn from yellow to golden brown rather quickly.
4. Take them out immediately with tongs on a paper towel and let the oil drain. Serve as an appetizer or with your meal.

Note: Lentil papad can be cooked on direct flame also but they have to be browned carefully with the help of tongs. They can be cooked also in the microwave. Papad bring very vivid memories of how my mother and her close friends used to get together in our courtyard to roll and make fresh papad, in the afternoons. They are not only made with *urad* and *mung* beans but are also made with potatoes and tapioca. Spiced just right according to your taste they have great flavour and aroma.

Namkeen Kaju

Cocktail Cashew Nuts

Serves: 6-8
Cooking Time: 5 Minutes

Ingredients

Fresh cashew nuts	2 cups
Oil	½ cup
Cumin powder ground, roasted	1 Tbs
Black salt	½ tsp
Regular salt	½ tsp
Red pepper	1 tsp
Black pepper	½ tsp

Cashew nuts deep fried and freshly flavoured with ground roasted cumin powder, black salt, red pepper, black pepper and regular salt are unbelievably tasty. They make a very tempting snack at the bar. A great party accompaniment, that go so well with your hot drinks or party drinks.

Method

1. Heat the oil in a medium size thick-bottom skillet for a minute. Add cashew and fry them stirring continuously on low flame to prevent burning until they are golden brown.
2. Take a large sieve, set it up on a large bowl and transfer the cashews along with oil on to this sieve.
3. Save the oil. Transfer the cashew on to a plate lined with a paper towel. Sprinkle them with a mixture of ground roasted cumin powder, black salt, regular salt, red pepper and black pepper. Toss them around well to coat them with spices and cool.
4. Serve them with drinks or soda.
5. They make an excellent appetizer.

Note:
Steps 1 and 2 can be avoided by using canned roasted cashew nuts. Do not use table salt and black salt.
Step 3: The fried cashew nuts can be coated with the spices in the following manner also:
Melt a packet of unflavoured gelatin in ¼ cup of water on low heat. Add all spices and stir well. Pour this mixture over the drained cashew and coat them well with this mixture. Heat the oven and set it on warm. Transfer the cashew onto a baking tray and let them dry in the warm oven. Once dry, remove them from the oven and serve when cool.

APPETIZERS AND SNACKS

Mathri

Crunchy Spicy Crackers

Serves: 4-6
Cooking Time: 10 Minutes

Ingredients

All purpose flour (*Maida*)	2 cups
Sesame seeds	½ tsp
Cumin seeds ground roasted	½ tsp
Ajwain (carom seeds)	½ tsp
Salt	½ tsp
Red pepper	½ tsp
Baking powder	¼ tsp
Vegetable oil or *ghee*	4 Tbs
Water as needed or	¼ cup
Oil (for frying) and more if needed	

Note: Sometimes whole black pepper corns are pressed into the discs or patties before frying to give them a spicy taste.

These crisp and crunchy spicy crackers are so yummy that it is hard to stop eating them once you start. When they are cut into one inch strips and fried, they are called *Nimki*. A great appetizer to go with drinks before the dinner, they make a perfect teatime snack too. They are very easy to make and can be enjoyed alone or with a pickle or sweet *chutney*.

Method

1. Mix all purpose flour, sesame seeds, ground roasted cumin seeds, *ajwain*, salt, red pepper, baking powder, and *ghee* or oil in a deep bowl and try to make a stiff but pliable dough with ¼ cup water. Add more water if needed.

For making Nimki:

2. Divide the dough into 2 inch balls and roll them real thin like a *chappati* about $1/8$ inch thick and prick them all over with a fork. Cut them into strips with a sharp knife 2–3 inches long and ½ –¾ inch wide and set them aside. Cover them with a plastic wrap until ready to fry.

For making Mathri:

3. Cut a piece of dough as small as a walnut and roll it into a small patty about $1/8$ inch thick with a diameter of 3 inches and prick it with knife or a fork at several places to prevent it from puffing up during frying. Set the patties aside covered with a plastic wrap.

4. Heat the oil to 300°F –340°F and deep-fry these strips and *Mathris* until golden brown and crisp on medium heat, few at a time. Drain them on to a paper towel and serve them with drinks or as a coffee snack.

5. Serve them with or without pickle or *chutney* of your choice, and chai or coffee.

Chakli

Spicy Saltine Crisps

Serves: 8-10
Cooking Time: 15 Minutes

Ingredients
For the dough flour

Rice flour	2 Cups
Mung dal	½ Cup
Urad dal	½ Cup
Gram dal	½ Cup
Cumin seeds	1 tsp
Coriander seeds	1 tsp

Spices

Asafoetida	½ tsp
Chili powder	1 tsp
Butter	2 tbsp
Salt to taste	
Sesame seeds	1 Tbsp
Water to make the dough as needed	
Oil to fry	

India is a country that is almost always bursting in celebration with so many sub-cultures in different parts of the country. People get together, share sweets and gifts and enjoy much fanfare observing some aspect of their heritage/religion. Padwa is celebrated as the New Year day by Maharashtrians. The festival falls generally in the month of March or April and is always celebrated with chakli along with other delicious foods. Since it is a popular snack it is usually made during this festive season in every house. They can be made from various kinds of flours, rice, wheat or ground mung. Chakli is a great saltine to counter balance sweets that are served in an Indian party. You can also buy readymade chaklis, Even readymade chakli flour (atta) is available in the market.

Method
Flour for chakli

1. Lightly brown the rice, mung dal, urad dal, channa dal, cumin seeds and coriander seeds.
2. Grind these ingredients coarsely and set this flour mixture aside.
3. In a bowl, combine the mixture of flours, asafoetida, chili powder, butter, and salt.
4. Wash sesame seeds and add them to the flour mixture prepared above.
5. Pour water and knead to make soft dough.
6. Heat oil in a wok.
7. Press bits of dough through a chakli mould on greased firm piece of parchment paper and shape them into chakli circles. Heat the oil to medium high.

33 APPETIZERS AND SNACKS

8. Fry the chakli in the oil till crispy and brown.
9. Drain with a perforated spoon and remove.
10. Put it on a towel paper for oil to be drained from the chakli.
11. Serve after it cools down a bit. Makes a excellent snack with or without tea or coffee.

Golgappa-Paanipuri

Flour Puffs Filled with Tamarind Water

Serves: 6-8
Cooking Time: 25 Minutes

Ingredients

Cream of wheat (3 oz)	½ cup
All purpose flour (3 oz)	½ cup
Urad flour	1 Tbs
Warm water to make pliable dough	1 cup
Vegetable oil (for frying)	
Flour (for dredging)	

To serve use:

Zeera paani	1 quart
Chick-peas (boiled) or from can	2 cups
Boiled potatoes chopped	2 cups
Tamarind sweet & sour *chutney*	1 cup
Mint *chutney*	½ cup
Yogurt	1 cup

Note: Ready made Golgappas are available at all small sweets and chaat shops now. All you have to do is make the jeera pani and golgappas are ready. Use the zeera pani recipe given in this book.

Hollow small wafers of flour and cream of wheat filled with delicious tamarind water are a definite party pleaser. Ready to eat *golgappas (paani poori)* are available at your local Indian grocery store. Here is a method to make them at home.

Method

1. Knead smooth dough with the three mixed flours using water. It takes a little time in kneading and making a smooth dough.
2. Leave it covered with a wet cloth for about 20 minutes.
3. Knead again for another 5 minutes and divide into 4 equal parts.
4. Knead one part as thin as possible and cut little circles of about 1–1½ inch diameter with the help of a round 1 inch cookie cutter.
5. Spread a piece of wet cloth and place these round circles or discs on this cloth and cover them with another wet cloth.
6. Deep-fry them in oil heated between 300°F–340°F, a few at a time. They become puffed up balls of light golden colour. Remove them from the hot oil onto a large baking sheet lined with tin foil.
7. Warm the oven and place the tray in the warm oven. Leave them until they are dry.

8. Take them out of the oven and store in a cool dry place in zip lock bags. They can be stored at room temperature in these bags for a month and can be stored in the refrigerator for a few weeks.

9. Serve them to the guests, few at a time, in small snack plates with *zeera paani,* in a small cup with 2 tbsp each of canned cooked chick-peas, boiled potatoes, and tamarind *chutney,* and/or mint *chutney* and yogurt.

10. *They are enjoyed as follows*: Make a small hole with your index finger at the top of the *golgappa* and add a small piece of cooked potato, couple of boiled chick-peas, and a slight bit of tamarind *chutney,* ½ tsp of yogurt and fill it up almost ¾ with *zeera paani.* Eat it whole without breaking it. They are a delicious appetizer and when served they always cheer up the crowd.

Chaat Papri

Tortilla Chips with Tamarind Sauce

Serves: 10-12
Cooking Time: 5-10 Minutes

Ingredients

Tortillas	12
Vegetable oil (for frying)	4 cups
Tamarind *chutney* chilled	1 cup
Boiled potatoes (small) chopped	2 cups
Chick peas washed and drained	1 can
Onions finely chopped	1 cup
Tomatoes chopped fine	1 cup
Mung bean sprouts	1 cup
Gram flour *bhiji*	1 cup
Coriander leaves chopped	1 cup
Yogurt whisked and smooth	2 cups

A spice container with roasted ground cumin powder, salt, *garam masala*, and red pepper

Or

Chaat masala in a bowl

Mint *chutney*	1 cup
Yogurt	1 cup

This appetizer is sure to please the crowd. These flour crispy chips are served with tamarind *chutney*, boiled chopped potatoes, yogurt, canned chick-peas, salt, red pepper, *garam masala*, and ground roasted cumin powder. A counterpart of the Tortilla chips of Mexico.

Method

1. Cut squares or circles from fresh uncooked tortillas. You can use a bottle cap with sharp edges as a cutter or cut them out with a knife in any shape but not bigger than one inch in size. Heat oil to about 180°C or 350°F in a deep skillet or a cooking pot and fry them until they are crisp and golden brown. Drain them on a paper towel and store them in a warm oven until ready to serve. They can be stored after cooling in zip lock bags for later use.

2. Serve them to the guests in a snack plate or large bowl as follows: 4 Tbs of the tortilla chips topped with 2 Tbs each of chopped boiled potatoes, washed and drained canned chick-peas, 1 Tbs each of chopped onions and tomatoes, *mung* bean sprouts, gram flour *bhiji*, chopped coriander leaves and 1 Tbs of yogurt.

3. Again top it all with *chaat masala,* salt, red pepper, ground roasted cumin powder, *garam masala* and tamarind *chutney* or any other *chutney* of your taste and serve.

4. Makes an excellent appetizer.

Note: *Papris* and *golgappas* are usually sold in special shops or by vendors in every region in India. To make uncooked tortilla, follow the method for preparing the dough as in the recipe for *samosa*. There are many variations in chaat in the chutneys and other contents in different states, towns and a home.

Bhelpoori

Crunchy Rice Puffs and Salad in Sweet and Sour Sauce

Serves: 10-15
Cooking Time: 10 Minutes

Ingredients

Rice puffs	6 cups
Tortillas deep fried and broken in pieces	2 cups
Gram flour *bhiji*	1 cup
Mung bean sprouts	2 cups
Channa dal soaked overnight	1 cup
Potatoes (boiled) chopped	2 cups
Raw mango chopped	½ cup
Onions chopped	2 cups
Tamarind *chutney*	2 cups
Tomatoes firmly chopped	2 cups
Yogurt	1 cup
Salt	1 tsp
Red pepper	1 tsp
Lemon juice	2 Tbs
Mint *chutney*	1 cup
Green chilies chopped	½ cup
Green coriander chopped	1 cup
Garam masala	1 Tbs
Chaat masala	2 Tbs

Note: It can have variations in its contents from place to place in the country.

A most common chaat sold in the streets of Mumbai. It has a Gujarati origin. All popular markets would have their own *Bhewala* with his own blends of chutneys and masalas. What makes the Bhelpoori most divine is the use of fresh curd which is made daily in every household.

From the beaches of Bombay comes this snack or appetizer. Made with a mixture of rice puffs, *mung* bean sprouts, chopped onions, tomatoes, green chilies, boiled potatoes, fine salted gram flour vermicelli, tossed in tamarind *chutney* and topped with mint *chutney*, yogurt, salt, red pepper, *garam masala* and chopped coriander leaves, this is now popular all over the country.

Method

1. In a large mixing bowl mix together rice puffs, crushed tortillas, gram flour *bhiji*.
2. Add *mung* bean sprouts, washed and soaked and drained *channa dal* and chopped boiled potatoes, chopped raw mangoes, onions and a cup of tamarind *chutney*. Toss the mixture well to coat everything in it.
3. Before serving to the guests, transfer 4 Tbs of the above mixture onto a snack plate and top it with chopped tomatoes, a little yogurt salt, red pepper, *garam masala*, lemon juice, mint *chutney* and more tamarind *chutney*, coriander leaves if desired. *Chaat masala* can be used instead of the individual spices. Serve it on the side for preference.
4. Serve it with your favourite drink. Makes a great afternoon snack with your tea or coffee too.

Phalon ki Chaat

Fruit Chaat

Serves: 4-6
Cooking Time: 15 Minutes

Ingredients

Guavas ripe – peeled and chopped into bite size pieces	2
Apples peeled and chopped	2
Bananas peeled and chopped	1
Pears peeled and chopped	2
Grapes	1 cup
Boiled peeled and chopped potatoes	1 cup
Tomatoes ripe and firmly chopped	1 cup
Cucumber peeled and chopped	1 cup
Cooked chick peas can (optional)	15 ozs
Lemon juice from fresh lemons	4
Chaat masala	¼ cup
Mint or Tamarind chutney	½ cup

India is known to have some of the most exotic fruits and vegetables. Vendors all over the country sell this mix (*chaat*) of fresh fruits like guavas, bananas, apples, pears, grapes, and fresh vegetables like cucumbers, tomatoes, boiled potatoes and boiled chick peas. The fruits and vegetables are chopped into bite size pieces and garnished with lemon juice, and *chaat masala* (black salt, ground roasted cumin, red pepper, *amchoor*, black pepper, *garam masala*) and the mint *chutney* or the tamarind *chutney*. This is a very healthy and delicious snack. *Chaat* is a term used for a snack and in this case the spices used make it a great appetizer too. This preparation brings back childhood memories when as a child or teenager, we looked forward to this snack from vendors near our homes.

Method

1. Wash and clean the fruits and the vegetables with fresh water and dry them.
2. Peel and chop the different fruits in bite size pieces in a large bowl. Cover and store in the refrigerator.
3. Chop the boiled potatoes, tomatoes, and cucumbers in different small size bowls and also transfer a can of washed and drained chick-peas in another bowl. Cover the bowls and also set them aside in the refrigerator. Just before snack time remove the bowls from the refrigerator and start serving as follows.
4. Transfer a cup of mixture of fruits onto the plate. Sprinkle a little *chaat masala* and mix it with tamarind *chutney* and serve. If you want to mix the vegetables with it, then follow steps 5 and 6.

Note: Ripe papaya, pomegranate, plums or peaches, kiwi fruits or *chikus* (sapodilla) can also be used for this salad.

5. Add 1 Tbs each of boiled potatoes, tomatoes and cucumbers and 1 tsp of the chick peas onto the top of the fruit.
6. Squeeze about a tablespoon of lemon juice over the fruits and vegetable mix and sprinkle a tablespoon of mixture of the *chaat masala* and add a teaspoonful of mint *chutney* or sweet tamarind *chutney* (some people only like tamarind *chutney*) and serve.

Shakarkandi ki Chaat

Spicy Sweet Potato Salad

Serves: 4
Cooking Time: 5 Minutes

Ingredients

Sweet Potatoes	2 Lbs
Chaat Masala	4 Tbs
Fresh Lemon juice	4 Tbs

Sweet and sour tamarind Chutney or mint Chutney to flavour

Chopped and baked sweet potato topped with spices and chutneys

Baked and chopped sweet potatoes (chaat) coated with spices and fresh sweet and sour chutney is available from vendors in India around the major shopping areas. Sweet potatoes are sometimes baked in hot sand right on the vendor stand. Sweet potatoes are extraordinarily rich in carotenoids (orange and yellow pigments) and they also play a role in helping the body respond to insulin. And as unlikely as it may seem, coffee (another Magic food) and sweet potatoes have something in common: They're both rich in the natural plant compound chlorogenic acid, which may help reduce insulin resistance but they're actually an excellent source of this compound. Abundant Vitamin C found in sweet potatoes may also help fight heart disease and complications of diabetes, such as nerve and eye damage.

Method

1. Bake the sweet potatoes in an oven at 400°F for 1hr or until they are completely soft as regular baked potatoes.
2. Peel and chop the baked sweet potatoes into ¾- inch pieces in a large bowl. Cover them and set them aside.
3. Transfer a cup of chopped sweet potatoes on to a serving plate and sprinkle with 1 Tbsp. of chaat masala and 1Tbs of lemon juice and garnish with the chutney of your choice.
4. Toss the pieces well to coat with juice and masala and serve.
5. Makes an excellent snack.

Bharwan Khumb

Stuffed Mushrooms

Serves: 4-6
Cooking Time: 10-15 Minutes

Ingredients

Mushrooms (large)	1 lb
Water	4 cups
Lemon juice	1 Tbs
Salt	1 tsp
Potatoes boiled and mashed	½ cup
Ricotta cheese or *Paneer* (completely drained of water)	½ cup
Salt	¾ tsp
Lemon juice (optional)	1 Tbs
Red pepper	½–1 tsp
Bread crumbs	1 Tbs
Fresh coriander leaves chopped	1 Tbs
Green chilies chopped	1 tsp
Ginger chopped	1 tsp
Garlic chopped	1 tsp
Vegetable oil or *ghee* as needed	
Garam masala	½ tsp

Note: Stuffed Mushrooms are a very desired appetizer in western cuisine with different kinds of fillings.

Mushrooms stuffed with mashed potatoes, spices and ricotta cheese make a tasty and a very quick fixing snack or an appetizer. They are light and delicious, and make great nibblers with a drink.

Mushrooms are classified as vegetables in the food world. They belong to the fungi kingdom but provide several important nutrients like any other vegetable. They contain just as high an antioxidant capacity as carrots, tomatoes, green and red peppers, pumpkins, green beans, and zucchini. Mushrooms like Truffles is a rare, yet edible mushroom that is considered a delicacy in most parts of the world. Shiitake in Japanese, Thai and other cuisines make several of their very elegant gourmet dishes. Mushrooms were rare to find in India at the time when I was growing up but now they have have taken their proper recognition in Indian cuisine Mushrooms are so rich in nutrients, their neglect is truly a pity. They are a substantial source of protein, while lacking in the toxins and fat that meat contains. Furthermore, they contain metallic salts and trace elements, both of which are essential within the healthy diet.

Method

1. Wash the mushrooms and remove the stems. Clean the cavities and set them aside.
2. Boil 4 cups of water with 1 Tbs of lemon juice and 1 tsp of salt and add the mushrooms. Boil for 2 minutes, drain the water and run cold water over the mushrooms and drain them and set them aside.

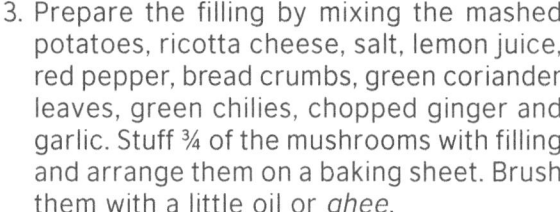

3. Prepare the filling by mixing the mashed potatoes, ricotta cheese, salt, lemon juice, red pepper, bread crumbs, green coriander leaves, green chilies, chopped ginger and garlic. Stuff ¾ of the mushrooms with filling and arrange them on a baking sheet. Brush them with a little oil or *ghee*.
4. Bake them at 400°F until the top starts to turn light brown and sprinkle a little garam masala. Serve with a *chutney*.

Rice, Pulav and Breads

India is one of the largest producers of grains and produces the best varieties of rice. Rice is the staple food of millions of Indians and is served daily in one form or another for breakfast, lunch or dinner.

In southern India it is served as *idli*, *dosa*, and *appam* besides as plain rice. Other states of India like Bengal, Maharashtra, Tamil Nadu, Karnataka, Gujarat use rice daily for their three major meals of the day.

From the South come rice dishes like Coconut Rice, Tamarind Rice, Yogurt Rice, Lemon Rice, Bisi Bele Bhaat, etc.

Northern India also has some very splendid rice preparations called *pulavs*. Among the famous *pulavs* are *Shahi Pulav*, *Navratan Pulav*, *Biryani*. These colourful aromatic *pulavs* decorated with nuts, fried onions, spices enhance the beauty of any dinner table when they are served surrounded by colorful curries, lentils and bread preparations. We know what to do with this versatile grain, and have transformed the plain grain of starch to beautiful aromatic and stylish dishes. Several appetizers like *Dhokla*, *Poha*, and some breads are the preparations using rice as the major component.

Rice is not only the staple food of the Indian sub-continent but feeds over three billion people all over the world. It is inexpensive, easily prepared, delicious and nutritious food. It is easy to digest and has non-allergic properties. It reduces hypertension and lowers cholesterol.

Breads are the staple food of millions of Indians. Several different grain flours like wheat, barley, millet, sorghum, gram, corn, garbanzo, lentils and rice are used in making these breads. Flours from these grains are easily available at Indian grocery stores or are sometime freshly ground at home.

There are unleavened flat griddle breads, like *chappatis*, *roghini roti* and *paranthas*. Then there are deep fried breads like *bhaturas, kachauris, luchhis* and *pooris*. Both types of these breads are the staple food of north India. These are made with whole wheat flour and are quite nutritious. They taste best when served hot and people like to eat them fresh. *Paranthas* are stuffed with grated or boiled vegetables, ground meats, cheese and lentils. Then there are rice and lentil flour griddle breads like *rava dosa, plain dosa, adais* and *appams*. These breads are the speciality of south India. They are normally served fresh with hot *sambhar* (a lentil preparation), chutney and potato stir-fry.

Then there are also clay oven (*tandoor*) baked leavened breads brought to India by the Mughals like plain *nan*, mint *nan*, or onion *nan* made from all purpose flour. These breads are usually served with non-vegetarian and vegetarian curries.

Cooking of Chappatis (Rotis)

Zeera Chawal

Plain Cumin Rice

Serves: 4-6
Cooking Time: 10 Minutes

Ingredients

Basmati rice	2 cups
Water	4 cups
Vegetable oil	2-4 Tbs
Cumin seeds	1 tsp
Salt	½ tsp

Note: Rice is the most consumed staple food of the world after corn especially in Asia and West indies. Actually it is more than a staple it is a synonym with life for millions on this earth. In Thialand the greeting is" have you had your rice today". It is also a grain with greatest verstality and can be changed into savories,and sweets at the same time can be boiled, steamed,pureed, fried baked, grilled, roasted. It is the ultimate comfort food and is missed by the major population of this worldwho have it 3 times a day. like China, Burma, Japan, Korea, major part of India, Philipines, Cambodia, Vietnam and many many more countries.

In North India it is served with all vegetable curries as an accompaniment but in South India it is a staple food and is always served in the meals plain or flavored with different ingredients. There are numerous varieties of rice found and consumed all over the country. Most varieties can be cooked using this recipe.

Method

1. Wash the rice and soak in water. Set aside.
2. Heat the oil in a heavy-bottom medium size saucepan. Add the cumin seeds, wait till they start popping.
3. Drain the water from soaked rice and transfer them to the cooking pan. Lower the heat and stir-fry the rice for a minute or so until the grains start sticking to the bottom. This frying is important as it hardens the outer covering of the rice and that prevents the grains from sticking to each other once they are cooked. Add 4 cups of water and salt. Boil it uncovered until almost all the water on the top of the rice is gone. Adjust the heat to low and cover with a lid.
4. Cook on low heat until rice has absorbed all the water. Turn the heat off, check the rice if it is not done, then cover it with a lid and again let it cook in its steam for another 5 minutes. Remove the lid and check the rice again. It should be done.
5. Serve it with any curry or *dal* and include it in a full meal with a stir-fry vegetable, *dal* and any kind of bread.

HINT

This rice can be made in a conventional rice cooker also.

Matar Chawal

Peas Pulav

Serves: 6-8
Cooking Time: 10-15 Minutes

Ingredients

Basmati rice	2 cups
Onion chopped	1 cup
Almonds chopped and slivered	2 Tbs
Vegetable oil or *ghee*	2-4 Tbs
Cumin seeds	1 tsp
Cinnamon stick	1
Cloves	6–8
Pepper corn	10–12
Bay leaves	4
Brown cardamoms	2
Peas frozen	2/3 cup
Raisins	1 Tbs
Water	4 cups
Salt	1 tsp
Boiled eggs (sliced or cubed)	1 or 2
Saffron	½ tsp

Slice of cucumber or Tomatoes and chopped optional Coriander leaves

A rice dish garnished with peas, onions, almonds and raisins. It is usually served with all curries and is one of most widely served rice dishes of North India served in Indian restaurants. It is simple but quite elegant.

Method

1. Clean and wash the rice and set them aside.
2. Fry ½ cup of onions and all the almonds in the oil using a frying pan till brown. Set these aside to garnish.
3. In the same oil add the remaining onion and fry till brown. Move the onion to one side and add the cumin seeds and wait until they start popping, then add cinnamon stick, cloves, peppercorns, bay leaves and the cardamoms.
4. Add the peas, raisins and stir-fry for a few minutes.
5. Then add the drained rice and continue stirring the rice for about 2–3 minutes in the spices.
6. Add salt and 4 cups of water to the rice. Stir to mix.
7. Cook on medium heat till half the water dries up. Reduce the heat to low and tightly cover the pan until the grains are soft and all the water dries up. If the rice is still not done then leave covered with the lid for a few more minutes so that the rice can cook in its steam.
8. Serve in an oval dish. Cover the centre with fried onions, almonds and garnish with saffron.
9. The *pulav* can be garnished with the slices of cucumbers, tomatoes, slices of boiled egg and coriander leaves. This is optional.

Matar-Paneer Pulav

Fried Cheese and Peas Pulav

Serves: 8-10
Cooking Time: 10 Minutes

Ingredients

Basmati rice washed and soaked in 2 cups of water	2 cups
Onions chopped	1 cup
Vegetable oil	2 Tbs
Ginger chopped	1 tsp
Garlic chopped	1 tsp
Green chilies chopped	½ tsp
Cinnamon sticks ½ inch piece	1
Brown cardamoms broken	2
Cloves	¼ tsp
Cumin seeds	1 tsp
Peas shelled or frozen	½ cup
Paneer cubes fried	1 cup
Water for cooking the rice	4 cups
Red pepper	½ tsp
Salt	½ tsp

To garnish:

Vegetable oil for frying	2 Tbs
Cashew nuts	2 Tbs
Onions chopped and fried	1 Tbs
Cucumber and tomato slices	½ cup
Small tomato sliced	1
Garam masala	½ tsp
Saffron (dissolved in 1 Tbs of water)	¼ tsp

Rice is a staple food in many parts of India and there are many preparations that involve use of spices and additional ingredients which bring it richness and palatability. Paneer rice or popularly known as paneer pulao, is one of the best rice recipes that is healthy, easy to prepare and can be served with various accompaniments and Indian curries. Unlike vegetable biryani, this rice *pulav* made with fried pieces of *paneer* is less cumbersome but wholesome and makes a beautiful presentation with peas and nuts. A popular rice dish.

Method

1. Wash and soak the rice in 2 cups of water and set aside.
2. Fry onions and cashew to garnish in 2 tablespoon of oil in a skillet on low heat and set aside.
3. Cook the onions in remaining 2 Tbs of oil in a thick-bottom saucepan of a medium size and add the ginger, garlic and green chilies, and wait till the onions are light brown. Add the cinnamon, cardamoms, cloves and cumin seeds. Wait till the cumin seeds start popping. Add the drained rice, and fry them with the spices for 2 minutes.
4. Add the peas and *paneer* cubes and stir-fry for 2 minutes.

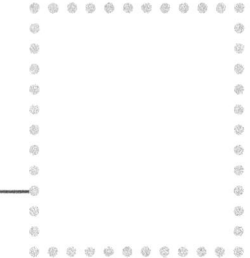

5. Add red pepper, salt and the water and mix. Raise the heat and bring the rice to a full boil and then reduce the heat. Cover and cook till the water is completely absorbed.

6. Remove from heat and leave covered with the lid. The rice cooks further in the steam, and 5 minutes later check the rice. It should be done.

7. Transfer the *pulav* to a serving dish and just before serving garnish the centre with cashew nuts, onions, and go around in a circle with tomatoes and cucumber slices alternating with each other. Sprinkle with little *garam masala* and dissolved saffron.

8. Serve just with yogurt, or as an accompaniment to a full meal with vegetable curry, salad and bread of your choice.

Note: Rice is one of the main staple foods in India. Many will say that a meal is not complete without rice. This grain gets disguised in many forms and ways. We even have our breakfast items done with rice, like the Idlis and Dosas. One cannot ignore the major part it plays in being the center of attraction.The typical thali from South India revolves around making dishes that one has to eat with Rice.Rice is a staple food of South India but in North India rice Pulav is made to make the meal look elegant and versatile.It is a great accompaniment in a North Indian meal.

Here is a way to make **Quick Pulav**. If you have left over plain rice and you do not have any thing to go with it go ahead and change it into a meal by heating some oil and add cumin seeds, chopped onion, ginger, garlic, green chilies, turmeric, coriander powder, red pepper and salt and some cooked frozen peas. Mix it well and stir and add the left over rice. Sprinkle lemon juice and serve with some yogurt and you have made yourself a meal.

Nariyalwale Chawal

Coconut Rice

Serves: 8-10
Cooking Time: 15 Minutes

Ingredients

Rice	2 cups
Water	4 cups
Onions to garnish light golden fried	1 cup
Clarified butter or oil	4-6 Tbs
Fresh coconut grated (whole)	1
Or	
Coconut powder dry (from an Indian grocery store)	1 cup
Mustard seeds	1 tsp
Curry leaves	6
Asafoetida	¼ tsp
Red pepper dried	4
Urad dal	¼ cup
Cashew nuts or peanuts raw chopped	⅓ cup
Green chilies chopped	2 tsp
Green coriander fresh chopped	⅓ cup
Salt	to taste

A delicacy of South Indian cuisine prepared with fresh coconut is a delicious, refreshing and crisp preparation of rice. Great for a meal as well as light lunch and a snack. It goes very well with meat curries and vegetable curries.

Method

1. Cook the rice in water part of which may be the water collected after breaking a coconut if available in case fresh coconut is used. (Follow instructions of collecting the coconut water after breaking it under 'Preparation of coconut milk' in the introduction). Follow the plain rice preparation recipe and cook the rice.

2. Now fry the onions in 2 Tbs of clarified butter until they are lightly brown and set them aside. Also fry the coconut in the same oil until it is light brown and set it aside.

3. Heat the remaining 2 Tbs of oil in a large heavy-bottom saucepan and add the mustard seeds, curry leaves, asafoetida, red pepper and *urad dal* and wait till the mustard seeds start popping and *urad dal* turns light brown.

4. In the same pan add the cashew nuts and the green chilies. Fry for few minutes until the nuts are light brown.

5. Stir in the cooked rice gently with the salt to taste and mix in ½ of the fried coconut and onion mixture.

6. Mix the coconut rice gently but thoroughly and serve topped with remaining fried onions and chopped coriander.

Gobhi Pulav

Cauliflower Pulav

Serves: 6-8
Cooking Time: 15 Minutes

Ingredients

Basmati rice	2 cups
Vegetable oil or *ghee*	¼ cup
Cardamoms green	½ tsp
Cloves and black pepper corns each	½ tsp
Cinnamon sticks ½ inch	1
Onions chopped	½ cup
Ginger chopped	1 Tbs
Garlic chopped	1 Tbs
Green chilies chopped	1 Tbs
Cumin seeds	1 tsp
Red pepper	½ tsp
Salt	1 tsp
Water	4 cups
Heavy cream	3 Tbs

To garnish:

Onions chopped	¼ cup
Roasted blanched almonds	1 Tbs
Cauliflower florets about 1 inch size	1 cup
Salt and black pepper to sprinkle	
Tomatoes and cucumber slices	2 Tbs
Saffron	¼ tsp
Potato vermicelli (optional) (available at an Indian grocery store)	½ cup

Another North Indian rice preparation flavoured with chunks of fried cauliflower florets, almonds and cooked with water and cream. It makes an elegant presentation and is very delicious and nutritious.

Method

1. Wash and soak the rice and set it aside.
2. Heat the oil in a large heavy-bottom saucepan and fry the onions and almonds for garnish. Remove them from oil and set them aside. In the same oil, fry the cauliflower florets by sprinkling salt and pepper over them. As soon as they turn light brown remove them from the oil and set them aside.
3. In the oil for making rice, add the cardamoms, cloves, black pepper and cinnamon, and fry for ½ minute and then add the onions, garlic, ginger and green chilies, and fry until onions turn light brown. Add the cumin seeds, and when they start to pop add the red pepper, salt, and the drained rice. Fry for a few minutes until the water dries up and rice begins to stick to the bottom. Add 4 cups of water and the cream.

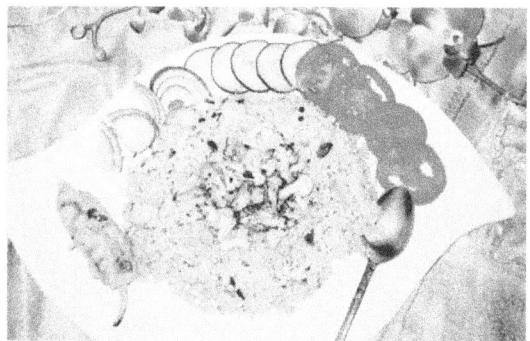

Note: Fried chopped jackfruit can also be used to make jackfruit pulav. It is delectable.

4. Cover and let it cook on medium to low heat. Partially cover with lid and cook till all the water is gone. Turn the heat off, and if the rice is not done, leave it covered with the lid for another 5–10 minutes to cook in its own steam.
5. Serve topped with fried cauliflower in the centre, and arrange chopped tomatoes and slices of cucumber, saffron, fried onions, almonds or fried potato vermicelli around it.
6. Serve with yogurt or a curry.

Nimbuwale Chawal

Lemon Rice

Serves: 8-10
Cooking Time: 10 Minutes

Ingredients

Basmati Rice	2 cups
Water (to make rice)	4 cups
Vegetable oil	2-4 Tbs
Green or yellow dry/split peas	½ cup
Cashew nuts or peanuts finely chopped	¼ cup
Mustard seeds	1 tsp
Red pepper (dry)	3
Curry leaves	10
Urad dal	2 tsp
Onions chopped	1 cup
Ginger chopped	1 tsp
Green chilies chopped	2 Tbs
Turmeric	1 tsp
Asafoetida	¼ tsp
Salt	to taste
Lemon juice	¼ cup
Coriander leaves chopped	2 Tbs
Garam masala	1 tsp
Green fresh onions chopped to garnish	½ cup

A splendid rice dish from South India that can be an accompaniment to any meal. It is flavoured with lemon juice, peanuts, *urad dal* and dried peas *dal*. It is crunchy and can also be served as a snack at teatime, coffeetime or lunchtime.

Method

1. Cook the rice following the plain rice recipe and set it aside.

2. Heat the oil and add to it the dry split peas. Brown them and remove them from oil and set them aside in a bowl. Add the cashew nuts or peanuts to the same oil and wait till they turn light brown. Remove them from oil and also set them aside in the same bowl.

3. In the same oil add the mustard seeds, red pepper, and curry leaves, and wait until the mustard seeds start popping. Add the *urad dal* and wait till it turns light brown.

4. Add the chopped green chilies, onions, ginger, green chilies and wait till onions are light brown. Add turmeric, asafoetida and salt also.

5. Remove from heat, gently add the cooked rice and softly fold into the rice all the contents very carefully so as not to crush the rice. Add the roasted split peas and cashew nuts and mix them in. Fold in the fresh lemon juice and stir the rice well.

6. Serve topped with fresh coriander leaves, *garam masala* and chopped green onions.

Imliwale Chawal
Tamarind Rice

Serves: 6-8
Cooking Time: 20 Minutes

Ingredients	
Basmati Rice	2 cups
Water	5 cups
Yellow or dry green split peas cup	¼ cup
Tamarind paste	2 tsp
Vegetable oil	¼ cup
Peanuts or cashew nuts (broken)	¼ cup
Red chili (whole)	2
Mustard seeds	1½ tsp
Asafoetida powder	¼ tsp
Coriander powder	1 Tbs
Fenugreek leaves	1 Tbs
Urad dal	1½ tsp
Turmeric powder	½ tsp
Red pepper to taste or	1 tsp
Salt	1 tsp
Curry leaves	4
Garam masala	½ tsp
Coriander leaves chopped	1 tsp

Note: This rice is very popular in South Asian kitchens. Tamarind contains many health benefiting essential volatile chemical compounds, mineral vitamins and dietary fibre.

A south Indian rice specialty that is made usually on festive occasions and for snack time.

Method

1. Cook the rice (refer to plain rice recipe) in 4 cups of water and set it aside.
2. Soak the dry split peas and the tamarind paste in remaining 1 cup of water in a bowl and let these sit for at least an hour. Strain the split peas from the tamarind water and save the water in a bowl.
3. Heat the oil in a pan and sauté the peanuts on medium low heat. Remove from the oil and set them aside. Also fry the strained split peas in the same oil and set them aside.
4. In the same oil fry the whole red pepper, mustard seeds, asafoetida powder, coriander powder, fenugreek leaves and the *urad dal* until the *dal* is light brown.
5. Add the tamarind water and mix keeping the heat on medium low.
6. Add turmeric powder, red pepper, salt, curry leaves, fried split peas and *garam masala* and gently stir the mixture. Cook till the water is almost absorbed.
7. Add the cooked rice and gently blend the spice mixture in to the rice. Add the peanuts or the cashew nuts and mix them gently into the rice. Serve topped with chopped green coriander leaves and *garam masala*.

Navratan Pulav

Multicoloured Rice Pulav

Serves: 8-10
Cooking Time: 15 Minutes

Multicoloured rice pulav from North India cooked with *paneer*, peas, nuts, and tomatoes. Another great dish inherited from the court of the great Mughal King, Akbar. It is colourful, delicious and unique. Though it is a little time consuming during preparation, it is a gem among the *pulavs*, and a complete meal by itself.

Ingredients

Vegetable oil or *ghee*	2-4 Tbs
Onions chopped	1 cup
Ginger chopped	1 tsp
Green chilies chopped	1 tsp
Garlic chopped	1 tsp
Cinnamon stick ½ inch	1
Cloves	½ tsp
Whole green cardamoms	½ tsp
Pepper corns	½ tsp
Cumin seeds	½ tsp
Rice	2 cups
Water	4 cups

To mix in rice:

Green food color	6 drops
Water	2 Tbs
Peas fried in 1 tsp of *ghee* with ¼ tsp each of salt and black pepper	½ cup
Tomato coloring	4 drops
Chopped tomatoes mixed with ¼ tsp each of red pepper, salt and *garam masala*	¼ cup
Fried *paneer* pieces or ricotta cheese + ¼ tsp each of salt and black pepper	¼ cup

Method

1. Heat the *ghee* and fry the onions, ginger, garlic and green chilies. When the onion mixture is light brown, add cinnamon sticks, cloves, cardamoms, black pepper corns, and the cumin seeds. When the cumin starts to pop, add the rice. Stir well and lower the heat and fry the rice in this mixture for 2–3 minutes. Add the water and cook the rice until all the water is absorbed. Turn the heat off and let the rice cook in its steam for another 2–5 minutes.

2. Divide the rice into three parts and set aside in separate bowls.

3. To the first part add the green colour by dissolving 6 drops of green food colour in 1 Tbs of water and mix it well. Use only few drops of this coloured water to give rice a light green colour. Add the fried peas to it and stir them in.

Matar Chawal - Page 46

Nariyalwale Chawal - Page 49

Khumbwale Chawal - Page 56

Methi Paranthe - Page 65

Paratha - Page 67

Onion Nan - Page 72

Puri - Page 75

Khasta Kachauri - Page 81

To garnish the *pulav*:	
Onions chopped	½ cup
Vegetable oil or *ghee*	1 Tbs
Almonds chopped	2 Tbs
Pistachio nuts	2 Tbs
Raisins	2 Tbs
Cashew chopped	2 Tbs
Green chilies finely cut	2–3
Full boiled eggs chopped	2
Saffron	¼ tsp
Red pepper	1 tsp
Coriander leaves chopped	2 Tbs

4. Colour the second part of the rice red by adding 4 drops of tomato colouring in 1 Tbs remaining of water. Use only few drops of this coloured water to turn the rice light red. Add the salted tomato cubes with *garam masala* and mix the rice well.

5. The third part can be left white and to that just add the cheese cubes with the salt and black pepper in it.

6. Fry the onions in 2 Tbs of oil until golden brown. Take them out of the *ghee* with slotted spoon and set aside. Now, fry the almonds, pistachio, raisins, cashew and chilies, and set them aside in a bowl.

7. Serve the rice by layering each colour on top of the other in a large and elegant serving dish and topping the three layers with chopped eggs in the centre and surround them with all the fried nuts and raisins, saffron, red pepper, chopped green coriander leaves and shredded green chilies. Serve with any vegetable curry of your choice.

Note: Moulds can be used to shape different coloured rice, instead of layering them as the layers tend to fall apart.

Khumbwale Chawal

Mushroom Pulav

Serves: 4-6
Cooking Time: 15 Minutes

Ingredients

Basmati Rice	2 cups
Vegetable oil or *ghee*	3 Tbs
Onions chopped	2 Tbs
Cardamom brown (whole) crushed	2
Cinnamon sticks (small)	2
Bay leaves	2–3
Clove whole	½ tsp
Black pepper corns	½ tsp
Cumin seeds	1 tsp
Mushrooms chopped into slices ½ inch thick and ½ long	1 cup
Fenugreek leaves freshly chopped	½ cup
Or dry leaves	2 Tbs
Peas frozen	¼ cup
Water or chicken broth	4 cups
Salt	¾ tsp
Red pepper	½ tsp
Garam masala to garnish	½ tsp
Saffron	¼ tsp
Coriander leaves chopped	2 Tbsp

Mughlai influence in Indian cuisine is very evident in this rice preparation. Royals used *guchhian** (a kind of lichen) similar to mushrooms. Actually in north India, lichens curry preparation was very popular. *Guchhians* are quite expensive and are considered a delicacy. It is hard to find a good quality in the market. Mushrooms make a good replacement.

Method

1. Wash and soak the rice. Set it aside.
2. Heat the oil in a thick heavy-bottom pan of at least 4–quart capacity.
3. Add the onions, and fry them till they are slightly brown. Add the cardamoms, cinnamon sticks, bay leaves, cloves and black pepper, and after a minute add the cumin seeds. When the seeds stop popping, add the mushrooms, fenugreek leaves and peas. Fry them for 5–10 minutes and add the rice.
4. Fry the drained rice stirring gently. Lower the heat. This frying is important because it prevents the rice from sticking to each other when fully cooked as the outer surface of rice gets a little hardened.
5. Add the water or broth. Add salt and red pepper and stir to mix. Let it cook partially open until all water on the top of the rice is gone. Lower the heat and cover the pan and simmer until all the loose moisture is gone and the rice grains are fluffy and non sticky. Turn the heat off and let them stay covered in the cooking pan for a few minutes before serving.
6. Serve garnished with a sprinkle of *garam masala*, saffron and freshly chopped coriander leaves. They will go well with any vegetable stir-fry and *raita*.

*Guchhian (a kind of lichen) can also be curried with peas and is mainly found in the valley of Kashmir.

Khichdi

Rice and Lentils with Vegetables

Serves: 4-6
Cooking Time: 20-25 Minutes

Ingredients

Ingredient	Amount
Rice	1 ½ cup
Mung dal (split and washed)	½ cup
Water	6 cups
Chopped small cubes of peeled potatoes	½ cup
Salt	to taste
Turmeric	½ tsp
Cauliflower florets or carrots	½ cup
Peas frozen	2 Tbs
Chopped Spinach	
Onions chopped	1 cup
Ginger chopped	1 Tbs
Garlic chopped	1 Tbs
Green chilies chopped	1 Tbs
Vegetable oil or *ghee*	4 Tbs
Cumin seeds	1 tsp
Coriander powder	1 tsp
Red pepper (or to taste)	½–1 tsp
Black pepper	½ tsp
Dry Fenugreek leaves	1 Tbsp
Garam masala	¾ tsp

Note: Khichdi makes a great meal for toddlers and children as it is very easy to digest and light on stomach. Use only ¼ tsp of red pepper and ¼ tsp of *garam masala* and don't use green chilies when cooking for infants.

When rice, lentils and few chopped vegetables are mixed and cooked it really turns out to be a delicious and complete dish. It is then garnished with onions, and spices and served topped with a little clarified butter along with milk, yogurt or pickle. It is a quick fixing and a very light family pleaser. *Mung* beans are easily digestible, therefore this preparation is served even to people recovering from illness. Try it on a busy day and you will like it.

Method

1. Wash the rice and *dal* in a couple of changes of water and soak in about 2 cups of water and set them aside.

2. Boil 6 cups of water in a medium size thick-bottom saucepan and add the drained mixture of rice, *dal* and the chopped potatoes, 1 tsp of salt and ½ tsp of turmeric, cauliflower, frozen peas, and chopped spinach. Cook over medium heat until all the water is absorbed and all the grains of rice and *dal* are softened and the mixture is smooth but still a little grainy. Add more water if needed. Set aside.

3. In a small saucepan cook the onions, ginger, garlic and green chilies in 4 Tbs of oil until the mixture is lightly brown.

4. Move the onion mixture aside in the saucepan and add the cumin seeds and wait till they pop.

HINT

To make the popular dish **'Bisi Bele Bhaat'** from Andhra Pradesh, use *toor dal* instead of *mung dal* and tamarind dissolved in a tsp of water. Add the tamarind water in step 6, along with onion mixture. Also add 1 tsp each of crushed mustard seeds and fennel seeds along with cumin seeds in step 4. Fry 1 tsp each of poppy seeds, fenugreek seeds and anise seeds in a pan, when light brown and aromatic, grind them and add in step 5. You can also add 2 Tbs of fried cashew nuts and coconut powder at the end.

Coriander leaves freshly chopped	1 tsp
Spinach fresh or frozen chopped (optional)	½ cup
Fenugreek leaves (dry)	2 Tbs

5. Add the coriander powder, red pepper, black pepper, dry fenugreek leaves, salt and mix into the onion mixture.
6. Transfer the spiced onion mixture into the rice and *dal* mixture and stir well. Move the saucepan back to the stove or cooking range on low heat and mix the spices and onion mixture well into the *khichdi*. Add more water, if needed.
7. Sprinkle with *garam masala* and chopped green coriander leaves and remove from heat. Mix and serve the *khichdi* topped with a dab of butter and with yogurt, pickle, or with a vegetable curry.

Chappati

Whole Wheat Griddle Bread

Serves: 4-6
Cooking Time: 5 Minutes

Ingredients

Whole wheat flour	2 cups
Water	1 cup + 2 Tbs
Wheat flour for rolling	¼ cup
Ghee or oil for brushing the *chappatis*	¼ cup

Caution: Tongs should be used to toss and turn *chappatis* on gas or electric stoves.

This whole wheat flour bread in Indian cuisine is very healthy. Whole wheat flour has good amounts of Protein, Fibre, Iron, B vitamins, Thiamin, Niacin, Magnesium, Phosphorus, Zinc. Use multigrain chappati flour. To make it healthier add powdered sesame and ajwain (Carom) seeds and make it extra nutritious. Ajwain and sesame seeds are effective remedy of ailments like paralysis, weakness of limbs, pain in chest, liver disease, hiccup, dyspepsia, and malfunctioning of kidney.

Method

1. Transfer 2 cups of flour to a deep mixing bowl and make a deep depression in the middle.
2. In the heap thus formed, pour water, mix it and knead it into soft dough.
3. Knead for a few minutes until the dough becomes smooth, sprinkle with 1–2 tsp of water and cover with a wet cloth and let it sit for about half an hour.
4. Butter your hands well and knead again for a few minutes and divide into 10 to 12 pieces and using a little dry flour shape them into

smooth round patties. Place them on the floured board and roll out with a rolling pin into thin pancake like forms (*chappati*) about 5-6 inches diameter and couple of millimetres in thickness.

5. Heat the griddle (medium heat) and transfer the rolled *chappati* on to it. When one side dries up and tiny bubbles began to appear, turn it over and cook until brown spots form on the under side.

6. Remove the griddle from the fire, place the *chappati* on direct heat *(see caution), if it is a gas stove, wait till it swells up into a shape similar to that of two saucers inverted over each other (If you have an electric stove, cover the gauge with a small wire grill and place the *chappati* on the wire grill). Keep turning using tongs, until it is browned on both sides. Remove from the fire and apply a little *ghee,* if you like, over one side. Serve immediately.

7. If the *chappatis* are made in advance, they should be placed one above the other, wrapped in a napkin and stored in a *chappati* container or tortilla container (this can be purchased at an Indian grocery store). If the *chappatis* container is not available then cover them in wax paper or paper towel and wrap them in aluminium foil and store them in a warm oven until ready to eat. Preferably serve hot.

Note: To make the *chappati* softer and proteinaceous add ½ lb of drained tofu and knead it into the dough. *Chappati* dough can be made ahead of time and refrigerated for a couple of days. They taste best when served fresh. Freeze them separated by wax paper and they would still be good for a week or two.

RICE, PULAV AND BREADS

Plain Parantha

Un-Stuffed Griddle Fried Bread

Serves: 6-8
Cooking Time: 5 Minutes

Ingredients

Flour	2 cups
Salt	a pinch
Red pepper	to taste
Vegetable oil or *ghee* for frying	¼ cup
Water	1 cup+1oz

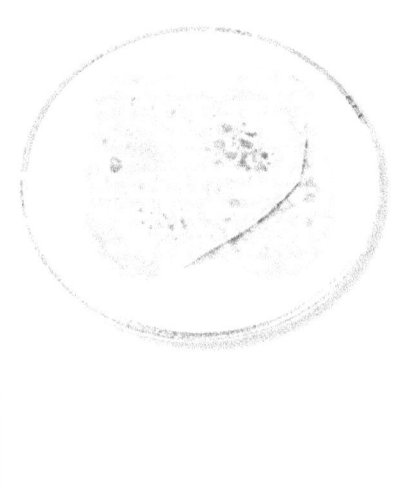

Plain *Paranthas* are nothing but pan-fried *chappati*. They are leavened with a little butter before you roll them which makes them fluffier, crisper and crunchy. They go very well with a vegetable curry or a meat curry or even stir-fry vegetable of your choice.

Method

1. Transfer the flour into a deep mixing bowl and add a pinch of salt and red pepper to it. Make a well in the middle. Add the water and knead to make pliable dough similar to *chappati* dough. Add more water, if needed.

2. Take a piece of dough and make a ball as big as plum and roll each ball into a round, about 4 inches in diameter. Coat the top with a little butter or *ghee* and fold the edges of the round over into half a circle and fold it one more time to make a triangle. Roll it gently with the help of the dry flour on a flat board or *chakla* (Indian *chappati* making board made of marble or wood) into a larger triangle with at least 4 inch sides.

3. Heat a 12–14 inch skillet or *tawa* (the Indian iron griddle for making *chappati*) for a minute on medium heat and transfer the *parantha* on to it. Turn over the rolled dough (*parantha*) when the surface is showing some bumps. Turn it over, and the turned side will show some brown spots. Coat it with *ghee* or oil and turn and cover the other side too with oil. Fry till the *parantha* is brown on both sides and turns crisp. Serve immediately with your favourite vegetable curry.

Note: Any leftover *dal* can be used to knead the flour into dough and *dal paranthas* can be made easily. No water or spices are needed to knead the dough as *dal* provides enough liquid to make pliable dough for making *paranthas*.

Lachhedar Parantha

Onion Stuffed Griddle Fried Bread

Serves: 4-6
Cooking Time: 10 Minutes

Ingredients

Whole wheat flour	2 cups
Onions chopped	½ cup
Green chilies chopped	2 Tbs
Ajwain (carom seeds)	1 tsp
Salt	1 tsp
Red pepper	½ tsp
Garam masala	½ tsp
Vegetable oil or *ghee*	½ cup
Water or milk (enough to make a pliable dough)	

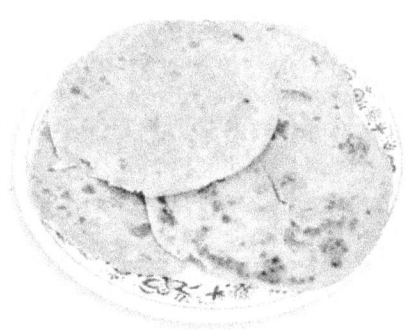

Note: A fast breakfast item that goes very well with Raita, Pickle and Chutney. Very common in North India.

In Punjab, *Lachhedar Paranthas* are very common for breakfast. In Rajasthan, they are called *Batia Roti*. Knead the dough with spices and chopped onions and make them nice and soft by coiling the dough and then rolling them into 6 inch circles. They are my favourites for breakfast.

Method

1. Transfer the flour to a deep mixing bowl and add chopped onions, green chilies, carom seeds, salt, red pepper, *garam masala* and 2 Tbs oil or *ghee*.
2. Add enough water and knead to make a pliable dough. Knead until it is smooth and leaves the sides of the bowl.
3. Cover with a slightly wet cloth and set aside.
4. Break a piece as big as a ball 2 inch in diameter and start to roll it on a floured surface with a rolling pin. Roll it into a 6 inch circle and brush it with oil or *ghee*. Lift dough from one side and roll up tightly into a tubular form. Change the tube into a coil. Roll the coil with a rolling pin into a 6 inch flat disc.
5. Heat *tawa* or non-stick frying pan on medium heat and transfer the rolled flat dough on to it.
6. Cook until brown spots start to appear on the under side. Turn over and brush the cooked side with the remaining *ghee* or oil and turn it over. Brush top with *ghee* or oil again and cook both sides until light brown. Repeat the same with other pieces of dough.
7. Serve them hot with tea at breakfast time or at teatime. They can also be served as a bread accompaniment with a stir-fry vegetable or a curry.
8. Wrap cooked bread in tin foil and store it in an oven at warm temperature, if it is going to be used later.

Gobhi ke Paranthe

Cauliflower Stuffed Griddle Fried Bread

Serves: 4-6
Cooking Time: 10 Minutes

Ingredients	
Flour	2 cups
Salt	a pinch
Vegetable oil or *ghee*	¼ cup
Use juices squeezed out of the vegetable stuffing+water for making the dough)	1 cup
Cauliflower florets grated	1 cup
Onions finely chopped	2 Tbs
Ginger finely chopped	1 tsp
Garlic finely chopped	1 tsp
Green chilies finely chopped	1 tsp
Coriander leaves chopped	1 Tbs
Salt	1 tsp
Coriander seeds crushed or powdered	1 tsp
Red pepper	½ tsp
Lemon juice (optional)	1 Tbs
Garam masala	½ tsp

Note: Cauliflower is low in fat, low in carbs but high in *dietary fibre, folate,* water, and *vitamin C,* possessing a high *nutritional density.* A high intake of cauliflower has been associated with reduced risk of aggressive *prostate cancer.*

A complete meal in itself, cauliflower stuffed bread is served for breakfast in India. This is yet another yummy *parantha* from the state of Punjab.

Method

1. Grate cauliflower and add onions, ginger, garlic, green chilies, green coriander and all the spices. Squeeze out all the juices and set it aside. The stuffing is ready.

2. Follow the recipe for making the dough similar to *chappati* dough. Instead of water use the mixture of squeezed juices and water. Knead to make a pliable dough. Cover and set it aside.

3. Take a piece of dough and make balls as big as a plum and roll each ball on a smooth flat surface using a rolling pin. You can use a slab of marble, fine smooth wooden chopping board or a traditional tawa. Dab the rolling surface first with dry flour and then roll the dough ball into a round, about 4 inches in diameter by using more dry flour.

4. Put about 2 Tbs of the stuffing in the centre of the round – fold the edges of the round over the stuffing and pinch them together making sure stuffing is completely covered with the dough from all sides. It is now a round patty with a diameter of 2–3 inches.

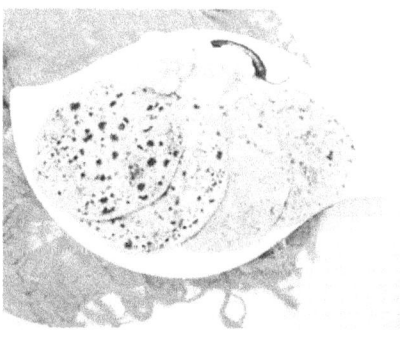

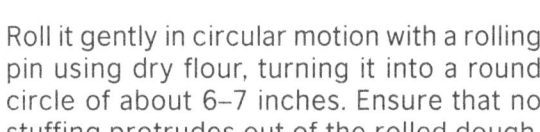

Roll it gently in circular motion with a rolling pin using dry flour, turning it into a round circle of about 6–7 inches. Ensure that no stuffing protrudes out of the rolled dough.

5. Heat a 12–14 inch skillet or *tawa* and transfer the stuffed rolled dough on to it. When the underside is a little crisp and shows some brown spots, turn it over. Coat it with *ghee* or vegetable oil. Turn it over again and coat this side also with the *ghee* or oil. Keep turning and frying until golden brown. Serve immediately with plain yogurt, *raita*, pickle or butter.

Methi Paranthe

Fenugreek Leaves Flavoured Griddle Fried Bread

Serves: 4-6
Cooking Time: 10-15 Minutes

Ingredients	
Chappati flour	3 cups
Fresh fenugreek leaves washed and finely chopped	1½ cup
Coriander leaves chopped	2 Tbs
Garam masala	½ tsp
Onions finely chopped	½ cup
Ginger finely chopped	1 Tbs
Garlic finely chopped	1 Tbs
Salt	¾ tsp
Red pepper	1 tsp
Green chilies finely chopped	1 tsp
Oil or clarified butter (for frying the *paranthas*)	½ cup
Water to make dough for making the *chappatis*	1½ cup
Vegetable oil or *ghee*	2 Tbs

Methi (Fenugreek flavoured) *paranthas* are a favorite in Punjab. These *paranthas* are wholesome, delicious and very healthy as fenugreek leaves have many health benefits. Easy to make too.

Method

1. Mix together the flour, chopped fenugreek leaves, coriander leaves, *garam masala*, onions, ginger, garlic, salt, red pepper, green chilies, and 2 Tbs of oil in a mixing bowl.
2. Add the water slowly and knead to make a smooth and pliable dough like the *chappati* dough.
3. Pinch off a piece of dough to make a ball of 1½ inch diameter.
4. Using dry *chappati* flour, roll the ball into 4 inch diameter disc and smear the centre with a dab of butter and fold the disc into a half circle and fold it again into a triangle and roll it into a triangle with 3–4 inch sides.
5. Heat an iron skillet (*tawa*) or any other medium size thick bottom skillet for a minute and keep the heat on medium.
6. Transfer the rolled dough (*parantha*) onto it. Soon little bumps start to appear on the surface of the *parantha*. Turn it over and you will see some brown spots on the turned side. Smear its surface with ¼ tsp of oil or *ghee* and turn it over. Smear this side also with a little oil.
7. Keep turning and frying until both sides turn light brown.
8. Serve with *Boondi Raita* or any other *raita* of your choice or plain yogurt. Makes an excellent breakfast or lunch. This bread can be served just with one curry or a stir-fry vegetable or served as a bread with any regular meal.

Note: To make *Paneer* or Onion *Parantha*, fenugreek leaves can be substituted with ½ cup of ricotta cheese, or with just a cup of chopped onions with 1 tsp each of green chilies, ginger and garlic. Make the dough in the same fashion as above. Use 1 cup of gram flour and 2 cups of wheat flour for making the dough. The *paranthas* will be more crisp and tasty.

Aloo ke Paranthe

Stuffed Potato Griddle Fried Bread

Serves: 2-4
Cooking Time: 10 Minutes

Ingredients

For the dough:

Wheat flour	2 cups
Salt	a pinch
Vegetable oil or *ghee*	1 Tbs
Water to knead the dough	1 cup +1 Tbs

For Potato stuffing:

Boiled and smoothly mashed potatoes	1 cup
Onions finely chopped	2 Tbs
Ghee or oil for frying the *paranthas*	¼ cup
Ginger finely chopped	1 tsp
Garlic finely chopped	1 tsp
Green chilies chopped	1 tsp
Cumin powder	½ tsp
Coriander powder	1 tsp
Coriander leaves chopped	1 Tbs
Red pepper	½ tsp
Garam masala	½ tsp
Salt	1 tsp
Lemon juice	1 Tbs

Note: Potato Paranthas are big favourite in Indian cuisine mainly as a breakfast or lunch item. It is served mainly with Raita and a pickle.

A superb treat, stuffed potato *Paranthas* are mostly served for breakfast in northern India. These are really a complete meal by themselves. Several different stuffings can be used.

Method

1. Boil the potatoes, peel them, mash them and set them aside.
2. Follow the recipe for making the dough, similar to *chappati* dough.
3. To the mashed potatoes, add the onions, 1 Tbs of *ghee*, ginger, garlic, green chilies, cumin powder, coriander powder, fresh chopped coriander leaves, red pepper, *garam masala*, salt and lemon juice. Mix well and set aside the stuffing.
4. Take a piece of dough and make a ball of 2 inch diameter and roll each ball on a smooth flat surface using a rolling pin and dry flour. You can use a slab of marble, fine smooth wooden chopping board or a traditional *chappati* making circular slab. Dab the rolling surface first with dry flour and then roll the dough balls into rounds about 4 inches in diameter by using more dry flour.
5. Put about 2 Tbs of the stuffing in the centre of the round and fold the edges of the round over the stuffing and pinch them together making sure stuffing is completely covered with the dough from all sides. It is now a round patty with a diameter of 2 to 3 inches. Roll it in gentle circular motion with the help of the dry flour into a round disc of about 6 to 7 inches diameter with the rolling pin or with your fingers, making sure no stuffing protrudes out of the *parantha*.
6. Heat a 12–14 inch skillet or *tawa* and transfer the *parantha* on to it. When the underside is a little crisp and shows some brown spots turn it over. Coat it with *ghee* or vegetable

oil. Turn it over again and coat this side also with the *ghee* or oil. Keep turning and frying until golden brown.

7. Serve immediately with plain yogurt, *raita*, pickle, or butter of your choice.

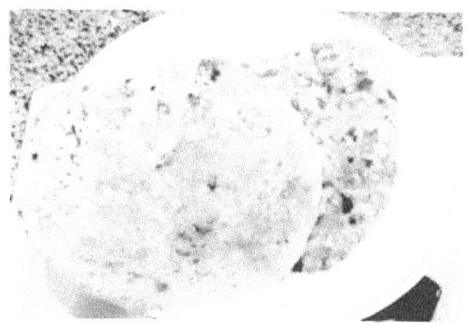

Mooli ka Paranthe

Daikon Stuffed Griddle Fried Bread

Serves: 4-6
Cooking Time: 10 Minutes

Ingredients

Grated daikon radish	1 cup
Ginger finely chopped	1 tsp
Garlic finely chopped	1 tsp
Green chilies finely chopped	1 tsp
Carom seeds (*Ajwain*)	½ tsp
Salt	1 tsp
Coriander powder	1 tsp
Garam masala	½ tsp
Lemon juice (optional)	1 Tbs
Red pepper	½ tsp
Wheat flour	2 cups
Coriander leaves chopped	1 Tbs
Salt	a pinch
Vegetable oil or *ghee*	¼ cup
Water (and juices squeezed out of the vegetable stuffing) to make the dough	1 cup

Note: In North India Daikon radishes are used raw in salads, shredded as Mooli ka Laccha and sprinkled with lemon juice and salt and becomes a favourite salad in winter time. It is used more extensively in south india in their Sambhars and as a stir fry. Daikon radish is eaten many ways in Japan. It is pickled, it is made into a dip with soy sauce and lemon juice. It used as a salad a garnish and even stir fried.

Stuffed Daikon *Paranthas* are mostly served for breakfast in India. These are delicious and really a complete meal by themselves. Several different stuffings can be used. These can be enjoyed for breakfast or lunch.

Method

1. Grate the daikon radish and add ginger, garlic, green chilies, all the spices and mix well. Squeeze well to take out all the juices and save in a bowl, this will be the water to knead the dough.

2. Follow the recipe for making the dough similar to *chappati* dough. Instead of water use the mixture of squeezed juices and water. Knead to make a pliable dough just like the *chappati* dough. Butter the dough, cover it and set it aside.

3. Take a piece of dough and make a ball as big as plum and roll each ball on a smooth flat surface using a rolling pin. You can use a slab of marble, fine smooth wooden chopping board or a traditional *chappati* making circular slab. Dab the rolling surface first with dry flour and then roll the dough ball into a round, about 4 inches in diameter by using a rolling pin and applying more dry flour.

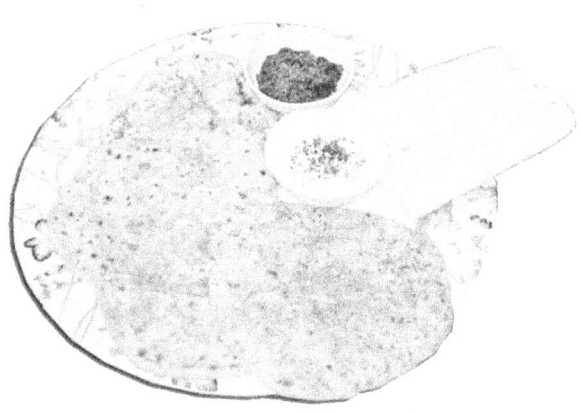

4. Put about 2 Tbs of the stuffing in the centre of the round and fold the edges of the round over the stuffing and pinch them together making sure stuffing is completely covered with the dough from all sides. It is now a round patty with a diameter of 2–3 inches. Roll it gently with the help of the dry flour into a round disc of about 6–7 inches in diameter with gentle circular motion, using a rolling pin, making sure no stuffing protrudes out of the dough.

5. Heat a 12–14 inch skillet or *tawa* and transfer the dough on to it. When the underside is a little crisp and shows some brown spots turn it over. Coat it with oil or *ghee* or vegetable oil. Turn it over again and coat it with *ghee*. Keep turning and frying until both sides are crisp and light brown. Remove serve with plain yogurt or a stir-fry vegetable of your choice or pickle.

Paneer aur Dal ke Paranthe

Cheese and Lentils Stuffed Griddle Fried Bread

Serves: 4-6
Cooking Time: 10 Minutes

Ingredients

Dough:

Chappati flour	2 cups
Water to make the dough	1 cup + 1 Tbs

Filling:

Water	2 cups
Masoor or *toor dal* washed	¼ cup
Salt	½ tsp
Turmeric powder	½ tsp
Coriander powder	½ tsp
Ginger chopped	1 tsp
Onions chopped	1 Tbs
Black pepper	¼ tsp
Red pepper*	¼ tsp
Garam masala	½ tsp
Vegetable oil or *ghee*	¼ cup
Paneer (or ricotta cheese completely drained of water) crumbled	1 cup
Coriander freshly chopped	2 Tbs
Dry flour to roll the *parantha*	¼ cup

Note: These Paranthas can be made by kneading the chappati flour in any leftover dal from the night before. They are just as good and delicious. Serve them with Yogurt and some pickle and they can add up to a quick vegetarian meal.

Cooked *dal* and crumbled *paneer* (or ricotta cheese – completely drained of water) flavoured with spices, is used as a filling to stuff the regular *chappati* dough in making these *paranthas*. These are nutritious and wholesome and make a very good meal or a finger food for children.

Method

Make the flour dough as described in the recipe for *chappati*.

Filling:

1. Heat 2 cups of water in a pressure cooker and transfer the washed *dal* into it.
2. Add salt, turmeric powder, coriander powder, ginger, onion, black pepper, red pepper and *garam masala*.
3. Cook until all the water is absorbed. Cool and set it aside. Add more water to cook, if needed.
4. Add 2 Tbs oil to the *dal* and stir it well. Mix it into *paneer*, add the chopped coriander leaves and mix well. Set aside.

Rolling:

5. Roll a piece of dough as big as a plum on a floured rolling surface into a 3 inch diameter circle. Place 2 Tbs of the filling in the centre of the rolled circle. Lift the edges of the circle and pinch them together to seal the

RICE, PULAV AND BREADS

filling inside the dough and make a ball. Lift the ball, flatten it a little and roll it on the floured board into a disc 5–6 inch in diameter and transfer it to the heated iron skillet (*tawa*) or a heavy-bottom non-stick pan. Keep the heat at medium-high.

6. Cook until the *parantha* is firm enough to turn. Once turned, smear it with ½ tsp of *ghee* or oil on the cooked side and turn it over. Do the same on the other side.

7. Cook both sides by turning the *parantha* till it turns light brown. Remove from the fry pan and serve hot.

8. Serve it with plain yogurt or *raita*. If you prefer, you can also serve it with a vegetable stir-fry of your choice.

*Omit red pepper if you are making this bread for children. Use ricotta cheese drained of water if *paneer* is not available.

Nan

All Purpose Flour Tandoori (Clay Oven) Bread

Serves: 4-6
Cooking Time: 10 Minutes

Ingredients

Yogurt	½–1 cup
Eggs (large)	2
Ghee or oil	¼ cup
Yeast dissolved (in ¼ cup of warm water)	2 tsp
Sugar	2 tsp
Salt	½ tsp
All purpose flour	4 cups
Baking powder	1 tsp
Flour for kneading	1 cup

Ingredients for basting over the *Nan*:

Melted *ghee*	4 Tbs
Poppy seeds	2 tsp
Kalonji	2 tsp

The popularity of *Nan* has reached many corners of the world and it is now served in United States, UK, Canada, Australia and served with kebabs and curry. It is one of the most popular varieties of South Asia Breads.

Leavened bread of Punjab made with all purpose flour, yogurt, yeast and eggs. Extremely delicious and soft.

Method

1. Beat the yogurt and stir in the eggs, and the melted *ghee*. Beat it with egg beater smoothly. Dissolve the yeast in water and add to it the sugar and stir it and set it aside.

2. Sift the flour in a large deep mixing bowl with baking powder, salt and sugar and make a depression in the middle. Pour the yogurt mixture and knead and mix it in. Add the dissolved yeast with sugar and salt in and start to knead the dough. Knead it well and make it as pliable as possible. Cover with a wet muslin cloth or any wet thin cloth and set it aside.

3. Leave it in a warm place for at least 4–6 hours to rise until it is more than double its size. Pat it down and knead it smooth again. Divide the dough into plum-sized balls and with the help of *ghee* make them smooth and set aside to rise for at least 15 minutes. Press them smooth again. Roll them into flat oblongs with the help of dry flour on a flat surface about 6–8 inch long and about 4–5 inch wide. They should be about ⅛ inch thick. Sprinkle with poppy seeds or *kalonji* (onion seeds). Set the oven at broil.

HINT

3-4 Nans can be cooked under the broil at the same time once you are to cook.

4. Transfer the *nan* on to a greased baking sheet and place the sheet under the broil. As the *nan* starts to cook and puff up, and shows brown spots, remove the tray from the oven, turn over the *nan* and cook again for half a minute under the broil. This side does not have to show brown spots. Remove it from the oven and brush it with butter. Keep them wrapped in foil and store them to keep warm.

5. *Nan* goes well with all meals but especially with meat curries, vegetable curries and vegetable stir-fries.

Note: The *Tandoor* (similar to *bhatti* in India), originated in Afghanistan and was introduced in India by the Mughals. A *tandoor* is fired by burning charcoal. It is an important fixture in Indian restaurants. It is more or less a shallow clay pit with fire at the bottom. Now there are *tandoors* that are transferable from one place to another and are heated by electricity. The temperature inside these ovens can reach upto 480°C or 900°F and it needs very specialized handling and care. The broil temperature of the conventional ovens works as well.

Bhatura

Deep Fried All Purpose Flour Bread

Serves: 6-8
Cooking Time: 10 Minutes

Ingredients

All purpose flour	4 cups
Baking powder	2 tsp
Vegetable oil or *ghee*	¼ cup
Yogurt beaten smooth cups	1¼
Yeast (dissolved in water)	2 tsp
Water enough to make the dough	
Sugar	1 tsp
Salt	1 tsp
Low fat oil for frying	4 cups

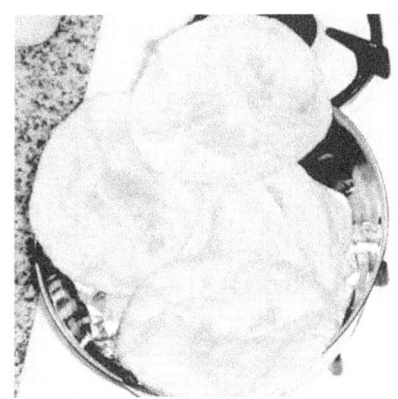

Note: A famous bread mostly made to go with tamarind flavoured Chickpeas (Chole). It makes a meal and is called on the menu of a restaurant "Chole Bhature."

Fried bread made with flour and yogurt is very soft and fluffy. They are served mostly with *chholey* (a spicy chick-pea preparation which is a speciality of Punjab) but you can serve them with any curry of your choice.

Method

1. Sift together flour and baking powder. Knead with oil, yogurt and yeast dissolved in 2 Tbs of water and sugar and salt. Add more water, if needed, to make a soft and pliable dough like a pizza dough.
2. Knead it smooth with the help of oil till it stops sticking to the sides of the pan.
3. Cover it with a wet cloth and let it rise in a warm place for a couple of hours. It will rise and double in size.
4. Press it down and take a piece of dough and shape it into a ball as big as a plum.
5. Using a little dry flour, roll the balls flat into rounds on a flat board or *chakla* (a round marble or stone pedestal for making *chappatis*) with a diameter of about 6–8 inches and about ½ of an inch thick.
6. Heat the oil at 350°F. Check the oil if it is ready for frying. (Drop a tiny ball of dough into the hot oil and if it rises to the surface immediately then the oil is ready for frying). Fry them till they are slightly brown and puffed up. Take them out of the hot oil with a slotted spatula and drain them on a plate lined with a paper towel.
7. This bread goes best when served with *chholey*, (Chick-peas curried, called *Khatta Kabuli Channa* in Punjab), make a complete meal with a little salad on the side.

Note: This bread can also be served with a potato curry or any other curry. For a quick recipe to make *bhaturas* omit yogurt, baking soda, salt, and use 2 tsp or 1 packet of yeast dissolved in water and enough club soda to make the dough.

RICE, PULAV AND BREADS

Puri

Deep Fried Whole Wheat Bread Puffs

Serves: 4-6
Cooking Time:
15 Minutes

Ingredient	
Whole-wheat flour	1½ cup
Cream of wheat	½ cup
Water as needed or	1 cup
Oil (for frying)	2 cups

Note: All over the country, it is made from the same ingredients regular wheat flour salt and water, but the stuffing of a pulse, herbs or a vegetable gives it a regional flavour and individuality. They can be made by kneading the dough with either pureed Tomatoes or Spinach or Potatoes or fresh coriander. Also add pureed ginger, garlic, green chilies, cumin powder, salt and red pepper to the mixture and knead the dough with the help of water. You can have deliciously flavoured puris that can be enjoyed as a snack or you can have them with a stir fry vegetable as a regular meal

Cream of wheat (*suji*) makes the *puris* crisper. If it is not available use all purpose or regular *chappati* flour only.

The word puri derives from the Sanskrit word पूरिका "filled." A light fried puffy bread used extensively at festive occasions and a popular bread all over India. It goes very well when served with potato curry and *raita*.

Method

1. Mix the flour and cream of wheat and knead it into a smooth dough with the help of water and set aside. (see pictures on facing page)

2. Heat the oil to 300°F–350°F in a fryer or thick bottom saucepan of a medium size or a wok. Check the oil, if it is ready for frying.

3. Pinch off a piece of dough as big as a walnut and roll it into a small ball. (See pix 2)

4. Flatten it and roll it with the help of some oil or dry flour into a small circle shape with a diameter of about 4 inches. (See pictures 3 and 4)

5. Drop these flattened discs one at a time into the heated oil. As the *puri* starts to rise to the surface pat it very gently a couple of times with the edge of the spoon. This helps in swelling and puffing up the *puri*. (See pictures 5 and 6)

6. Turn it over and after a couple of seconds turn it over again. (See pictures 7)

7. Cook a few seconds, if you want a crisper *puri*. Take it out with a slotted spoon, and drain it on a paper towel before serving. Makes approximately 15–20 *puris*.

8. Serve with a vegetable stir-fry or any other curry.

Makki ki Roti

Griddle Corn Flour Bread

Serves: 4-6
Cooking Time: 10 Minutes

Ingredients

Fine ground corn tortillas flour	2 cups
Butter or melted *ghee* (for brushing the bread before serving)	¼ cup
Dry flour for rolling	
Warm water to make the dough	

Note: If corn meal is being used then mix 2 cups of it with ½ cup wheat flour and add boiling water to the mixture. Stir it with a large spoon and as soon as it is cool enough to handle, knead it into a dough. Wet your hands slightly and make 8–10 equal parts and pat each part into 4-5 inch diameter discs and lay them down on a piece of plastic wrap. Heat the griddle and transfer each disc onto the hot griddle and wait till brown spots start to appear on the underside. Turn it over the disc and cook until brown spots appear on this side too. Cook the disc on direct flame. Follow and refer to the recipe of *chappati* making for this particular step. Enjoy with a dab of butter with mustard greens (*saag*).

This bread goes specifically with mustard greens (*saag*) and is a popular bread of Punjab. Hot corn bread topped with butter is delicious with any curry. In western countries corn bread is made with milk or butter milk sometimes has spices like green chilies, onions and is served with plenty of butter.

Method

1. Transfer the flour into a bowl. Make a depression in the middle and add 1-2 Tbs of *ghee* and water into it. Mix in the water with clean hands and knead to make a pliable dough so it can be rolled into *chappati* or Tortilla shapes.

2. Take pieces of dough slightly bigger than a plum and roll them into 3 inch diameter discs with a rolling pin on a flat rolling stone or a board (*chakla*) or any clean flat surface.

3. Heat a *tawa* or heavy-bottom iron skillet. Sometimes the bread starts to fall apart while transferring. In that case use a large spatula to transfer the rolled bread onto the *tawa* and cook on medium heat till light brown spots appear on the underside of the bread. Turn it over and cook for a few minutes until this side also has light brown spots. Remove the bread from the skillet or *tawa* and holding with tongs put it directly on the flame that is covered with a little grill or a frame to hold the pots and pans. Leave it on the flame for a few seconds till it gets lightly roasted on both sides. Serve it hot topped with butter or *ghee*. It is mostly served with mustard greens preparation but can be served with any other curry of your choice.

Rava Dosa

Cream of Wheat Crepes

Serves: 4-6
Cooking Time: 5-8 Minutes

Ingredients

Cream of wheat (Rava)	1 1/3
Rice flour	2–3 cup
All purpose flour	½ cup
Yogurt	1 cup
Water	3 cups
Vegetable oil or *ghee* (for making *dosa*)	4 Tbs
Green and red bell pepper finely chopped	1 cup
Garlic chopped	1 tsp
Green chilies chopped	1 tsp
Green onions finely chopped	1 cup
Cumin seeds	1½ tsp
Urad dal	1 Tbs
Red pepper	½ tsp
Coriander powder	1 tsp
Asafoetida	1/8 tsp
Salt	to taste
Green coriander finely chopped	1 Tbs

These thin cream of wheat pancakes from south India are among my favourites. Garnished with fresh green peppers, onions, coriander leaves, *ghee*, fresh cumin, red pepper and salt, they really get the appetite going. The smell of fresh spices makes them a favourite of everyone and they are quick to fix too. Serve them with a *chutney* and *sambhar*. Taste best when made fresh.

Method

1. Mix the cream of wheat, rice flour, and all-purpose flour in a deep mixing bowl and add the yogurt, 1 Tbs of the oil and water.

2. Beat as smooth as possible with a fork. Set it aside for the cream of wheat to soften.

3. Take a thick bottom skillet and add remaining 3 Tbs of oil and heat it. Add the bell pepper, garlic, green chilies and green onions in to the oil, and fry them about 2–3 minutes. Move them to one side and add the cumin seeds, *urad dal* and wait till they pop. Then, add the red pepper, coriander powder, asafoetida, salt and cook the spices as they change colour. Add the mixture to the cream of wheat batter and stir it in the batter evenly. Add the chopped green coriander and mix it in.

4. Wipe the skillet clean and heat it. Coat the surface with a thin film of oil and pour a ladle full of the batter and spread it evenly by tilting the skillet back and forth. Cook until the underside is light brown, adding more oil if needed (for about 2 minutes) and turn it over with a turner. Cook the other side also for as long as it takes to get it cooked. Remove with a turner from the skillet on to a plate and serve warm with coconut *chutney* or eggplant *chutney* or *channa dal chutney*, or plain yogurt.

5. Serve them warm, as they are cooking, for breakfast, lunch or dinner.

Idli

Steamed Rice Cakes

Serves: 6-8
Cooking Time: 10 Minutes

Ingredients

Rice long grain	4 cups
Urad dal	1 cup
Cooked rice	1 cup
Salt	4 tsp

Water as needed
Vegetable oil or *ghee* as needed

These are tender steamed rice cakes that are served for breakfast, lunch or dinner and go best with coconut *chutney* and *sambhar*. This speciality from south India is popular everywhere in India and abroad.

Method

1. Soak the rice and *urad dal* in separate containers for 6–8 hours.
2. Grind the rice by adding a little water in an electric blender and add the cooked rice while grinding to make a creamy but grainy batter. Set aside.
3. Grind the *urad dal* to a creamy mixture. Mix the two batters and add the salt and let it stand to ferment overnight in a warm place.
4. The following morning the batter would rise. Press down the dough with a spatula and beat it smooth with an eggbeater or your hand. It should have the consistency of a pancake batter.
5. Prepare the *idli* maker to make the *Idlis*. It is a special kind of steamer pot with inserts. Each of these inserts or plates has depressions to put *idli* batter. These plates get fitted into their respective slots in this pot, layered over one another, with enough room for the steam to go around them to cook the *idli*.

HINT

Fresh *idli* batter and *Idli* mixes are also available. They are a very good way to fix *Idlis* quickly. Follow the instructions on the package carefully and enjoy the *idlis*. If you want to save yourself a trip to the store and fix *idli* quickly at home here is a recipe: Cook 1 cup of cream of wheat in a Tbs of oil until light brown, cool and mix with ¼ tsp each of salt and baking soda and 1½ cup of yogurt and if the mixture is too thick, add 2–4 Tbs of water. Use this mix to make *idlis* in an *Idli* maker. This is an another way to cut down all the cumbersome work needed in preparing the batter by grinding and fermenting.

6. Remove the empty plates from the pot and pour water into the pot to fill only enough to stay 1 inch below the surface of the lowest plate. Grease the circles in the insert plates with oil and pour the batter into the circles making sure the circles are only two-third full. After filling the circles with the batter put the plate inserts back carefully into the steam pot layering them over one another. Cover the pot with the lid. Turn the heat on and start boiling the water. It takes about 8–10 minutes for the *idlis* to cook once the water starts to boil. Keep the heat low.

7. Remove the cover and check the *idlis*. Stick a toothpick in the middle of the *idli* and if it comes out clean that means it is done. Take the plate inserts out of the pot very carefully. Gently take out the *idlis* from the circles with a spatula. Serve them hot with *sambhar* and coconut *chutney, channa dal chutney* or peanut *chutney*.

Note: An easily disgestible food taken with sambher, Idli provides a mix of proteins and carbohydrates to the body. The cakes are usually two to three inches in diameter and are made by steaming a batter consisting of fermented black lentils (de-husked) and rice. The fermentation process breaks down the starches so that they are more readily metabolized by the body.

Aadai

Spicy Rice and Lentils Pancakes

Serves: 4-5
Cooking Time: 15 Minutes

Ingredients

Toor dal	⅓ cup
Mung beans split (washed or unwashed)	⅓ cup
Urad dal	⅓ cup
Split peas yellow or green	⅓ cup
Basmati rice	⅔ cup
Red dried peppers broken in pieces	2
Cumin seeds	½ tsp
Water to grind the mixture of lentils and rice	2 cups
Salt	½ tsp
Fennel seeds (optional)	1 tsp
Green Serrano chilies finely chopped	½ tsp
Ginger chopped	1 Tbs
Garlic chopped	1 Tbs
Fresh grated coconut	½ cup
Or	
Dry coconut powder	¼ cup
Asafoetida powder	⅓ tsp
Fresh cilantro chopped	⅓ cup
Shallots or yellow onions finely chopped	⅓ cup

These rice pancakes are made with a batter of ground soaked lentils, rice and spices. A refreshing and nutritious pancake served with podi powder, stir-fried potato curry, peanut or red pepper *chutney*. It can also be served for lunch with a little salad and pickles or *raita*. It is very versatile in its preparation. Oats powder can subsituted for rice and channa dal can replace any of the lentils in the recipe.

Method

1. Wash and soak *toor dal*, *mung* beans, *urad dal*, split peas, rice, red peppers and cumin seeds in water for atleast 3–4 hours.

2. Drain the water and grind them in a blender coarsely to a consistency of pancake batter by adding 2 cups of water as needed and grind the batter to a desired consistency. Add more water, if necessary.

3. Add salt, fennel seeds, green chilies, ginger, garlic, grated coconut or dry coconut powder, asafoetida powder, fresh cilantro and onions, and mix well.

4. Heat a nonstick *tawa* (Indian skillet) or a thick bottom 12 inch skillet or a skillet to make *dosa* and cover it with 1 tsp of oil. Drain the excess oil and pour a ladle full of batter spreading thin by going in circular motion, starting from the centre on the hot surface of the skillet. Spread about 6–8 inch in diameter or larger, keeping the heat on medium-low. As the batter is browning on one side brush the top side with cooking oil. It takes a couple of minutes. Cover and let it cook until the underside is light brown. Turn it and cook the other side until the batter is lightly brown and crisp.

5. Serve it hot with red pepper *chutney* or peanut *chutney* just like *dosa*. Boiled potatoes, onions stir-fry and *sambhar* can also be served along with the *chutney*.

Khasta Kachauri

Crisp Pastries Fried

Serves: 4-6
Cooking Time: 15 Minutes

Ingredients	
All purpose flour	2 cups
Baking powder	a pinch
Clarified butter to make the dough	4 Tbs
Salt	1 tsp
Water	½ cup
Filling ingredients	
Oil for making the filling	2 Tbs
Ginger	1 tsp
Green chilies chopped	1 Tbs
Cumin seeds	1 tsp
Fennel seeds crushed	½ tsp
Coriander seeds crushed	½ tsp
Oil for frying	
Asafoetida	¼ tsp
Mung or *urad dal* soaked overnight and coarsely ground	½ cup
Ajwain	½ tsp
Black pepper	½ tsp
Red pepper	1 tsp
Salt	1 tsp
Amchoor	1 Tbs
Gram flour	2 Tbs
Water	½–1 cup
Coriander powder	1 tsp

Deep-fried leavened bread stuffed with spiced ground lentils make a great snack and can also be served for breakfast. These go well with a potato curry or *raita*. They are delicious and crisp especially when served hot. An alltime favourite for breakfast mostly in the northern parts of India. Excellent snack any time.

Filling:

Method

1. Make smooth and tight dough by kneading together flour, baking powder, *ghee*, salt and about ½ cup of water. Add more water, if necessary. Cover with wet cloth and set it aside.

2. Heat the oil in a deep saucepan and add the ginger, chopped chilies and fry them. Then add the cumin seeds, fennel seeds, coriander seeds and coriander powder, and wait till they all crackle. Now add the asafoetida powder – wait till it sizzles and then add the ground *dal*, salt, red pepper, black pepper and gram flour. Mix and fry for few minutes until the flour and *dal* start turning slightly brown. Simmer with 1½ cups of water until the *dal* is softened but is not mushy (about 10–15 minutes) on medium heat. Add more water, if needed necessary. *Urad dal* will take

a little longer to cook and may require more water to soften. Make sure that the water is completely gone and the *dal* is dry enough to be used as a filling. Set it aside.

3. Divide the dough into 16 equal parts and roll each into a 2½ inch disc. Put 1 tsp of the filling in the centre and bring the sides of the circle over the filling and seal firm. Roll them a little with a rolling pin and set them aside covered with a wet paper towel.

4. Heat the oil at about 300°F in a deep wok. Keep the temperature steady around 300°F only and fry them few at a time, making sure the seam side of the *kachauri* is down. Fry until golden brown. Slow frying is very necessary to make them crisp and cooked inside. It take a few minutes to get that result. Take them out with a slotted spoon and drain them on a paper towel. Serve them with tamarind chutney, potato curry or *raita*.

Note: Kachauri probably originated in Rajasthan. Cooking was influenced by both the war-like lifestyles and food that could last for several days and could be eaten without heating was preferred. Rajasthan is also famous for *Bikaneri Bhujia, Mirchi Bada* and *Pyaaj Kachauri*. In *Gujarat*, it is usually a round ball filled with a stuffing of yellow *moong dal, black pepper, red chilli powder,* and *ginger* paste. Also Delhi has this other kind of kachori called 'Khasta Kachauri' or 'Raj Kachori'.

Exotic Vegetables

Indian culinary traditions are rooted in vegetarianism, mainly because of religion and of the cornucopia of vegetables available to the cook. With this incentive they have generated a great treasure of beautiful aromatic vegetable dishes. There is a major emphasis on freshness in Indian cooking. People cook fresh bread, use fresh vegetables, fresh lentils, and fresh yogurt for every meal each day. Vegetables and legumes substitute for the staple meat of the west. There is a great effort made to make at least two vegetable dishes for a fairly decent meal every day in an Indian household. Vegetables are ornamented with spices in as many different ways as you can imagine. They are stir-fried, curried, roasted as in eggplant (*bharta*), grilled like in *kebabs*, or steam cooked like in *undiya*. Sometimes several of these vegetables are curried together. Vegetables are immersed in a spicy batter to make delicious *fritters* and *koftas* (croquettes). Several kinds of croquettes are curried in exotic, aromatic and creamy gravies to be served with *nans* and home made fresh *chapattis*. The gravy of these vegetable curries is similar to the meat curries in terms of appearance and content.

Even the most ordinary vegetable can be turned into a delightful and appetizing accompaniment to a meal. Many different kinds of spice powders are used to make the vegetable curries like *podi masala* in the south, *panchphoran masala* in Bengal, *garam masala* and *achari masala* in north India, *tandoori masala* for making vegetable *kebabs*, *goda masala* mix in Maharashtra, *malwani masala* in the Malabar coast of India and *pathare prabhu masala* in Bombay. All vegetables in the north of India are cooked with tempering of cumin seeds and flavoured with *garam masala* (a mixture of 5 spices) and freshly chopped coriander leaves whereas in the southern and western regions tempering is done with mustard seeds and their regional spice powders.

Vegetables should always be washed before chopping. They can be steam cooked with salt and pepper for a few minutes on the stove and frozen for future use. The seasoning of onions, ginger, garlic and green chilies for a vegetable stir-fry can be prepared ahead of time by chopping them in the food processor and can be frozen or refrigerated till the day of use. You can also make the curry masala-mixture of chopped onions, garlic, ginger, green chilies, tomatoes and the spices ahead of time and stored in the freezer in small bags. These will stay good for a couple of weeks and can be used as needed for making curries. All cooking should be done on medium to low heat in a heavy-bottom, preferably nonstick, metal pan. High heat usually destroys the flavour and nutritive value.

According to ayurvedas and modern scientific research we should have atleast 3 servings of vegetables per day. Vegetables, like fruits, are low in calories and fats but are full of vitamins and minerals. All the Green-Yellow-Orange vegetables – like mustard greens, pumpkin, okra, beans, bitter melons and bell peppers are a rich source of calcium, magnesium, potassium, iron, beta-carotene, vitamin B-complex, vitamin-C, vitamin-A, and vitamin K. As in fruits, vegetables too are home for many antioxidants. They help protect the human body from oxidant stress, diseases, and cancers, and secondly; help the body develop the capacity to fight against these by boosting immunity. Living raw foods or fresh vegetables have the highest biophoton energy. The greater your store of light energy from healthy raw foods the greater the power of your overall electromagnetic field, and consequently the more energy is available to you for healing and maintenance of your optimal health. Vegetables also provide you with omega-3 fats and B vitamins, proven to help reduce anxiety and depression. Green leafy vegetables, such as kale, spinach, and Swiss chard, are loaded with magnesium, which helps balance your cortisol, one of your "stress hormones." Low magnesium levels have been linked with anxiety disorders and migraines, both of which are typically aggravated by stress.Magnesium and potassium also relax blood vessels, helping keep your blood pressure low. Magnesium also plays an important role in calcium absorption.helping you maintain good muscle and nerve function and a healthy immune system. your Vegetables are your REAL comfort foods, with nutrients that actually improve your resilience to stress. I must empasize here that makin vegetables a major part of your daily diet is the wisest decision you will make to prolong your life. Our forefathers were thinking far ahead when they even spiced the vegetables so that we could eat them with delight and also gain all the healthful benefits as a bonus.

EXOTIC VEGETABLES

Navrattan Curry

Mixed Vegetable Curry

Serves: 8-10
Cooking Time: 15 Minutes

Ingredients

Onions chopped	2 cups
Ginger chopped	1 Tbs
Garlic chopped	1 Tbs
Green chilies chopped	1 Tbs
Vegetable oil	¼ cup
Cumin seeds	1 tsp
Curry leaves (small)	6
Mustard seeds	1 tsp
Whole red pepper broken	2 or 3
Tomatoes fresh chopped	2 cups
Turmeric powder	1 tsp
Coriander powder	1 Tbs
Red pepper	1 tsp
Salt	to taste
Potatoes chopped	1 cup
Carrots chopped	½ cup
Cauliflowerets	1 cup
Beans chopped	½ cup
Pieces of fried paneer	1 cup
Peas fresh or frozen	½ cup
Zucchini* chopped	½ cup
Cashew Nuts	2 Tbs
Water	2 cups
Heavy cream	1–2 Tbs
Or coconut milk	½ cup
Green coriander leaves chopped	3 Tbs
Garam masala	1 tsp

This delicious Mughlai curry gets its name (navratna) from 9 (gems) different vegetables with or without paneer and nuts.

Several vegetables can be mixed to make a delicious colourful curry with a creamy sauce of tomatoes and small amount of coconut milk or heavy cream. It is mouth-watering, flavoury and appetizing.

Method

1. Cook the onions, ginger, garlic, green chilies in the oil till light brown on medium heat in a deep heavy-bottom saucepan or a *Dutch oven.
2. Add the cumin seeds, curry leaves, mustard seeds and whole red pepper broken into pieces and wait till the cumin and mustard seeds start popping.
3. Lower the heat and add the tomatoes, turmeric powder, coriander powder, red pepper, salt and stir well.
4. Add the potatoes and carrots first and let them cook for 5 minutes and then add all the vegetables, paneer pieces, cashew nuts

and stir well to coat them with all the spices. Add 2 cups of water and cover with the lid. Simmer for 10 minutes stirring in between by removing the lid. Add the coconut milk. Mix the curry well and let it simmer by occasionally stirring to check that there is no sticking to the bottom of the pan.

5. Cook until the potatoes get tender and carrots look softened.
6. Sprinkle with *garam masala* and chopped coriander leaves and simmer for another 2 minutes and serve.

Note: Vegetables are packed with soluble as well as insoluble dietary fiber known as non-starch polysaccharides (NSP) such as cellulose, mucilage, hemi-cellulose, gums, pectin...etc. These substances absorb excess water in the colon, retain a good amount of moisture in the fecal matter, and help its smooth passage out of the body. Thus, sufficient fiber offers protection from conditions like chronic constipation, hemorrhoids, colon cancer, irritable bowel syndrome, and rectal fissures. Besides eating cooked vegetables, salads are also a great source of nutrition. Among the vegetables used here zucchini, a vegetable originating from the Americas, has a variety of benefits Zucchini being a good source of vitamin C, is considered a good food for fighting asthma. Vitamin C, a powerful anti-oxidant, plays a huge role in keeping the immune systems healthy and fighting respiratory problems. The anti-inflammatory properties help keep the lungs open and clear. Zucchini also contains calcium that helps the nervous system to function properly and gives strength to the bones and teeth. It improves eyesight, helps in reducing blood pressure and is great for your heart because it is rich in pottasium. Zucchini is extensively grown in Argentina, Mexico, Turkey, Egypt China, Japan, Italy and India, besides other countries.

Zucchini and tomatoes give the curry a tangy taste and make it delicious

---
HINT

Instead of paneer and nuts you can add In this preparation ½ cup each of chopped daikon, radish, brocolli or red, green or yellow bell peppers. Two Tbs each of chopped fenugreek leaves and coconut powder will really enhance the flavour of the curry. If frozen vegetables are used in the cooking, then use less cooking time. "Dutch" oven is a deep heavy bottom cooking pan with an opening and is used in the west for cooking stews and chilli.

Ghia Kofta Curry - Page 91

Milijuli Subjion ke Kofoton ki Curry - Page 95

Aloo ki Subzi - Page 98

Bharwan Baingan - Page 100

Dum Aloo - Page 135

Palak aur Aloo ki Subzi - Page 142

Matar Paneer - Page 145

Khatte Meethey Baingan - Page 151

EXOTIC VEGETABLES

Undiya

Grilled Mixed Vegetable Curry from Gujarat

Serves: 8-10
Cooking Time: 25 Minutes

Ingredients

Ingredient	Amount
Potatoes peeled and chopped in 4 pieces	2 small
Plantain (raw banana) peeled and chopped	½ cup
Beetroot chopped	½ cup
Sweet potatoes peeled and chopped	½ cup
Carrots peeled and chopped	½ cup
Green frozen *toovar* or snow pea pods	1 cup
Eggplant chopped	1 cup
Spinach washed and chopped	1 cup
*Fenugreek leaves (kasuri methi)	1 cup
Onions chopped	2 cups
Ginger chopped	2 Tbs
Garlic chopped	2 Tbs
Green chilies chopped (mild)	2 Tbs
Salt	2 tsp
Red pepper	1 tsp
Roasted ground peanuts	¼ cup
Kashmiri chilies dry, broken	2-3
Turmeric powder	½ tsp
Vegetable oil or *ghee*	6 Tbs
Coriander powder	2 Tbs
Cumin powder	1 tsp
Ground roasted sesame seeds	1 Tbs

Undiya is popular in Gujarat. It is a mixed vegetable dish which has great flavour because it used to be baked in a clay pot. A group of selected vegetables are mixed with different spices, onions, ginger, garlic, green chilies which are then baked in a inverted claypot called *undu* with burning coal on top of it and around it. The pot is completely sealed and the vegetables cook in their own steam under pressure.

Vegetables like plantains add a nice creamy taste to undiya. Plantains, "potatoes of the air" or "cooking bananas" are more starchy than sweet and must be cooked before being eaten. They are a staple crop in much of Africa, and are served boiled, steamed, baked, or fried. Plantains grilled over a charcoal fire are popular street food in many African cities. In the Congo river region, plantain bananas—peeled, sliced, and boiled, or cut into rondelles and fried in oil—are called makemba. Their attractiveness as food is that they fruit all year round, making them a reliable all-season staple food. Curries made out of plantain are popular throughout the world. A sour, spicy and sweet curry known as pazham pachadi is made out of ripe bananas, coconut and curd is quite popular in Kerala.

Method

1. Chop all the vegetables from 1-9 in large pieces. Mix the vegetables together in large deep baking dish and add onions, ginger,

Sugar	1½ Tbs
Water	1 cup
Tomatoes chopped	2 cups
Muthias	1 cup
Mustard seeds	1 tsp
Cumin seeds	1 tsp
Curry leaves	8–10
Carom seeds	1 tsp
Fresh coconut grated	½ cup
Or	
Coconut powder	2 Tbs
Asafoetida	½ tsp
Green coriander leaves chopped	2 Tbs
Garam masala	1 tsp

garlic, green chilies, salt, red pepper, Kashmiri chilies, ground roasted peanuts, turmeric, 4 Tbs of *ghee*, ground roasted sesame seeds, coriander powder, cumin powder, sugar, water, and mix well until blended. Cover the pan with a lid.

2. Bake covered in an oven at 425°F for 30 minutes or microwave until the vegetables are tender. Add the *muthias* and tomatoes and bake for another 15 minutes or until all the vegetables are tender and cooked. Add more water, if needed.
3. Heat the remaining 2 Tbs of oil in a large thick-bottom cooking pan and add the mustard seeds, cumin seeds, curry leaves and carom seeds. Wait till the seeds start to pop, then add the fresh coconut or dry coconut powder and asafoetida powder. Stir and transfer the tempering on cooked vegetables into the pan. Stir to mix.
4. Top it with chopped coriander leaves and *garam masala*.
5. Undiya serves best with *poori*.

Bread Kofta Curry

Bread Croquettes Curried in Gourd Sauce

Serves: 6-8
Cooking Time: 35 Minutes

Ingredients

Pureed squash for the curry sauce:

Bottle gourd (*ghia*) or pumpkin grated	½ lb
Water	2 cups

Koftas:

Fresh yogurt	½ cup
Bread slices	6–8
Coriander leaves chopped	2 Tbs
Green chilies chopped	1 Tbs
Ginger chopped	1 tsp
Garlic chopped	1 tsp
Onion	½ cup
All purpose flour as needed	
Baking soda	$1/8$ tsp
Salt	½ tsp
Vegetable oil (for frying)	4 cups

For the Sauce

Onions chopped	1 cup
Ginger and garlic chopped	2 Tbs
Green chilies	1 Tbs
Vegetable oil or *ghee*	3 Tbs
Ghee or oil	3 Tbsp
Cumin seeds	1 tsp
Tomato sauce	1 cup
Turmeric powder	1 tsp
Cumin powder	1 tsp

Here is Ghia or gourd in its more subtle form. Add a little extra poise to your cooking by making these bread dumplings in a sauce of ghia. These koftas called croquettes in western cuisine are sure to make your meal looking special. Koftas an offshoot of Persian cuisine are delicacy now of Indian cuisine. Usually kofta are made of paneer/cottage cheese, and vegetables for the vegetarian version and meat for non-vegetarian version. The word *kofta* originated from Persian and means, beat/grind/meat ball. Here is a great example of fusion of foreign culinary specialities into the cuisine of India.

Bread *koftas* in a delicious white gourd sauce with tomatoes and curd are mouth watering. The bottle gourd is high in dietary fibre, vitamin C, riboflavin, zinc, thiamin, iron, magnesium and manganese. It also contains moderate amount of vitamin-B complex. The dish makes an excellent accompaniment to any dinner.

Method

For the Pureed Squash for the Curry

1. Boil the chopped or grated *ghia* (bottle guard) in 2 cups of water with ½ tsp of salt. As soon as the *ghia* becomes transparent and soft, purée it in a blender. Set it aside.

2. Prepare the *koftas* by mixing together yogurt, pieces of bread slices (remove the crust), chopped green coriander, chopped green

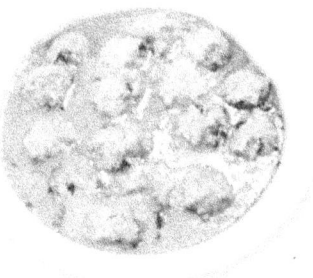

Red pepper	1 tsp
Coriander powder	1 Tbs
Salt	1 tsp
Sour cream or heavy cream	½ cup
Potatoes small cooked and peeled	1 cup
Water	½ cup
Garam masala	1 tsp
Coriander leaves chopped	½ cup

chillies, chopped ginger, garlic, onions, all purpose flour, baking soda, and salt in a deep salad bowl. Knead it well to make a soft dough and make small balls of the size of a walnut. Add more flour if needed.

3. Heat the oil in a wok at 325–350°F and fry the *koftas* light brown. Do not overheat the oil. Drain them on a paper towel and set them aside.

For the Sauce

4. Grind onions, ginger, garlic and green chilies together in a blender.

5. Heat 3 Tbs of *ghee* in a medium size thick-bottom cooking pan and add the puréed onions, ginger and garlic mixture. Add the cumin seeds and when they start to pop, add the tomato sauce, turmeric, cumin powder, red pepper, coriander powder and salt. Mix and fry the *masala* until the *ghee* separates from the *masala*. Add the puréed squash, sour cream, cooked potatoes and ½ cup of water and cook for 5 minutes on medium heat.

6. Just before serving, make sure the sauce is not too thick because after adding *koftas* it is going to thicken as the *koftas* will absorb water. Add more boiling water, if needed, and mix it well. Add the *koftas* to the sauce and bring it to a boil and simmer for 2 minutes. Remove from heat. Wait till the *koftas* swell up (15 – 20 minutes) and then serve by first ladling out the *koftas* in a serving dish. Serve them sprinkled with green coriander and *garam masala*.

Ghia Kofta Curry

Bottle Gourd Croquettes Curry

Serves: 4-6
Cooking Time: 25 Minutes

Ingredients for the *koftas*:

Bottle gourd (*ghia*) peeled and grated or finely chopped	2 cups
Salt	½ tsp
Ginger chopped	1 tsp
Garlic chopped	1 tsp
Green chilies chopped	1 tsp
Red pepper	½ tsp
Coriander powder	1 tsp
Gram flour	1 cup
Garam masala	½ tsp
Baking soda	a pinch
Pistachio very finely chopped	1 Tbs
Raisins	1 Tbs
Anaardana powder	1 tsp
Amchoor	1 Tbs
Vegetable oil for frying	3 cups

Ingredients for the curry sauce:

Onions chopped	1 cup
Ginger chopped	1 Tbs
Garlic chopped	1 Tbs
Green chilies chopped	1 tsp
Oil	as needed
Cumin seeds	1 tsp
Red pepper (dry) broken	2
Turmeric powder	1 tsp
Coriander powder	1 Tbs
Red pepper	1 tsp
Salt	to taste

Indians love vegetables and they can transform any vegetable with spices and curry sauce into a delicacy. This curry is a perfect example of that. Bottle gourd or Chinese squash is grated and mixed with gram flour and spices to make balls. These balls called koftas are then deep fried and cooked in a creamy tomato sauce.

Koftas are prepared all over India in every state with the vegtables that are more prevalant of that particular state. Ghia koftas are particularly prepared in Punjab and Northern part of India. Other famous names bottle gourd is known for according to different culture are white gourd and bottle squash for the US, doodhi for China, Lauki and ghia for India, Labu for Indonesia, Hyotan and yugao for Japan, Upo for Philippines, Bau for Vietnam, Buap Khaus and nam tao for Thailand.Oozing with health and cosmetic benefits, the bottle gourd is a blessing in disguise many are unaware.

Method

1. Mix 1 tsp of salt into the 2 cups of grated *ghia* or bottle gourd and let it sit for 1 hour. Squeeze the *ghia* and save the squeezed juices to be used later for the sauce. Add to the drained *ghia*, ginger, garlic, green chilies, red pepper, coriander powder, garm flour, *garam masala*, baking soda, chopped pistachio, raisins, *anaardana* powder or 1 Tbs of *amchoor* and knead with help of gram flour into balls (*koftas*). Add more gram flour if needed. Fry them, few at a time, in a deep wok or *karahi* in oil heated to about 300°F until golden brown (about 5 minutes). Take them out on a plate lined with paper towel with a slotted spoon. Keep the heat low to maintain steady temperature.

Tomato sauce	1 cup
Fresh tomatoes chopped	2 cups
Water	2 cups
Cream	2 Tbs
Garam masala	1 tsp
Coriander leaves chopped	2 Tbs

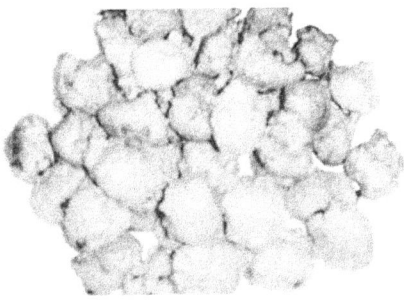

Note: Ayurveda highly recommends this food for diabetic patients and young children. Ayurveda the juice of the gourd can be used for the treatment of acidity, indigestion and ulcers as it serves as an alkaline mixture. *Lotus root, cauliflower and spinach are also very frequently used to make *koftas*. Same procedure as *ghia koftas* will work very well for spinach but lotus root and cauliflower after chopping would have to be boiled in water until soft.

For the Curry Sauce

2. In a heavy bottom 2–3 quart cooking pan, fry the onions, ginger, garlic, and green chilies in oil and wait till they turn light brown. Add the cumin seeds and whole red pepper. Wait for the cumin to start popping and add the turmeric powder, coriander powder, red pepper, salt, and mix well. Add the tomatoes, tomato sauce and mix the sauce in.

3. Cook on low heat for 3–5 minutes and add the water and the saved liquid from the grated *ghia*. Simmer the sauce for 15–20 minutes. Add gently the *koftas* and stir them in.

4. Cover with a lid and let it simmer for another 2 minutes. Turn off the heat, check to see if *koftas* are soft and plump but not broken. Add the cream and mix it in. Let the *koftas* sit in hot sauce for at least 20–30 minutes before serving.

5. Heat for another 2 minutes and add the *garam masala*, chopped coriander leaves and gently stir.

6. Remove from fire and serve by ladling out the *koftas*.* They can be served with rice, *pulav* or bread of your choice or any other meal. This dish is always a special addition to any meal.

Malai Kofta Curry

Creamy Cheese Croquettes in Curry Sauce

Serves: 6-8
Cooking Time: 25 Minutes

Ingredients

For *Koftas*:

Potatoes boiled and mashed	2 cups
Paneer or ricotta cheese completely drained of moisture	1 cup
Bread crumbs	1 cup
Ginger	1 tsp
Garlic	1 tsp
Green chilies	1 tsp
Salt	½ tsp
Baking soda	a pinch
Red pepper	½ tsp
Coriander powder	1 tsp
Coriander leaves chopped	1 Tbs
Garam masala	½ tsp
Amchoor	1 Tbs
Almonds or pieces of pistachio chopped	2 Tbs
Oil for frying	

For the curry:

Onions chopped	2 cups
Ginger, garlic and green chilies (each) chopped	1 Tbs
Oil	3 Tbs
Cumin seeds	1 tsp
Red pepper (whole) broken	2 or 3
Turmeric powder	1 tsp
Red pepper	1 tsp

Malai koftas, A dish of ultimate food seduction. Koftas originated from persian cuisine. An American statesman John Adams once wrote in a letter some where in early 19th century that the "The shortest road to men's hearts is down their throats." Remember, it s just one of the things that can take you close to man's heart! Not the ultimate one...Cooking is not just chopping, grinding or mashing and throwing everything into a pot and stirring but it reflects how much care and love you have put into it because it becomes evident once you taste it. Try cooking these once and see your taste buds falling head over heels in love with this tempting Malai Kofta.

These deep fried balls of mashed potatoes and cheese are curried and usually served with rice *pulav* but can be served with *chappati* or *nan*. It is one of the gourmet dishes in Indian cooking and takes a little effort to make than the regular curry but it is all worth it.

Method

1. Boil the potatoes and mash them.
2. Mix the cheese and the bread crumbs into the mashed potatoes.
3. Add ginger, garlic, green chilies, a pinch of baking soda, salt, red pepper, coriander powder, green coriander leaves, *garam masala* and *amchoor*. Mix well to make thick dough.
4. Make small 1 inch diameter balls/croquettes (*koftas*) and insert a piece of pistachio or a piece of almond in the centre of each of them and fry few at a time in oil heated at 325–350°F on medium low heat until light brown. Do not overheat the oil. Takes about 2–3 minutes.

Coriander powder	1 Tbs
Salt	1½ tsp
Tomatoes chopped	1 cup
Tomato sauce	1 cup
Plain whipped yogurt	1 cup
Water	2 cups
Heavy cream	2 Tbs
Garam masala	1 tsp
Coriander leaves chopped	2 Tbs

5. Take *koftas* out with slotted spoon. Drain on a paper towel lined bowl and set them aside.

For the curry:

6. Grind the onions, ginger, garlic, and green chilies in a blender. Fry the ground *masala* in 2 Tbs of oil in a heavy-bottom 2 quart cooking pan on medium low heat.

7. Move the onions mixture to one side and add the cumin seeds and wait till they start popping.

8. Add the whole red chili peppers, wait till they start sizzling. Add turmeric powder, red pepper, coriander powder, salt, tomatoes and tomato sauce. Keep frying until the tomatoes become soft, and the oil separates from the *masala*. Lower the heat.

9. Add the yogurt and stir well on low heat.

10. Add the 2 cups of water and cook the sauce for 5 minutes.

11. Add the *koftas* and stir them gently in the sauce.

12. Cover the pan with a lid and simmer on low heat for 2 minutes. Add the heavy cream and stir it in gently. Cook a minute longer. Let the *koftas* sit in the gravy for at least ½ hour before serving.

13. Sprinkle with *garam masala* and coriander leaves and serve with *pulav*, *nan*, *chappati* or *poori*.

Note: Instead of bread crumbs, 1–2 Tbs of arrow-root flour can be mixed with mashed potatoes and *paneer* to make the *koftas* or croquettes.

EXOTIC VEGETABLES

Mixed Vegetable Kofta Curry

Vegetable Croquettes Curry

Serves: 8-10
Cooking Time: 30 Minutes

Ingredients

Peas cooked and mashed	½ cup
Cauliflower florets boiled and mashed (medium size head)	½
Potatoes boiled and mashed (medium)	3
Ginger chopped	2 Tbs
Garlic chopped	2 Tbs
Green chilies chopped	1 tsp
Onions chopped	1½ cup
Gram flour	2 cups
Baking soda	a pinch
Cumin seeds ground roasted	1 tsp
Coriander seeds ground roasted	1 Tbs
Garam masala	1 tsp
Red pepper powder	1 tsp
Salt	1½ tsp
Coriander leaves chopped	2 Tbs
Raisins (lightly pan-fried in a tsp of oil)	1 cup
Pistachio chopped (lightly fried 1 Tbs in a pan along with raisins)	
Vegetable oil (for frying)	2–4 cups

For the Sauce

Ghee or oil	3 Tbs

Completely made of vegetables these koftas are especially flavorful and nutritious.

Cooked vegetable when mashed with gram flour can be formed into balls and deep-fried. These balls when curried make a dish, which is called *Kofta* Curry. It is usually served with rice or your favourite bread. Highly recommended for a formal occasion. This classic dish of Moghul origin is a rich dish usually prepared during special occasions. Deep fried vegetable balls are prepared and simmered in a special creamy sauce/curry and served along with rice and rotis/Naans (Indian flat bread).

Method

1. Boil peas and cauliflower in 2 cups of water until soft. Drain the water from the vegetables and save to be used later. Mash the vegetables. Store them. Boil the 3 potatoes until soft (the skin starts to break on the potato) and peel them. Mash potatoes and mix them with mashed vegetables in the mixing bowl.

2. Add 1 Tbs each of ginger, garlic, 1 tsp of green chilies, ½ cup of onions, gram flour, a pinch of baking soda, ground roasted cumin and coriander, ½ tsp of *garam masala*, ½ tsp of red pepper, ½ tsp of salt, 2 Tbs of chopped coriander leaves and mix well. Make

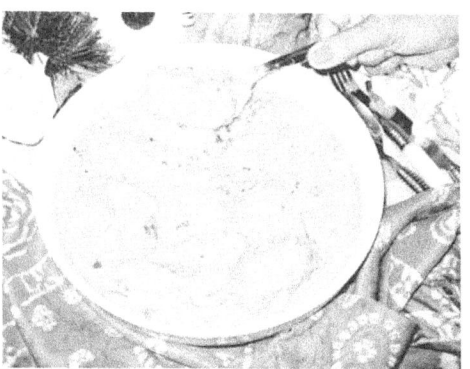

Tomato sauce	1 cup
Tomatoes chopped	1 cup
Turmeric powder	1 tsp
Coriander powder	1 tsp
Red pepper	1 tsp
Salt	to taste
Cream	½ cup
Water from the boiled vegetables	1½ cups
Garam Masala	as needed
Coriander Leaves chopped	1 Tbsp

    1 inch balls (*Koftas*) from the mixture. Add more gram flour, if needed.

3. Make a depression in the centre and place a raisin and $1/8$ tsp of pistachio in each ball. Heat the oil to 325–350°F. Do not overheat. Fry *koftas* until light brown and remove them from oil with a slotted spoon. Drain them on a paper towel and set aside.

4. Grind remaining 1 cup of onions, remaining ginger, garlic and green chilies in a blender and fry in 3 Tbs of oil for sauce in a deep, thick-bottom saucepan. Cook till the oil starts to separate from the onion mixture.

5. Add the tomato sauce, tomatoes, turmeric, coriander powder, 1 tsp each of red pepper, salt and fry till the tomatoes are completely soft. The mixture should look like a sauce and the oil separates from the sauce. Add 1½ cups of water plus the saved water from the boiled vegetables and boil the sauce for 5–10 minutes. Gently add the *koftas* and cover the pan and let it simmer on low heat for 2 minutes. Add the cream and stir it in gently. Turn off the heat and leave the *koftas* in sauce for ½ an hour before serving.

6. Add the *garam masala* and chopped coriander. Remove the *koftas* onto the serving dish first and then pour the gravy over them. It can be served with rice, *pulav*, *nan* or *chappatis*.

EXOTIC VEGETABLES

Arbi ki Curry
Yam Curry

Serves: 8-10
Cooking Time: 15 Minutes

Ingredients

Yams boiled, peeled, chopped into cubes	2 cups
Vegetable oil for frying the yams	4 Tbs
Vegetable oil for cooking	2 Tbs
Cumin seeds	1 tsp
Carom seeds	1 tsp
Onions chopped	1 cup
Ginger chopped	1 Tbs
Garlic chopped	1 Tbs
Green chilies chopped (mild)	1 Tbs
Turmeric powder	1 tsp
Coriander powder	1 tsp
Red pepper	1 tsp
Salt to taste or	1 tsp
Tomato sauce	1 cup
Water	2 cups
Heavy cream	2 Tbs
Garam masala	½–1 tsp
Coriander leaves chopped	2 Tbs

Here is another example of a very ordinary vegetable turned into a delicious preparation by cooking it in a creamy tomato sauce and flavouring it gently with spices.

It is considered sacred and is one of the single most well-known, important, and reliable plants in all of Polynesia, and the locals take a deep pride in its profound history.

Method

1. Wash the yams in tap water and boil them in water in a saucepan.
2. As soon as you see a spilt in the skin on the yams turn the heat off and cool them in running water. Peel the skin, chop them and slightly pan-fry them for 2 minutes in oil for frying in a skillet. Set aside.
3. In the same saucepan heat the oil for cooking. Add the cumin seeds and the carom seeds. As soon as they start to pop, add the onions, ginger, garlic and green chilies. Fry till the onions start to turn light brown.
4. Lower the heat and add the turmeric powder, coriander powder, red pepper and salt. Stir to mix. Add the tomato sauce and mix it in. Cook until the oil separates from the sauce. Add the chopped fried yams. Stir them in the sauce and add the water. Cover the saucepan with a lid and let it simmer for 5–10 minutes or until the sauce becomes creamy and thick. Add the cream and heat it through.
5. Sprinkle with *garam masala* and chopped coriander leaves and serve it with your favourite bread.

Aloo ki Subzi

Potato Curry

Serves: 4-6
Cooking Time: 20 Minutes

Ingredients

Onions chopped	½–1 cup
Ginger chopped	1 Tbs
Garlic chopped	1 Tbs
Green chilies chopped	1 tsp
Vegetable oil	2-3 Tbs
Cumin seeds broken and crushed	1 tsp
Mustard seeds	1 tsp
Red pepper whole	2 tsp
Curry leaves	5–6
Tomatoes chopped	2 cups
Red pepper powder	1 tsp
Turmeric powder	1 tsp
Coriander powder	1 Tbs
Dried fenugreek leaves (optional)	2 tsp or more
Salt	to taste
Coconut milk canned and unsweetened (optional) or ½ cup of Yogurt	½ cup
Boiled potatoes chopped into cubes	2 lbs
Water	1 cup
Garam masala	1 tsp
Cilantro leaves chopped	2 Tbs

Whenever you are short of vegetables and in need of a curry, prepare this spicy potato curry. It has lots of taste and a great presentation.

A perfect accompaniment with *poori* for a Sunday lunch. Quick and delicious, in fact it is a perfect side dish for any occasion.

Method

1. Cook the onions, ginger, garlic and green chilies in oil in a deep thick-bottom saucepan and wait till the onions turn light brown.
2. Add the cumin seeds, mustard seeds, whole red pepper and sauté until the seeds crackle.
3. Add the curry leaves and tomatoes.
4. Add the red pepper, turmeric powder, coriander powder, dry fenugreek leaves and the salt. Stir-fry for 5 minutes until the tomatoes are soft and the oil separates from the sauce. Lower the heat. Add ½ cup of coconut milk or Yogurt and mix it in.
5. Add the potatoes and mix them well into the mixture. Add the water and simmer for 10–15 minutes or until the potatoes are tender. The amount of water to be used is at your own decision depending on how thick a curry you want.
6. Top it with *garam masala* and the chopped cilantro leaves. Mix well into the curry and boil once.
7. Serve with *raita* and *poori* or as a side dish with any meal.

EXOTIC VEGETABLES

Bhindi ki Subzi

Okra Curry

Serves: 6-8
Cooking Time: 15 Minutes

Ingredients

Oil for frying	4 cups
Okra chopped in 1 inch pieces	1 ½ lbs
Vegetable oil or *ghee*	3–4 Tbs
Onions chopped	1 cup
Ginger chopped	1 Tbs
Garlic chopped	1 Tbs
Green chilies (mild)	1 Tbs
Mustard seeds	1 tsp
Cumin seeds	1 tsp
Split yellow or green peas	1 tsp
Curry leaves	6–8
Turmeric powder	1 tsp
Coriander powder	1 Tbs
Red pepper	½ tsp
Fenugreek dry leaves (*Methi*)	1 Tbs
Coconut dry powder	1 Tbs
Tomato sauce	1½ cup
Tamarind pulp or *kokum* powder	½ tsp
Frozen okra chopped pkg	16 oz
Coconut milk	1½ cup
Salt	1 tsp

Usually okra is served as a dry vegetable stir-fry but in the southern parts of India it is also served as a curry. Here is a recipe I acquired from a friend of mine. A curry made from tomatoes, tamarind and coconut milk.

Method

1. Heat the oil in a wok and fry the okra until light brown for about 10 minutes and set aside.

2. In the same pan heat another 1 Tbs of the oil and add the onions, ginger, and fry till the onion is brown. Add the chopped garlic. Fry for 2 minutes and move the onion mixture to one side and add the mustard seeds, cumin seeds and the split peas and fry till they start to pop and start to turn slightly brown. Add the curry leaves. Stir them in.

3. Add the turmeric powder, coriander powder, red pepper and fenugreek leaves and fry for a minute or two. Add the coconut powder and fry until it turns slightly brown. Add the tomato sauce and the tamarind pulp dissolved in water and stir to mix. Keep stirring until the oil begins to separate from the sauce (5 minutes).

4. Add the okra. Coat it gently in the sauce and lower the heat.

5. Add the coconut milk and salt, and stir it in well. Cover the pan and let the curry simmer for another 5–10 minutes or until the okra is cooked. Remove from heat and serve as a vegetable accompaniment to any meal.

Note: *Kokum* powder can be substituted for Tamarind pulp.

Bharwan Baingan

Stuffed Eggplants

Serves: 8
Cooking Time: 15 Minutes

Ingredients

Indian eggplants	2 lbs
Onions ground	1 cup
Ginger ground	1 Tbs
Garlic ground	1 Tbs
Green chilies ground	1 tsp
Turmeric powder	1½ tsp
Goda masala	4 Tbs
Tamarind pulp	1 tsp
Salt to taste or	1 tsp
Oil	½ cup
Green coriander leaves chopped	4 Tbs

Small Indian eggplants are stuffed with a mixture of spices, ground onions, ginger, garlic, tamarind pulp and pan-fried or baked in the oven. They make a very tasty, great looking vegetable presentation. There are many varieties of egg plants but these are best for making stuffed eggplant dish.

Method

1. Wash the eggplants and make two crosswise slits on the smooth side of the eggplants, ¾ inch down the length of the eggplant. Set them aside.

2. Mix the onions, ginger, garlic, green chilies, turmeric powder, salt, 4 Tbs of *goda masala* and 1 tsp of tamarind pulp dissolved in 1 Tbs of water in a small bowl. Add 2 Tbs of the oil to a skillet and heat it a little and transfer everything from the bowl into it. Fry for 5 minutes or until the water dries up. Set it aside.

3. Cool and stuff the *masala* mixture in between the slits of the eggplants and press to close them. Put them in a shallow baking dish that has already been greased generously with oil.

4. Cover the dish with a foil and bake at 425°F for 30 minutes. Remove the foil and bake them open for another 15–20 minutes turning them once or twice or until the skin turns golden brown. Remove them to a serving dish and sprinkle with coriander leaves and serve.

Note: Japanese eggplant are slender with thinner skins and a more delicate, sweeter flavour and can be green, pink, white, lavender and purple. One American eggplant equals about 3 Japanese eggplants.

Bharwan Bhindi

Whole Stuffed Okra

Serves: 8-10
Cooking Time: 45 Minutes

Ingredients

Onions chopped	1 cup
Ginger chopped	1 Tbs
Garlic chopped	1 Tbs
Green chilies	2–3
Turmeric powder	1 tsp
Red pepper	1 tsp
Cumin powder	1 tsp
Coriander powder	1 Tbs
Salt	1 tsp
Garam masala	¾ tsp
Amchoor or *Anaardana* powder	1 Tbs
Fenugreek leaves (dry)	1 tsp
Oil (for frying)	5 Tbs
Whole okra washed and ends trimmed	2 lbs
Coriander leaves chopped	2 Tbs

It is a very special north Indian preparation and is one of the very popular vegetables to be served in a formal setting. Regularly eating okra reduces risk of colon cancer. It has insulin-like properties that help to reduce blood sugar level. The fiber helps improve the population of beneficial bacteria in the gut. The high antioxidants and vitamin C content makes it a good immune booster food that reduce your catching the cough and cold. With good bowel movements, skin health will improve. Helps reduce acne, psoriasis and other skin conditions. Okra contains beta-carotenes (precursor of vitamin A), xanthin and lutein, all antioxidant properties that are helpful for vision health, preventing eye problems like cataract and glaucoma.

Method

1. Grind the onions, ginger, garlic and green chilies in a blender. Add turmeric powder, red pepper, cumin powder, coriander powder, salt, *garam masala* and *amchoor* or *anaardana* powder and dry fenugreek leaves. Mix and fry the *masala* in 2 Tbs of oil for 5 minutes and set it aside.

2. Make a single lengthwise slit into the okras. Fill up the opening with 1 tsp of the fried *masala*. Set them aside.

3. Take a large cookie sheet and oil it generously. Arrange the stuffed okra in single layer on the cookie sheet and bake them at 425°F for 40–45 minutes until they are dark brown and crisp. Turn them once or twice and brush them with oil or *ghee*.

4. Remove from the oven, sprinkle *garam masala* and chopped coriander and bake again for 2 minutes. They should be crunchy and delicious.

5. Serve them with a meat curry, *dal* and any bread of your choice.

Bharwan Shimla Mirch

Stuffed Green Bell Peppers

Serves: 6-8
Cooking Time: 25-30 Minutes

Ingredients

Green bell pepper (small size)	8
Onions chopped	½ cup
Ginger chopped	1 Tbs
Garlic chopped	1½ tsp
Green hot chilies chopped	1 Tbs
Cumin seeds	1 tsp
Boiled potatoes, peeled and cubed or small fried *paneer* cubes	2 cups
Cooked rice	½ cup
Turmeric powder	1 tsp
Vegetable oil	¼ cup
Poppy seeds	1 tsp
Red pepper	1 tsp
Ground coriander	1 Tbs
Salt	to taste
Lemon juice	2 Tbs
Coriander leaves chopped	2 Tbs
Garam masala	1 tsp
Cream of coconut	¼ cup

Stuffed vegetables are usually made when the meal is special. They are easy to make and look elegant too. The stuffing is made of cooked mixture of boiled potatoes, onions, core of the peppers, fresh herbs, rice and spices. Bell peppers are an outstanding source of antioxidants and anti inflamnatory phyto nutrients.

Most often bell peppers are green, yellow, orange, and red. Bell peppers are sometimes called "sweet peppers." Peppers are native to Mexico, Central America and northern South America. Peppers were carried to Spain in 1493 and from there they spread to other European, African and Asian countries. Today, China is the world's largest pepper producer, followed by Mexico and Indonesia. Bell Peppers or capsicums are very nutritive and are high in antioxidants and vitamin C. Christopher columbus who brought them to Europe, named them pepper after newly discovered black pepper from India. In India Australia and Newzland it is known as capsicum. Compared to green peppers, red peppers have more vitamins and nutrients. The level of carotene, like lycopene, is nine times higher in red peppers. Red peppers have twice the vitamin C content of green peppers. Red and green bell peppers are high in para-coumaric acid- a nutrient that helps in the growth and heath of your stomach bacteria.

Method

1. Wash and dry the peppers. Boil them in water for 5 minutes, drain the water and dry them. Remove the top – going in a circle with a sharp knife, so that the top comes out like a cap with a little handle that is the stem of the pepper. Set it aside for use later. Remove the seeds and centre flesh and brush the outside of the pepper with oil. Set them aside.

2. Cook the onions, ginger, garlic and green chilies in 2 Tbs of oil until light brown and

add the cumin seeds. Wait till they pop and add the chopped potatoes, or small paneer cubes, fried and freshly chopped flesh from the interior of the peppers leaving any firm seeds behind. Add also ½ cup of cooked rice. Stir well.

3. Add the turmeric powder, poppy seeds, red pepper, coriander powder and salt, and mix well. Lower the heat and cook while stirring for 2 minutes.

4. Add the lemon juice, chopped green coriander, *garam masala* and the cream of coconut. Stir and cover the pan with a lid and let it simmer for 3–5 minutes or until the potatoes become a little soft. The stuffing is ready. Let it cool and set it aside.

5. Fill the pepper shells with the stuffing leaving a little space at the top and cover them with the top of the pepper that was removed and stored for this purpose only.

6. Bake at 425°F in an 8–10 inch baking dish that has been greased with the remaining oil. Cover the pan for the first 15 minutes and then remove the cover and bake open for another 10 minutes. Remove them from the oven and serve. Great vegetable accompaniment to any meal.

Note: If large size peppers are used, cut them in half and fill the cavities in the same way and bake them.

Shimla Mirch, Aloo Tamatar ki Subzi

Bell Pepper, Potatoes and Tomatoes Stir-Fry

Serves: 8
Cooking Time: 15 Minutes

Bell peppers and potatoes go very well together and the tomatoes give it the extra tangy taste needed to make this a delicious stir-fry vegetable special.

Ingredients

Onions chopped	1 cup
Vegetable oil	as needed
Ginger chopped	1 Tbs
Garlic chopped	1 Tbs
Green chilies chopped	1 tsp
Cumin seeds	1 tsp
Potatoes peeled, washed and chopped	1 cup
Turmeric powder	1 tsp
Red pepper	1 tsp
Salt	to taste
Cumin powder	½ tsp
Coriander powder	1 Tbs
Water	¼ cup
Bell pepper fresh, medium size washed, deseeded and chopped	4
Tomatoes chopped	1 cup
Tomato sauce	½ cup
Garam masala	1 tsp
Coriander leaves chopped	1 Tbs

Method

1. Cook the onions in oil and add the ginger, garlic and green chilies. Fry until light brown in a deep-heavy bottom saucepan or a wok.
2. Add the cumin seeds and wait till they pop. Add the potatoes and all the spices – turmeric powder, red pepper, salt, cumin powder, coriander powder, and stir well. Add ¼ cup of water, lower the heat and cover and cook for 10 minutes.
3. Add the chopped peppers, the tomatoes and the tomato sauce, stir well. Cover with a tight lid on a low heat and simmer for another 5 minutes or until the potatoes are tender.
4. Keep stirring to make sure the vegetables do not stick to the bottom of the pan.
5. Sprinkle with *garam masala* and chopped coriander leaves and mix.
6. Cook for another 2 minutes and serve.

Note: 1 tsp of Amchoor or mango powder can be substituted for tomatoes. 2 Tbs of soaked and ground channa dal or 1 Tbs each of crushed peanuts and sesame seeds can be added along with the bell pepper to give a thicker gravy. In some parts of India couple of teaspoons of gram flour are added along with spices and stir fried to make a creamier gravy.

Bharwan Tamatar

Stuffed Whole Tomatoes

Serves: 6-8
Cooking Time: 20 Minutes

Ingredients

For stuffing:

Tomatoes (medium) fresh, firm	8
Onions chopped	½ cup
Ginger finely chopped	1 Tbs
Green chilies finely chopped	1 Tbs
Vegetable oil	¼ cup
Garlic finely chopped	1 Tbs
Cumin seeds	1 tsp
Carom seeds	1 tsp
Potatoes boiled chopped	2 cups
Peas and finely diced carrots (fresh or frozen)	½ cup
Tiny fried cheese (*paneer*) cubes	½ cup
Turmeric powder	1 tsp
Red pepper	1 tsp
Coriander powder	1 Tbs
Coconut powder	1 Tbs
Salt	to taste
Garam masala	1 tsp
Green coriander leaves chopped	2–4 Tbs

Note: Prepare the filling and even fill the tomatoes ahead of time and cook when ready for serving. Many different fillings are used. Instead of the potatoes, fried cheese cubes, peas and carrots, fresh corn and chopped bell peppers with bread crumbs can be used or beans, onions and grated paneer with bread crumbs and lemon juice can be used or you can even use cooked rice, peas and onions. Either way the stuffed tomatoes are always a welcome dish.

Tomato, a pulpy nutritious fruit commonly eaten as a vegetable, is another wonderful gift of the Mayans. This humble vegetable of Central America has seized the attention of millions of health seekers for its incredible phyto-chemical properties. Interestingly, it has more health-benefiting compounds than that of an apple! This exotic vegetable of all seasons is native to the Central America and was cultivated by the Aztecs centuries before the Spanish explorers introduced it to the rest of the world. It was introduced to India by the portuguese and other colonian powers.

Tomatoes are an excellent sources of antioxidants, dietary fiber, minerals, and vitamins. On account of their all-round qualities, dieticians and nutritionists often recommend them in cholesterol controlling and weight reduction diet programmes.

Tomatoes stuffed with mashed boiled potatoes, diced carrots, peas, onions and spices and tiny fried cheese cubes baked in oven makes a delicious preparation with a beautiful presentation.

Method

1. Wash and dry the tomatoes. Remove the top of each tomato by going in a circle around the top with a sharp knife so as to make a cap with any stem it may have and brush the outside of the tomato with oil and set it aside.

2. Scoop out the centre pulp of the tomato and store in a bowl, leaving the sides intact.

3. Fry the onions in a thick-bottom skillet in 2 Tbs of oil. Add the ginger with green chilies in two tbs or more of oil, and wait till the onions turn a shade of brown. Add the garlic. Stir and add the cumin seeds, carom seeds and wait till they start popping. Add the potatoes, peas and carrots, the centre of the tomato pulp and the tiny fried cheese (*paneer*) cubes and mix well.

4. Add the turmeric powder, red pepper, coriander powder, coconut powder, salt, and stir to cook. Lower the heat, cover the skillet with a lid and cook the stuffing for 8–10 minutes.

5. Add the chopped up coriander leaves, *garam masala* and mix these in.

6. Remove from heat and cool.

7. Stuff the shell of the tomatoes with the stuffing leaving a little space at the surface and place the cap on top.

8. Pour the remaining oil into an 8–10 inch baking dish and arrange the tomatoes in the pan. Bake at 425°F in a conventional oven for 10–15 minutes. Sprinkle the remaining chopped coriander leaves. Remove from the baking dish gently with a spatula and serve as a vegetable accompaniment to any dinner or a meal. Make sure that you do not overcook the tomatoes.

Note: Either potatoes or cheese from the stuffing can be replaced by chopped cabbage that has been drained of all moisture. Water can be removed by sprinkling salt over the cabbage. Let it sit for an hour or so and squeeze out the water.

EXOTIC VEGETABLES

Bharwan Tinda

Stuffed Round Gourd

Serves: 6-8
Cooking Time: 25 Minutes

Ingredients	
Salt	1½ tsp
Turmeric powder	1 tsp
Coriander powder	2 Tbs
Garam masala	1½ tsp
Red pepper	1 tsp
Garlic powder (or chopped garlic)	1 tsp
Ginger powder (or chopped ginger)	1 tsp
Cumin powder	1 tsp
Amchoor	2 Tbs
Round gourd fresh (*Tinda* medium size)	10–12
Vegetable oil	3–4 Tbs
Coriander leaves chopped	1 Tbs
*Cooked rice	½ cup
Or	
Grated *paneer*	½ cup

Note: For stuffing the round gourd (*tindas*), scoop out the centre of the gourd. Chop the centre flesh finely. Heat some oil, add cumin seeds and when they stop popping add cooked rice, chopped central flesh of the *tindas* and all the spices. Cook for 5 minutes stirring. Fill the empty shells of round gourd with the filling and follow step 3 onwards. You can also add crumbled paneer, boiled channa dal or Mung dal to the filling instead of cooked rice to make it more delicious. Tinda can be curried with potatoes using the curry masala. (The recipe for curry masala is in the introduction of the book). They can be stir fried just like the recipe of Potatoes and Egg Plant Stirfry.

It is regarded as super food due to its numerous health benefits. It contains antioxidants like carotenoids and many anti-inflammatory agents, which are effective for controlling blood pressure, heart diseases, and strokes and prevent cancer formation. It is very mild and soothing vegetable for intestinal tract. A lot of fiber helps in digestion, helps in diarrhea by increased water absorption, relieves stomach acidity, and prevents constipation. Some researches indicate that they are good food for healthy skin and hairs, its consumption result in very long and healthy hairs. It increases the urinary flow and excretes toxins from the kidney. Tinda is also called Indian round gourd or apple gourd or Indian Baby Pumpkin.

Native to India, this vegetable is from the cucumber family. It has a soft very green and tender exterior and is rich in vitamins. It is cooked in many different ways but Stuffed with spices and pan-fried, they make a delicious and pleasing presentation.

Method

1. Mix all the spices salt, turmeric powder, coriander powder, 1 tsp *garam masala*, red pepper, garlic powder, ginger powder, cumin powder and *amchoor* in a small mixing bowl and set them aside.

2. Cut and peel fresh round gourd (*tinda*) and cut them twice crosswise from the top with one-third bottom intact. Brush the outside with oil or *ghee*. *Tindas* can be stuffed as described in the Note.

3. Coat the cut sides of each *tinda* with mixture of spices (at least using ½–1 tsp) using a spoon and set them on a plate.

4. Heat the remaining oil in a wok or a heavy-bottom skillet on medium low heat. Arrange the round gourd in a layer in the skillet. Cook them, covered on low heat for 5–8 minutes. Remove the cover, turn them over and cook them uncovered until the sides and the bottom starts to turn dark brown. Keep turning them to avoid burning (about 15–20 minutes).

5. Instead of cooking on direct heat, bake them in an 8–12 rectangular 2 inch deep baking pan at 425°F in the oven. Bake covered for 5–10 minutes and then uncovered for another 15–20 minutes until they turn golden brown. Turn them once or twice in between to avoid burning the bottom of the round gourd. Remove them from heat and serve them with any meal as a vegetable accompaniment. Brush them with a little *ghee* during baking.

6. Serve, sprinkled with chopped coriander leaves and *garam masala*.

Note: This unique squash-like gourd is very popular in Indian and Pakistani curries and many gourmet dishes. The green coloured, apple sized fruits are flattish round in shape and 50-60 grams in weight and are called baby pumpkins. Over all this vegetable has a magical effect on the body if used regularly.

Bharwan Karela

Stuffed Bitter Gourd

Serves: 6
Cooking Time: 35 Minutes

Ingredients

For soaking to remove bitterness:

Bitter gourds medium sized	6
Salt	2 tsp
Lemon juice	2 tsp

Ingredients for stuffing:

Onions chopped	½ cup
Ginger chopped	1 Tbs
Green chilies (mild) chopped	1 Tbs
Garlic chopped	1 Tbs
Ghee (for frying)	2 Tbs
Ghee (for frying the stuffing)	as needed
Turmeric powder	1 tsp
Coriander powder	1 Tbs
Cumin seeds	1 tsp
Anise seeds ground	1 Tbs
Red pepper	1 tsp
Salt	1 tsp
Tamarind pulp	1 tsp
Mashed potatoes	½ cup
Or	
Crumbled up ricotta cheese or *paneer*	½ cup
Garam masala	1 tsp
Coriander leaves chopped	1–2 Tbs

Peeling them and soaking them in lemon juice and salt for an hour ahead of cooking takes out the bitterness of bitter gourd. This vegetable has tremendous health benefits, helps cure diabetes, high blood pressure and increases body's resistance against infection. They taste best when stuffed with a mixture of mashed potatoes, or crumbled up ricotta cheese, ground onions, garlic, ginger, tamarind pulp and all the other spices used in the curries. This makes them really delicious and palatable. This is one of the typical North Indian way of cooking bitter gourd.

Bitter melon originated on the Indian subcontinent, and was introduced into China in the 14th century. It is very popular in Japanese, Indonesian, Vietnamese, and Philipino cuisine. In Turkey it is used as a folk remedy for various stomach ailments when consumed in raw or juice form, can be efficacious in lowering blood glucose levels.

Method

1. Peel the bitter gourds and make a slit lengthwise in them and soak in lemon juice and salt at least an hour or overnight. Wash them well the next morning and scoop out the pulp and any tough seeds you may have. Squeeze to take out all the bitterness from the bitter gourds and set them aside.

2. Fry the onions, ginger, garlic and green chilies in *ghee* until light brown. Add the turmeric powder, coriander powder, cumin seeds, ground anise seeds, red pepper and salt. Stir well and add the tamarind pulp. Fry till the water dries up.

3. Add the crumbled up cheese or mashed potatoes and mix. Cook another 2 minutes and add the *garam masala* and chopped coriander leaves. Stir the mixture well and let it cool. Stuff the *karelas* with this stuffing

and wrap a thin thread around it 3–4 times to cover the opening of the bitter gourd.

4. Grease generously an 8 or 10 inches wide, two inches deep baking dish and arrange the bitter gourds in a layer. Bake them in an oven at 425°F and cover them for 20–25 minutes. Spray them with oil again. Remove the lid and bake for another 15–20 minutes. Keep turning them occasionally to brown all sides. It may take more or less time depending on the number and size of bitter gourds. They can be pan fried in the oil coated frying pan, turning them occasionally until light brown.

5. Serve them with any wet curry, *dal* and bread of your choice. Remove the thread before eating.

EXOTIC VEGETABLES

Bhuni hui Bhindi

Okra Stir-Fried

Serves: 6-8
Cooking Time: 10 Minutes

Ingredients

Fresh okra cut and trimmed in ¼ inch pieces	2 lbs
Vegetable oil	3–4 Tbs
Onions chopped	½ cup
Ginger chopped	1 Tbs
Green chilies chopped	1 Tbs
Garlic chopped	1 Tbs
Cumin seeds	1 tsp
Curry leaves	6–8

Spice mixture:

Turmeric powder	1 tsp
Red pepper	1 tsp
Coriander powder	1 Tbs
Salt	to taste
Amchoor (dried mango powder) or *anaardana* powder	1 Tbs
Garam masala	1 tsp
Coriander leaves	

Note: Baking the okra in the oven is done only because the okra pieces will not crush. Okra can be fried gently in the frying pan on direct heat. Making sure it is done gently.

Okra is really full of numerous vitamins including vitamins A, C, B1 B2 and B6. Okra has also been advised for expectant mothers simply because of its high vitamin B folic acid content that is crucial during the formation of the neural tube from the fetus. It brings the blood sugar down of a diabetic patient if taken regularly.

Okra is widely enjoyed all over India. It is mostly stir-fried with onions, green chilies and spices and it becomes crunchy and very flavourful. It is also served whole stuffed with spices on special occasions.

Method

1. Wash and dry the okra and chop them horizontally into ¼–½ inch pieces. Coat an 10–13 inch baking dish with 2 Tbs of the oil or use oil spray to coat the pan with grease and spread the okra evenly in the dish in a layer. Bake at 425°F in the oven for 15–20 minutes or until they start to turn brown. Turn them occasionally during baking with a spatula for even browning.

2. Fry the onions, ginger and green chilies in a wok or large heavy-bottom skillet in 2 Tbs of oil until the onions are a shade of brown and then add the garlic. Fry till the garlic turns light brown.

3. Add the cumin seeds and curry leaves and wait till the cumin seeds stop popping. Mix it well. Transfer the baked okra into the wok and stir gently to mix it with the onion mixture. Making sure that okra pieces do not get crushed.

4. Add the turmeric powder, red pepper, coriander powder and the salt, and gently fold in the spices.

5. Turn the heat low and add the *amchoor* and the *garam masala*. Mix it in gently.

6. Serve topped with chopped green coriander leaves.

Bhune hue Karele

Bitter Gourd Stir-Fried

Serves: 4-6
Cooking Time: 20 Minutes

Ingredients

Bitter gourd (*karela*) peeled, sliced and salted	1 lb
Salt	1½ tsp
Onions chopped	½ cup
Oil	as needed
Ginger chopped	1 tsp
Garlic	1 tsp
Green chilies chopped	1 tsp
Turmeric powder	1 tsp
Red pepper	1 tsp
Salt	to taste
Cumin seeds	1 tsp
Cumin powder	½ tsp
Coriander powder	1 tsp
Amchoor (dried mango powder)	1 tsp
Lemon juice	1 Tbs
Garam masala	½ tsp
Green coriander leaves chopped	2 Tbs

Bitter gourd stir-fry is very easy to make. It is crunchy, and its hot and sour taste makes it very appetizing. The natural bitterness is removed by sprinkling salt over it before cooking and then squeezing out the bitter water. Bitter gourd lowers blood sugar and maintains normal body functions. This vegetable is rich in all the essential vitamins and its regular use prevents hypertension and increases the body's resistance against infection. Particularly recommended, if you have diabetes.

Method

1. Peel and slice the bitter gourd (*Karela*) in ¼ inch thick slices and sprinkle 1 Tbs of salt on them and leave them in a bowl for 2–3 hours or longer. It can be covered and can be left in the refrigerator overnight.
2. Remove from the bowl, wash and squeeze the bitter water out and put them aside.
3. Fry the onions in the oil until golden brown and set them aside.
4. Heat the same oil in a deep skillet and fry the bitter gourd on medium heat until light brown and add the ginger, garlic and green chilies and keep stirring until the ginger turns brown too. Add the turmeric powder, red pepper, salt, and cumin seeds and wait till they start to pop. Add the fried onions, the cumin powder, and coriander powder. Stir and add the lemon juice, or the *amchoor*, *garam masala* and chopped coriander leaves.
5. Cook while stirring for 2 more minutes. Serve with *dal* and *chappati*.

EXOTIC VEGETABLES

Oven mein Bhuni hue Gobhi

Baked Cauliflower

Serves: 8-10
Cooking Time: 45 Minutes

Ingredients

Cauliflower head medium size	1
Onions chopped	1 cup
Ginger chopped	1 Tbs
Garlic chopped	1 Tbs
Green chilies chopped (mild)	1 Tbs
Turmeric powder	1 tsp
Red pepper	1 tsp
Ground coriander	1 Tbs
Salt	1 tsp
Cumin powder	½ tsp
Amchoor	1 Tbs
Vegetable oil or *ghee*	3–4 Tbs or more
Garam masala	1 tsp
Lemon juice	1 tsp
Coriander leaves chopped	2 Tbs

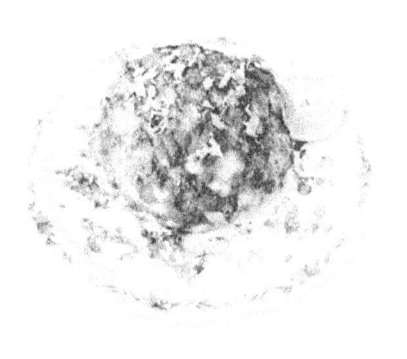

Cauliflower, coated with spices and butter and baked whole. Makes a great presentation.

Cauliflower is an excellent source of vitamin C, vitamin K, folate, pantothenic acid, and vitamin B6. It is a very good source of choline, dietary fiber, omega-3 fatty acids, manganese, phosphorus, and bioti. Additionally, it is a good source of vitamin B2, protein, vitamin B1, niacin, and magnesium. It has the ability to eliminate cancer enzymes. Regular cauliflower consumption can help decrease the risk of inflammation-mediated diseases such as arthritis, obesity, diabetes mellitus, inflammatory bowel disease and ulcerative colitis. a substance called glucoraphin present in cauliflower appears to have a protective effect on your stomach lining. With glucoraphin, your stomach is not prone to the bacterium helicobacter pylori, thereby reducing your risk for stomach ulcer and cancer.

Method

1. Wash and remove the loose leaves of the head of the cauliflower and dry it with a paper towel and set it aside.
2. Grind the ginger, onions, garlic and green chilies in a blender and grind it. Remove the mixture from the blender into a bowl and add the turmeric powder, red pepper, coriander powder, salt, cumin powder and *amchoor,* and mix well.
3. Coat the cauliflower head with this *masala* mixture completely and pour 2 Tbs of *ghee* or oil over it and bake at 425°F in the oven in a shallow baking pan.
4. Cover the pan for 30–40 minutes. Remove the cover and pour 2 Tbs of remaining melted butter or *ghee* over the cauliflower again and bake for another 10–15 minutes or until it starts to turn brown.
5. Remove from the oven and sprinkle *garam masala*, lemon juice and chopped coriander leaves and serve as a vegetable accompaniment to any meal.

Bhune hue Baingan ki Subzi/ Baingan Bharta

Grilled Egg Plant Curried

Serves: 8-10
Cooking Time: 35 Minutes

Ingredients

Eggplants (large)	2
Onions chopped	1½ cup
Ginger chopped	2 Tbs
Garlic chopped	2 Tbs
Green chilies chopped	2 tsp
Vegetable oil	3 Tbs
Cumin seeds	1 tsp
Tomatoes chopped	2 cups
Tomato sauce	1 cup
Turmeric powder	1 tsp
Red pepper	1 tsp
Coriander powder	1 Tbs
Cumin powder	½ tsp
Salt	to taste
Peas frozen	1 cup
Water	¼ cup
Heavy cream	1 Tbs
Cream (optional)	2 Tbs
Garam masala	1 tsp
Green coriander or cilantro leaves chopped	2 Tbs

An eggplant preparation made by roasting the eggplant under broiler in the regular oven until soft and the skin is dark brown. The skin is then peeled off and pulp of the eggplant is mashed and cooked with spices, tomatoes and some cream, topping it with butter and cilantro. Here is a delicious vegetable addition to any meal.

Long prized for its deeply purple, glossy beauty as well as its unique taste and texture, they are full of host of vitamins and minerals, Eggplant is a very good source of dietary fiber, vitamin B1, and copper. It is a good source of manganese, vitamin B6, niacin, potassium, folate, and vitamin K. Eggplant also contains phytonutrients such as nasunin and chlorogenic acid. Nasunin is a potent antioxidant and free radical scavenger that has been shown to protect cell membranes from damage. In animal studies, nasunin has been found to protect the lipids (fats) in brain cell membranes that are almost entirely composed of lipids. The famous Eggplant parmagiana from Italian cuisine is famous all over the world.

Method

1. Rub a little oil over the eggplants before wrapping them in aluminum foil. Transfer them to a regular oven in a rectangular

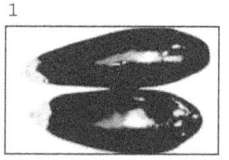

baking pan and broil for 30 minutes or longer until they turn brown and get soft. Turn them a couple of times to get uniform browning. Remove from the oven. The eggplants will shrink considerably. Wait until they cool down. Peel the skin and mash the pulp with a fork or a potato masher.

2. In a large skillet, fry the onions, ginger, garlic, in 3 Tbs of oil and green chilies in oil until the onions turn light brown.
3. Add the cumin seeds and wait until they pop and then add the tomatoes and the tomato sauce.
4. Cook for a few minutes stirring on low heat. Add the turmeric powder, red pepper, coriander powder, cumin powder and salt, and cook till oil separates from the sauce mixture.
5. In ¼ cup of water boil peas separately for 5 minutes and draw.
6. Add peas to the sauce mixture.
7. Mix well and add the mashed eggplants. Mix thoroughly. Cook on low heat until the mixture is absolutely smooth (about 20–25 minutes) stirring occasionally. Cooking time will depend on how well roasted are the eggplants.
8. Add the cream and cook another 2 minutes.
9. Top it with *garam masala* and green coriander leaves.

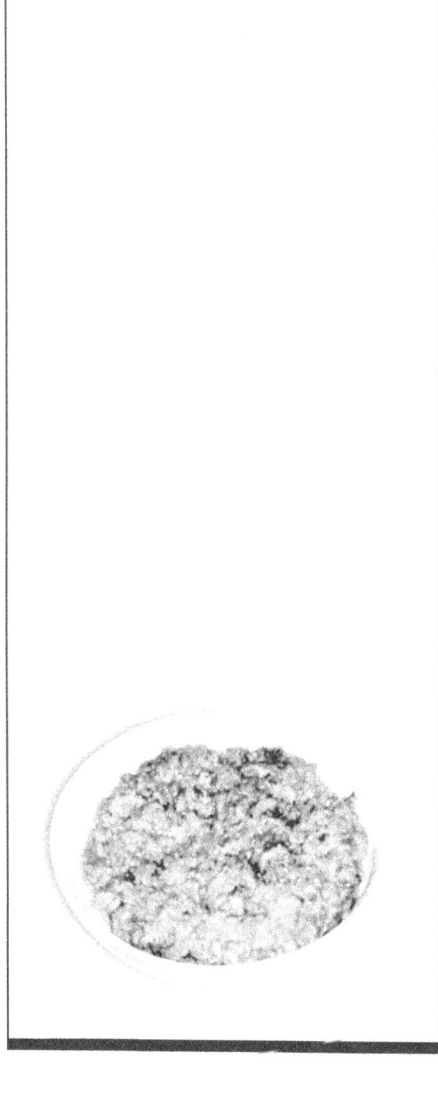

Gobhi aur Aloo ki Subzi

Cauliflower and Potatoes Stir-Fry

Serves: 8
Cooking Time: 20 Minutes

Ingredients

Onions chopped	1 cup
Vegetable oil	3 Tbs
Ginger chopped	2 Tbs
Garlic cloves chopped	1 Tbs
Green hot chilies chopped (mild)	1–2 tsp
Cumin seeds	1 tsp
Medium potatoes chopped into 1 inch cubes	2
Cumin powder	¾ tsp
Coriander powder	1½/2 tsp
Salt	1 tsp
Red pepper	1 tsp
Turmeric powder	1 tsp
Cauliflower head chopped into 1 inch florets	2 lbs
Garam masala	¾ tsp
Coriander leaves chopped	3 Tbs

Note: Cauliflower is one of the most loved vegtables anywhere in the world. It is anti cancer and full of antioxidants. It contains 320 milligrams of potassium, approximately 7 per cent of the recommended daily required in one cup. The brain relies on potassium to send electrochemical signals required for nerve signalling and it also has choline which is a very essential vitamin for the brain. It is rich in phosphorus for healthy cell membranes and is rich in vitamin-B-C.

This is the most popular cauliflower preparation in Indian cuisine. The cauliflower florets are flavoured with onions, cumin and *garam masala* and the potatoes give it an extra creamy taste. Truly a delicious vegetable preparation.

Method

1. Fry the onion in a Dutch oven or a deep saucepan in oil. Add ginger, garlic and green chilies. Fry until light brown, move onion mixture to one side with a large serving spoon.

2. Add 1 tsp of cumin seeds and wait until they start popping and then add the potatoes. Stir-fry them for 5 minutes.

3. Add cumin powder, coriander powder, salt, red pepper and turmeric. Stir the mixture well and add 3 Tbs of water. Cover it tight with a lid for about 8–10 minutes. During cooking turn the heat on medium-low. Add the washed cauliflower florets after draining them well. Stir gently to coat them with spices and cover the stir-fry with lid again for 5 minutes. Stir gently not to break the florets. Remove the lid and cook open for few minutes so that any extra moisture will evaporate, about 5 more minutes.

4. If the potatoes or cauliflower are still firm, cook for a few more minutes on low heat while covering the stir-fry with the lid.

5. Sprinkle with *garam masala* and chopped coriander leaves and heat through before serving.

6. This is a side dish suitable to serve with main course with rice or *chappatis,* or any other kind of dinner.

HINT

½ cup of fresh or frozen peas can be added to this stir-fry.

Gobhi aur Anjeer ki Subzi

Cauliflower with Figs Stir-Fry

Serves: 6-8
Cooking Time: 15 Minutes

Ingredients

Cauliflower head separated into small florets (large head)	1
Oil to fry the florets	2 cup
Figs dried (small)	8–10
Yogurt	1 cup
Onions chopped	1 cup
Ginger chopped	1 Tbs
Garlic chopped	1 Tbs
Green chilies chopped	1 tsp
Vegetable oil or *ghee*	3 Tbs
Cumin seeds	1 tsp
Turmeric powder	1 tsp
Red pepper	1 tsp
Coriander powder	1 Tbs
Salt	2 tsp
Garam masala	1 tsp
Coriander leaves chopped	2 Tbs

Cauliflower coated in sauce of chopped onion *masala* and ground figs is it crunchy, with sweet and sour taste and is it very appetizing.

Delicious, sweet fig fruit is one of the prime fruits enjoyed since antiquity in the human history. Fig is naturally rich in much health benefiting phyto-nutrients, anti-oxidants and vitamins. Dried figs, indeed, are highly concentrated source of minerals and vitamins. A fully developed fig features bell or pear shape with succulent flesh inside. figs and and cauliflower make a excellent combination. Figs are a good source of dietary fiber, vitamin B6, copper, potassium, manganese, and pantothenic acid, has full array of nutrients, including carbohydrates, sugar, soluble and insoluble fiber, sodium, vitamins, minerals, fatty acids, amino acids and more. Figs were also revered in ancient Rome where they were thought of as a sacred fruit.

Method

1. Pan fry the cauliflower florets in 2 Tbs of oil. Remove them with a slotted spoon and set them aside.
2. Grind the figs with yogurt in a blender and set aside.
3. Fry the onions with ginger, garlic and green chilies in a large wok or a frying pan in 3 Tbs of *ghee* or oil till the onions turn light brown.
4. Add the cumin seeds and wait till they start popping. Add the turmeric powder, red pepper, coriander powder and salt. Mix well and add the ground figs and yogurt mixture. Keep stirring and cooking till the sauce gets a little thick and the oil separates from the sauce.
5. Add the fried cauliflower florets and stir to coat them well with the spicy fig sauce. Serve hot as an accompaniment of a vegetable dish at a dinner.
6. Sprinkle with *garam masala* and coriander leaves before serving.

Baingan, Aloo aur Tamatar ki Subzi

Eggplants, Potatoes and Tomatoes Stir-Fry

Serves: 8
Cooking Time: 15-20 Minutes

Ingredients

Onions chopped	1 cup
Ginger chopped	1 Tbs
Garlic chopped	1 Tbs
Green chilies chopped	1 Tbs
Vegetable oil	¼ cup
Cumin seeds	1 tsp
Fresh eggplants chopped	2 lbs
Potatoes peeled and chopped	1 cup
Turmeric powder	1 tsp
Salt	1 tsp
Coriander powder	1 Tbs
Cumin powder	1 tsp
Red pepper	1 tsp
Fresh tomatoes chopped or canned chopped tomatoes	1 cup
Garam masala	1 tsp
Sesame seeds ground, dry roasted	1 Tbs
Green coriander leaves chopped	2 Tbs

This eggplant, potatoes and tomatoes stir-fried dish is a delicious vegetable accompaniment to any dinner. Fresh eggplants are cooked with onions, tomatoes, green chilies and flavoured with fresh coriander and *garam masala*. This dish goes with any meal. Eggplants are rich source of phenolic compounds that function as antioxidants.

Eggplant is of such a versatile nature and is used so widely that it is often described (under the name brinjal) as the "King of Vegetables". It can be fried, it can be roasted, to make Bharta, It can be stir fried. You can make fritters of it or a dip, chutney or a Raita.

Method

1. Cook the onions, ginger, garlic and green chilies in a deep skillet or a wok in oil and wait till they are light brown. Add the cumin seeds, and wait till they pop, and then add the chopped eggplant, potatoes and stir the mixture well.
2. Add the turmeric powder, salt, coriander powder, cumin powder and the red pepper, and coat the vegetable mixture.
3. Add the tomatoes and stir them well into the curry.
4. Lower the heat and cover the vegetable tight with a lid. Cook for 15 minutes or more and stir two or three times in between by removing the lid to make sure there is no sticking. If the stir-fry is too dry, add a couple of Tbs of water and stir in it.
5. Cook until the potatoes are tender.
6. Add the *garam masala,* dry roasted sesame seeds and sprinkle with green coriander leaves. Stir and serve as a side dish with lentils, bread, rice and meat curry.

EXOTIC VEGETABLES

Aloo aur Pyaz ki Subzi

Potatoes and Sliced Onions Stir-Fried

Serves: 6-8
Cooking Time: 15 Minutes

Ingredients

Potatoes boiled	2 lbs
Onions medium sliced	2 cups
Ginger chopped	1 Tbs
Green chilies chopped	1 Tbs
Cooking oil	2–3 Tbs
Red pepper (whole) dry, broken	2
Cumin seeds	1 tsp
Mustard seeds	1 tsp
Urad dal	1 tsp
Garlic chopped	1 Tbs
Turmeric powder	¾ tsp
Red pepper powder	1 tsp
Coriander powder	1½ tsp
Fenugreek leaves (dry)	2 Tbs
Asafoetida powder	⅛ tsp
Tomatoes chopped	2 cups
Salt	1 tsp
Water	1-2 cups
Green coriander leaves chopped	2 Tbs
Garam masala	½ tsp

Note: 1 quart is equal to 4 cups.

Boiled, peeled and chopped potatoes when stir-fried with chopped onions, tomatoes and spices make a very delicious accompaniment to go with any meal but specifically with *masala dosa*. It is quick to fix and quite yummy.

Method

1. Boil the potatoes in a 4 quart saucepan with plenty of water to cover the potatoes. Cover and cook until the skin on the potato tears open (about 25–30 minutes). Slowly drain the water from the potatoes into the sink and cover them with cold water. Wait to peel until they are cool and easy to peel. Chop them into about one inch cubes. Set them aside in a bowl.

2. On medium heat, cook the sliced onions, chopped ginger and pepper in oil in a deep large skillet and wait until they turn light brown. Move the onion mixture to one side and add the whole dry red pepper, cumin seeds, mustard seeds and *urad dal,* and wait till the seeds start to pop.

3. Add the chopped garlic, turmeric powder, red pepper, coriander powder, dry fenugreek leaves, and the asafoetida powder. Stir and cook for half a minute and mix them into the onion mixture.

4. Add the chopped tomatoes and the salt. Stir and cook for few minutes until the tomatoes get mixed into the onion and spices mixture and oil starts separates from the sauce. Add the chopped potatoes and mix and coat them with the spice mixture. Add 1–2 cups of water and lower the heat. Cover them with a lid and cook for 5 minutes. Remove the lid and sprinkle with the chopped coriander leaves and stir.

5. Transfer to a serving bowl and sprinkle garam masala and serve it with your favorite meal.

Aloo aur Beans ki Subzi

Green Beans and Potatoes Stir-Fried

Serves: 4-6
Cooking Time: 15 Minutes

Ingredients

Onions chopped	1 cup
Vegetable oil or *ghee*	6 Tbs
Ginger chopped	1 Tbs
Garlic chopped	1 Tbs
Green chilies chopped (mild)	1 Tbs
Turmeric powder	1 tsp
Red pepper	1 tsp
Cumin powder	1 tsp
Coriander powder	1½ tsp
Salt to taste or	1 tsp
Potatoes washed peeled chopped into 1 inch cubes	1 cup
Water	½ cup
Green beans cut in ½ inch pieces (washed) Or	2 lbs
Frozen French cut beans	15 oz pkg
Channa dal	¼ cup
Urad dal	2 Tbs
Sesame seeds	2 Tbs
Mustard seeds	1 tsp
Asafoetida	¼ tsp + 2 Tbsp
Garam masala	1 tsp
Green coriander leaves chopped	2 Tbs

This is one of those vegetables that is universally loved and cooked most frequently in every home and restaurant. Green beans curried and stir-fried with potatoes make a great vegetable side dish.

Green beans, while quite low in calories (just 43.75 calories in a whole cup), are loaded with nutrients. They are an excellent source of vitamin K, vitamin C, Manganese, vitamin A, dietary fibre, potassium, folate, and iron.

Method

1. Fry the onions in 2 Tbs oil and add the ginger, garlic and green chilies. When the onions start to turn light brown add the turmeric powder, red pepper, cumin powder, coriander powder and salt. Add the chopped potatoes. Stir well and add ¼ cup of water.

2. Turn the heat low and cover it tight with the lid. Cook for about 10 minutes. Remove the lid to stir and check if the potatoes are sticking to the bottom of the pan and add a couple of teaspoons of water. Add the beans and stir well and cover the pan again. Cook for another few minutes until the potatoes are tender.

3. In a wok heat remaining ¼ cup of oil, add the *channa dal*, *urad dal*, sesame seeds and fry till golden brown. Add the mustard seeds and asafoetida powder and wait till the mustard seeds start to pop. Add this tempering over the cooked beans.

4. Sprinkle with the *garam masala* and the chopped coriander leaves and mix well. Heat again for a minute and serve.

Makki aur Palak ki Subzi

Corn Curry with Spinach

Serves: 4-6
Cooking Time: 8-10 Minutes

Ingredients

Onions chopped	½ cup
Ginger, garlic and green chilies chopped	1 Tbs each
Coconut powder	1 Tbs
Poppy seeds	1 Tbs
Vegetable oil	3 Tbs
Cumin seeds	1 tsp
Mustard seeds	1 tsp
Fenugreek leaves (dry)	1 Tbs
Salt	1 tsp
Red pepper	1 tsp
Coriander powder	1 tsp
Tomato sauce	1 cup
Spinach chopped frozen or fresh	8 ozs
Corn frozen or fresh	2 cups
Coconut milk	1 cup
Garam masala	1 tsp
Green coriander leaves	2 Tbs

Sweet corn comes alive in this delicious sauce of ground poppy seeds, green chilies, coriander leaves and coconut milk.

Recent research has shown that bacteria in our large intestine transforms the corn fiber into short chain fatty acids, or SCFAs, that supply energy to our intestinal cells and thereby help lower the risk of colon cancer. According to Ayurveda, corn is diuretic and very good for people with high blood pressure. It is specially beneficial when taken with legumes. It is gluten free and goes perfect with nutriton rich Spinach for your overall health.

Method

1. Grind together chopped onions, ginger, garlic, green chilies, coconut powder and poppy seeds.
2. Heat oil or *ghee* in a heavy-bottom saucepan on medium-heat. Add the cumin and mustard seeds. When they stop popping add the ground onions mixture, fenugreek leaves, salt, red pepper and coriander powder. Add the tomato sauce. Stir well. Cook till the oil separates from the mixture. Lower the heat.
3. Add the spinach and cook for 3–4 minutes. Add the corn and mix well. Add the coconut milk and mix it again. Let it simmer for 10–15 minutes.
4. Add the *garam masala*. Mix it in and bring it to a boil again. Add the coriander leaves and serve as a vegetable accompaniment to any meal.

Kele ki Subzi

Raw Bananas Curry

Serves: 8
Cooking Time: 15 Minutes

Ingredients

Raw bananas (plantain) deep fried	2 cups
Oil for frying	2 cups
Paneer cubes or ricotta cheese cubes	1 cup
Onions chopped	1 cup
Ginger chopped	1 Tbs
Garlic chopped	1 Tbs
Green chilies chopped	1 tsp
Vegetable oil or *ghee*	3 Tbs
Cumin seeds	1 tsp
Curry or Bay leaves	4–6
Turmeric powder	1 tsp
Coriander powder	1 Tbs
Cumin powder	1 tsp
Red pepper	1 tsp
Salt	to taste
Tomato sauce	1 cup
Water	2 cups
Yogurt beaten smooth	1 cup
Garam masala	1 tsp
Coriander leaves chopped	2 Tbs

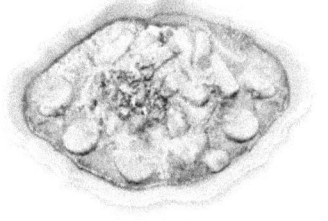

Bananas grow in abundance in India and raw bananas (plantains) make a wonderful curry. Sliced plantains are first deep fried and then curried in a sauce of tomatoes and cream. It is a north Indian preparation. We also eat them as fritters, chips, koftas or make stir-fry as below.

Method

1. Peel the plantains and slice them about ½ inch thick.
2. In a skillet heat the oil to about 300°F–340°F and fry them light brown. Drain them on a paper towel and set them aside. Fry the *paneer* cubes in the same oil and set them aside.
3. In a thick-bottom saucepan fry the onions, ginger, garlic and green chilies in 3 Tbs of oil until the onions are light brown and add the cumin seeds. When they start to pop, add the curry leaves and stir.
4. Add the turmeric powder, coriander powder, cumin powder, red pepper, and salt. Mix well and add the tomato sauce and stir the mixture. Cook till the oil separates from the sauce. Add water. Mix and bring it to a full boil.
5. Add the fried bananas and fried cheese cubes. Lower the heat. Let it simmer on low heat until the bananas are tender but still firm and not mushy (10–15 minutes).
6. Lower the heat and add the yogurt. Mix well and cook for 3–5 minutes. Bring the curry to a boil.
7. Add the *garam masala* and the chopped coriander leaves. Mix well and remove from heat and serve with rice, *chappati* or any bread of your choice.

Note: Yogurt can be replaced by 2 Tbs of cream.

Shakarkandi ki Subzi

Sweet Potato Curry

Serves: 4-6
Cooking Time: 25 Minutes

Ingredients

Large sweet potatoes peeled and cut into cubes	2 cups
Vegetable oil or *ghee*	3 Tbs
Onions chopped	2 Tbs
Ginger chopped	1 tsp
Green chilies chopped	1 tsp
Urad dehusked *dal* or *channa dal*	2 Tbs
Mustard seeds	1 tsp
Sesame seeds	2 Tbs
Asafoetida powder	¼ tsp
Curry leaves chopped	2 Tbs
Salt	1 tsp
Turmeric powder	¾ tsp
Coriander powder	1 Tbs
Red pepper	1 tsp
Water	¼ cup
Spinach chopped	1 lb pkg
Fresh coriander leaves chopped	1 Tbs
Garam masala	½ tsp

Sweet potato is very common among Gujarati and south Indian stir-fries and mixed vegetable curries. In north India, it is mostly enjoyed as a baked vegetable with lemon, spices and *chutney*.

They are featured in many favorite dishes in Japan, Taiwan, Philippines. Indonesia, Vietnam, India, and some other Asian countries. Sweet potato not only sweetens your taste buds but also good for your cardiovascular health! A large one contains more than 100 percent of the daily recommended intake, of vitamin A according to the U.S. Food and Drug Administration. Vitamin A is an antioxidant powerhouse, and is linked to anti-aging benefits, cancer prevention and the maintenance of good eyesight . For as sweet as they are, sweet potatoes have a low glycemic index and therefore help control diabetes and someday provide a less expensive treatment with fewer side effects.

Method

1. Peel and chop the sweet potatoes in cubes and set them aside. Heat the oil in a wok or frying pan on medium heat.
2. Add the onions, ginger and green chilies. Brown them a little and add the *urad dal*, mustard seeds and the sesame seeds. As they start popping add the asafoetida powder and the curry leaves. Wait for a few seconds and add chopped sweet potatoes, and cook. Stir well.
3. Add salt, turmeric powder, coriander powder, red pepper and mix. Add the water. Cover tight with a lid and keep the heat on low.
4. Let it cook and simmer for 15–20 minutes and add the chopped spinach and cook until the sweet potatoes are tender but not mushy. Garnish with the fresh chopped coriander leaves and *garam masala* and serve.

Kamal Kakadi, Khumb, Paneer aur Matar ki Subzi

Lotus Roots, Cheese Cubes, Mushrooms and Peas Curry

Serves: 4-6
Cooking Time: 20 Minutes

Ingredients	
Vegetable or sesame oil	3 Tbs
Onions chopped	½ cup
Ginger chopped	1 Tbs
Garlic chopped	1 Tbs
Green chilies chopped	1 Tbs
Lotus roots chopped or frozen but cooked	8 oz
Cumin seeds	½ tsp
Tomato sauce	1 cup
Turmeric powder	½ tsp
Coriander ground	1 Tbs
Red pepper	½ tsp
Salt	1 tsp
water	1 cup
Peas frozen	¼ cup
Mushrooms chopped	1 cup
Tomatoes fresh chopped	1 cup
Garam masala	1 tsp
Coriander leaves chopped	2 Tbs
Heavy cream	1–2 Tbs

Crunchy lotus roots with creamy and soft mushrooms together make two perfect ingredients to make a curry. They are very popular and can be curried in many different ways. Lotus root croquettes curry is a delicacy in northern India. Lotus roots are also pickled with raw mangoes and other vegetables to make a great mixed vegetable pickle.

Lotus root has a wide range of health benefits owing to its rich nutritional composition, and some of the benefits include its ability to improve digestion, reduce cholesterol, lower blood pressure, boost the immune system, prevent various forms of cancer, balances mood and relieves depression, increases circulation, and maintain proper enzymatic activity in the body. Kashmir is the home of a myriad lotus root dishes as the supply is abundant from the many lakes in this region Nadeir yakhean is a lotus root preparation from the state of Kashmir. This vegetarian recipe is a mandatory dish in all important feasts. This unique Kashmiri cuisine is prepared in earthen pots.

The lotus flower has been a powerful element of numerous Asian countries for thousands of years, and represents purity, sexual innocence, and divine beauty. Lotus root is used in cooking in Japan, China, Korea, and Vietnam, Srilanka and many other countries in Asia.

The lotus plant has long stem with very beautiful aromatic flowers with floating leaves. It can regenerate after thousands of years untouched by the mud and muddy water it grows in. Therefore, it symbolizes the triumph and purity of heart and mind. It has been an auspicious symbol of Indian culture since time immemorial. It also represents long life, honour, good fortune, divinity, knowledge and enlightenment for the people of India. Founding fathers enshrined it as the national flower of India.

Method

1. Heat the 3 Tbs of oil in a heavy-bottom saucepan and add the chopped onions, ginger, garlic and green chilies. If using fresh, them boil the lotus roots in a separate pan until tender and set aside.

2. After the onions are light brown, add the cumin seeds and when they stop popping, add the tomato sauce, turmeric powder, coriander powder, red pepper and salt .

3. Stir to mix. Fry the sauce on low heat until the oil separates from the sauce. Add one cup of water and stir to mix. Boil the sauce for 5 minutes and add the cooked lotus roots. Mix well. Cover the pan and cook for 5–10 minutes. Add the peas and mushrooms. Stir to mix. Simmer for 5 minutes and add the fresh tomatoes, *garam masala* and the chopped coriander. Lower the heat.

4. Cook for 3–5 minutes more. Remove from heat and add 1 Tbs of cream. Stir to mix and serve with any meal as a vegetable accompaniment.

Soya ki Subzi

Tofu Curry

Serves: 4-6
Cooking Time: 15 Minutes

Ingredients

Vegetable oil (for frying the Tofu)	1 cup
Tofu firmly drained and cubed in 1 inch cubes	2 lbs
Onions chopped	1 cup
Ginger chopped	1 Tbs
Garlic chopped	1 Tbs
Green chilies	1 Tbs
Vegetable oil	3 Tbs
Red pepper (dry)	2–3
Curry leaves	5–6
Cumin seeds	1 tsp
Tomatoes chopped	1 cup
Turmeric powder	1 tsp
Red pepper	½ tsp
Salt	1½ tsp
Coriander powder	2 tsp
Cumin powder	½ tsp
Tomato sauce	½ cup
Potatoes peeled and cubed	½ cup
Peas frozen	¼ cup
Water	1 cup
Yogurt whipped	½ cup
Or	
Coconut milk	½ cup
Coriander leaves chopped	2 Tbs
Garam masala	1 tsp

Tofu is a biproduct of Soybean. Soybean cultivation was long confined chiefly to China and Manchuria but gradually spread to other East Asian countries such as Korea and Japan. The Chinese invented tofu. Soy protein is the nutritional equivalent of meat, eggs, and casein for human growth and health. It is essentially identical to the protein of other legume seeds and pulses. Soy beans are now a major crop in the United States, Brazil, Argentina, India, and China. Tofu is cooked in several ways in Indian cuisine. It is sometimes curried and sometimes stir-fried. It is also being used in the *pulavs*.

Method

1. In a skillet pour 1 cup of oil and heat it to pan-fry the Tofu cubes. Fry them until they are slightly brown. Remove and drain them on a paper towel.
2. Fry the onions, ginger, garlic, and green chilies in 3 Tbs of oil and add whole dry red pepper, curry leaves and cumin seeds.
3. When the cumin seeds start to pop, add the tomatoes, turmeric powder, red pepper, salt, coriander powder, cumin powder and the tomato sauce.
4. Mix well and cook for 5 minutes on low heat. When the oil starts to separate, add the potatoes, and fry stirring constantly for 2 minutes.
5. Add the peas and 1 cup of water and simmer for 5–10 minutes and add the Tofu gently and mix. Lower the heat.
6. Let it simmer until the potatoes are tender. Lower the heat a little more and add the yogurt and stir gently on low heat and slowly bring to a boil.
7. Remove from heat and add the chopped coriander leaves and *garam masala* and serve with plain rice or any *pulav* and *chappati*.

EXOTIC VEGETABLES

Parwal aur Aloo ki Subzi
Pointed Gourd Curry

Serves: 4-6
Cooking Time: 15 Minutes

Ingredients

Vegetable oil or clarified butter	2–3 Tbs
Cumin seeds	1 tsp
Onions chopped	1 cup
Ginger and garlic chopped each	1 Tbs
Green chilies chopped	1 Tbs
Potatoes peeled and cubed	1 cup
Salt	1 tsp
Coriander powder	1 tsp
Turmeric powder	½–1 tsp
Red pepper	1 tsp
Pointed Gourd (*parwal*) washed and cut length wise into ½ inch strips	2 cups
Water	¼ cup
Coconut fresh grated	½ cup
Or	
Coconut powder	2 Tbs
Garam masala	¾ tsp
Coriander leaves chopped	2 Tbs

Parwal are cooked only in north Indian or Punjabi style of cooking, but in other parts of the country they are stuffed with spiced mashed potatoes or grated coconut. Pointed Gourd belongs to the squash or zucchini family.

It is high in calories and is full of Vitamin A, C, Magnesium and other nicronutrients. It is four to 5 inches long and blunt on one side robust in the middle and pointed at the other end. Grows in eastern and Northern part of india like Orrisa, Bengal, Assam, Bihar, and U.P. The vegetable is known for its digetibility and nutritinal value. In Ayurvedas it has high profile. A extract of its seeds lowers cholestrol and blood sugar levels. It used to treat digestive dosorders, skin conditions and fevers. It can grow in any tropical country.

Method

1. Heat the oil or clarified butter in a wok or a thick-bottom frying pan on medium heat and add the cumin seeds. As they stop popping add the chopped onions, ginger, garlic and green chilies.

2. Fry until the onions start turning light brown and then add the chopped potatoes. Lower the heat. Stir them well and add the salt, coriander powder, turmeric powder, red pepper and stir well again. Cook covered for 5 minutes.

3. Add the chopped round gourd and mix. Add ¼ cup of water and stir well. Cover the vegetable with a tight lid and keep the heat medium low. Add the coconut after 5 minutes. Let it cook for another 5–10 minutes or until the potatoes are soft. Stir in between to prevent stocking.

4. Sprinkle the *garam masala* and the coriander leaves. Mix well and serve. A welcome vegetable accompaniment to any meal.

Kaddu ki Subzi

Pumpkin Stir-Fried

Serves: 6-8
Cooking Time: 15 Minutes

Ingredients

Vegetable oil or *ghee*	3–4 Tbs
Onions chopped	1 cup
Green chilies chopped	1 Tbs
Ginger chopped	1 Tbs
Brown cardamom pods half open	2
Cinnamon sticks (small)	2
Curry leaves	4–6
Nigella seeds	½ tsp
Fenugreek seeds	½ tsp
Turmeric powder	1 tsp
Red pepper	1 tsp
Coriander and cumin powder mixture	1 Tbs
Asafoetida powder	½ tsp
Salt	1 tsp
Tomato sauce	1 cup
Water	½ cup
Pumpkin peeled and grated	4 cups
Sugar	1 Tbs

Note: Pumpkins are also cooked into Koftas. Pumpkin Kofta curry is very popular with the Jews of India. It is an Indian cuisine delicacy. A lip-smacking side dish. Kofta are essentially an Indian form of gnocchi, an Italian Pasta.

In India, pumpkin is usually served highly flavoured with spices and a little sugar. The flavour and aroma of spices makes this one of my very favourite dishes. The sweet and sour taste of this dish goes very well with *pooris.* In the state of Bengal the pumpkin is absolutely adored. It is said that they can use every part of the plant except the stem. Pumpkins favourably effect the insulin and Glucose levels in lab animals.

In the United States and Canada, pumpkin is a popular Halloween and Thanksgiving staple. it is a very important, traditional part of the autumn harvest, eaten mashed and making its way into soups and purees. Often, it is made into pie, a traditional dessert staple of the Canadian and American Thanksgiving holidays. In Canada, Mexico, the United States, Europe and China, the seeds are often roasted and eaten as a snack.

Pumpkins are commonly carved into decorative lanterns called jack-o'-lanterns for the Halloween season in North America. Throughout Britain and Ireland, there is a long tradition of carving lanterns from vegetables, particularly the turnip, mangelwurzel, or swede. The practice of carving pumpkins for Halloween originated from an

Coconut fresh grated	1 cup
Or	
Coconut dry powder	2 Tbs
Yogurt	½ cup
Garam masala	1 tsp
Fresh coriander leaves chopped	2 Tbs

Irish myth about a man name "Stingy Jack". The turnip has traditionally been used in Ireland and Scotland at Halloween, but immigrants to North America used the native pumpkin, which are both readily available and much larger – making them easier to carve than turnips. Not until 1837, does jack-o'-lantern appear as a term for a carved vegetable lantern and the carved pumpkin lantern association with Halloween was first recorded in 1866.

Method

1. Heat the oil in a deep, thick-bottom cooking pan of medium size and add the onions, green chilies and ginger. Wait till they turn slightly brown. Add the cardamoms, cinnamon sticks and curry leaves. Cook for a minute. Add the nigella seeds, and fenugreek seeds. When the seeds start to crackle, add the turmeric, red pepper, coriander powder and cumin powder mixture, asafoetida, and salt. Lower the heat. Stir well and add the tomato sauce.
2. Mix all the ingredients well and fry for 2–3 minutes on medium low heat.
3. Add ½ cup water and stir. Cover the pan and let the sauce cook for 2 minutes. Add the chopped pumpkin. Cover it with a lid and let it simmer and cook until the pumpkin gets soft. Add the sugar, coconut powder and the yogurt. Stir well and cook until the sugar completely mixes in. Heat it through.
4. Remove from heat. Sprinkle a little *garam masala*, chopped coriander leaves and serve.*

*Discard the whole spices before serving.

Musli ki Subzi

Asparagus Stir-Fry

Serves: 4-6
Cooking Time: 10 Minutes

Ingredients

Tender sprigs of chopped asparagus	1 lb
Vegetable oil or mustard oil	2 Tbs or more
Onions chopped	½ cup
Ginger chopped	1 tsp
Garlic chopped	1 tsp
Green chilies chopped	1 tsp
Sesame seeds	1 tsp
Or	
Sesame dry leaves	2 Tbs
Cumin seeds	½ tsp
Fenugreek leaves fresh	1 cup
Or	
Fenugreek leaves dry	2 Tbs
Turmeric powder	½ tsp
Salt	1 tsp
Coriander powder	1 tsp
Red pepper	½ tsp
Water or more as needed	2 Tbs
Mushrooms chopped in ½ inch pieces	½ cup
Coriander leaves chopped	1 Tbs
Garam masala	½ tsp

You will not find Asparagus (*Musli*) easily with vegetable vendors in India. It grows in the Himalayas, in Nepal and is abundant in Europe and North America in spring time. When curried like any other vegetable, it is delicious and creamy. It can be served as a vegetable accompaniment to any meal of your choice.

Asparagus has been used as a vegetable and medicine in Egypt, Syria and Spain. The Greeks and Roman also used it as a beneficial herb. It is rich in vitamin B6, calcium, magnesium, protein, claromium, and is good for diabetes. Asparagus became available to the new world around 1850.

Method

1. Slice the asparagus into ½ inch pieces after cutting off the lower harder part of the asparagus shoots. Set it aside.

2. Heat the oil in a saucepan and add the onions, ginger, garlic and green chilies. Cook until the onions turn light brown and then add the sesame seeds. Wait till they stop popping and add the cumin seeds. Give it a minute and add the fenugreek leaves. Stir to mix.

3. Add the asparagus and stir well. Add the dry spices, turmeric powder, salt, coriander powder and red pepper. Stir-fry on low heat until the asparagus is well coated with spices. Add the water, cover the saucepan, and cook for 5–7 minutes or until the asparagus is soft. Add the mushrooms and stir. Cook for 5 more minutes. Sprinkle with green coriander leaves, *garam masala* and serve.

Patta Gobhi aur Matar ki Subzi

Cabbage and Peas Stir-Fried

Serves: 8-10
Cooking Time: 10 Minutes

Ingredients

Ginger chopped	1 Tbs
Garlic chopped	1 Tbs
Green chilies chopped	1 Tbs
Vegetable oil	3 Tbs
Mustard seeds	1 tsp
U*rad dal* (dry)	1 Tbs
Asafoetida powder	$\frac{1}{8}$ tsp
Cabbage (*patta gobhi*) washed chopped and shredded	4 cups
Or	
A bag of fresh Cole Slaw	4 cups
Coriander powder	1 Tbs
Salt	1 tsp
Turmeric powder	1 tsp
Red pepper	1 tsp
Frozen peas	½ cup
Curry leaves chopped	2 Tbs
Fresh grated coconut	1 cup
Or	
Dry unsweetened coconut powder	¼ cup
Coriander leaves	2 Tbs
Garam masala	½ tsp
Lemon juice	1 Tbs

HINT

Gujarati style cabbage stir-fry will use 2 Tbs of sugar and substitute the peas with ½ cup roasted chopped peanuts.

This widely popular vegetable plays a unique role in cancer prevention and cancer treatment as it is very rich in three different types of nutrients. It is antioxidant, anti-inflammatory and it is rich in glucosinolates. Cabbage has a long history of use both as a food and a medicine. It was developed from wild cabbage, a vegetable that was closer in appearance to collards and kale and introduced in India by the Portuguese. Koftas and cabbage soup are commonly made from cabbage in Indian cuisine beside making stir fries with peas, potatoes or just by itself. But in western cuisine it is used extensively as cole slaw and many other dishes. Convert the ordinary cabbage into a great vegetable side dish. Serve it with bread, rice, or lentils.

Method

1. Fry the ginger, garlic, and green chilies in a thick-bottom skillet on low heat in 3 Tbs of oil. Wait till they are light brown and then add the mustard seeds, and the *urad dal*. Wait till they start popping and *urad dal* starts to turn brown. Add the asafoetida powder. Mix well.

2. Add the cabbage and mix completely to coat the cabbage with the spice mixture. Lower the heat.

3. Add salt, turmeric powder, coriander powder, red pepper and stir the vegetable well. Cover it tight with a lid and cook for 5 minutes. Add the peas and mix them in. Again cover with a lid and cook another 2 minutes, stirring in between to prevent sticking to the bottom of the pan.

4. Add the curry leaves and coconut and fry the vegetable on low heat till the moisture is somewhat gone.

5. Remove from heat and sprinkle chopped coriander leaves, *garam masala* and lemon juice. Stir well and serve. Makes an excellent vegetable accompaniment to any meal.

Shalgam ki Subzi

Turnips Stir-Fried

Serves: 8-10
Cooking Time: 10 Minutes

Ingredients

Turnips washed, peeled and chopped	2 lbs
Vegetable oil or *ghee*	3 Tbs
Onions chopped	1 cup
Ginger chopped	1 Tbs
Garlic chopped	1 Tbs
Green chilies chopped	1 Tbs
Cumin seeds	1 tsp
Turmeric powder	1 tsp
Salt	1 tsp
Red pepper	1 tsp
Coriander powder	1 Tbs
Cumin powder	½ tsp
Fennel seeds	½ tsp
Tomatoes chopped	2 cups
Brown sugar	1 Tbs
Yogurt	½ cup
Garam masala	1 tsp
Sesame seeds, poppy seeds, coconut powder ground, roasted	1 tsp each
Coriander leaves chopped	1 Tbs

Turnips are very low calorie root vegetables; Nonetheless, they are very good source of anti-oxidants, minerals, vitamins and dietary fibre. They are one of those fresh root vegetables that are rich in vitamin C. Vitamin-C is a powerful water-soluble anti-oxidant required by the human body for synthesis of collagen. It also helps the body scavenge harmful free radicals, in prevention from cancers, inflammation, and helps boost immunity. Originated in India they were well established in Europe by the 7th century BC. Large turnips were used in Europe for making carved out lanterns at Halloween. Mostly used as a vegetable in Punjab and Kashmir regions of India and Pakistan in variety of stirfries, pickles.

Method

1. Wash peel and chop the turnips into small cubes and set aside.

2. In a wok or non-stick skillet heat the *ghee* and add the chopped onions, ginger, garlic, and the green chilies, and fry the onions until light brown.

3. Add the cumin seeds and wait till they start to pop and then add the chopped turnips. Stir and add the turmeric powder, salt, red pepper, coriander powder, cumin powder and the fennel seeds. Mix and coat the turnips with these spices.

4. Add the tomatoes and stir-fry for 2 minutes. Lower the heat and cover the turnips tight with a lid. Cook until the turnips are tender. Mash the turnips and add sugar and yogurt. Mix well.

5. Remove from heat and add the *garam masala*, roasted ground mixture of sesame seeds, poppy seeds and coconut powder and the chopped coriander leaves and mix well. Adjust seasonings. Heat it through and serve.

Chukandar ki Subzi

Beetroots Stir-Fry

Serves: 4-6
Cooking Time: 15 Minutes

Ingredients

Beetroots julienne strips	1 lb
Carrots julienne strips	2 Tbs
Water (for boiling the vegetables)	4 cups
Sesame oil	3 Tbs
Onions red	½ cup
Green chilies	
Ginger chopped	1 Tbs
Garlic chopped	½ tsp
Mustard seeds	1 tsp
Fenugreek seeds	1 tsp
Jalapenos chopped	2
Salt	1 tsp
Sugar	1 tsp
Rice vinegar	1 Tbs
Water	½ cup
Coconut milk canned	½ cup
Curry leaves	6–8
Garam masala or	To taste
Ceylonese spice powder	2 Tbs

Beets are a great source of minerals and vitamins. As I remember, they used to ornament salads but in this dish from Sri Lanka, they are curried with hot pepper and coconut milk. The dish is colourful, delicious and makes a healthy addition to any meal.

Beet roots are quite high in carbohydrates but low in fat. They also contains phosphorus, sodium, magnesium, calcium, iron, and potassium, as well as fibre, vitamins A and C, niacin, and biotin. it is a vegetable of great amount of nutrition and healthful benefits. Recently beet root has been gaining popularity as a new super food due to recent studies claiming that beets and beetroot juice can improve athletic performance, lower blood pressure and increase blood flow.

Method

1. Boil the beet roots and carrots in 4 cups of water until tender. Set aside.
2. Heat the oil in a wok or heavy-bottom saucepan of medium size. Add the red chopped onions, green chilies and ginger and garlic. Stir to cook until the onions are slightly brown.
3. Add the mustard seeds and as they start to pop add the fenugreek seeds, and as the fenugreek seeds change colour, add the chopped salapeno. Lower the heat and add the salt, sugar and vinegar. Slowly stir and add the cooked vegetables along with water.
5. Cover the pan and let it cook (about 10 minutes).
6. Add the coconut milk and the curry leaves. Cook for another 5 minutes and bring it to a boil. Sprinkle the *garam masala* before serving. Serve it as a vegetable accompaniment with any meal.

Tori ki Subzi

Flavourful Zucchini

Serves: 6-8
Cooking Time: 15 Minutes

Ingredients

Ingredient	Amount
Onions chopped	½ cup
Vegetable oil	2 Tbs
Ginger chopped	1 tsp
Garlic chopped	1 tsp
Green chilies chopped	1 tsp
Cumin seeds	1 tsp
Tomatoes chopped	1 cup
Dill leaves chopped (optional)	1 tsp
Turmeric powder	¾ tsp
Red pepper	1 tsp
Coriander powder	1½ tsp
Cumin powder	½ tsp
Salt	as needed
Fresh zucchini peeled and chopped	2 lbs
Garam masala	1 tsp
Coriander leaves chopped	2 Tbs

Note: To make this dish special, in step 1, as soon as the onion is done, add *badian* (dried spiced lentil balls) and fry them in oil until light brown. Addition of *badian* will make it much more appetizing. Badians are available at your local Indian grocery store.

This simple but delicious dish is a delight in itself. Enjoy its delicate taste. When it is cooked with fresh tomatoes, onions and spices. Makes a very rich and flavourful accompaniment to any dinner.

Stuffed Zucchini Flowers are part of the family of stuffed vegetable dishes in the cuisines of the former Ottoman Empire. The most popular use of Zucchini in the western world is Zucchini Bread to go with tea and coffee. It is also one of the most versatile summer vegetables.

Method

1. Heat the oil and cook the onions, ginger, and the green chilies on medium low heat until the onions are tender and then add the garlic. Fry for another minute.
2. Add the cumin seeds and fry them until they crackle.
3. Add the tomatoes and the dill leaves and stir-fry until the tomatoes are softened. Lower the heat.
4. Add the turmeric powder, red pepper, coriander powder, cumin powder and the salt and stir the mixture well. Add the chopped and sliced (¼ inch pieces cut horizontally or into cubes) zucchini and again stir well and cover the pan.
5. Let it simmer until the zucchini is tender (about 10–15 minutes). Stir and remove the lid and cook for another 5–10 minutes so that some of the moisture dries up.
6. Add the *garam masala* and green coriander leaves and mix.
7. Cook for another 2 minutes and serve.

Note: Zucchini is made in many ways in Italian Cuisine. It is stuffed with a cooked mixture of onions, ginger, garlic, tomatoes and scooped flesh from the cavity of Zucchini, all the spices. Once the Zucchini is stuffed with this mixture, it is baked, topped with Mozarella cheese, bread crumbs and parsley. It is made into fritters also and can be baked as Zucchini chips by coating them in a mixture of bread crumbs, spices and grated Parmesan cheese. It is delicious every way.

Aloo Dum

Fried Potato in Creamy Sauce of Yogurt

Serves: 8-10
Cooking Time: 15 Minutes

Ingredients

Potatoes small peeled and washed 1–1½ inch diameter	2 lbs
Salt	½ tsp
Vegetable oil or *ghee*	¼ cup
Cumin seeds	1 tsp
Poppy seeds	1½ tsp
Almonds	1 Tbs
Black peppercorns	½ tsp
Cloves	½ tsp
Brown cardamom seeds	½ tsp
Coconut powder unsweetened	1 Tbs
Ginger chopped	1 Tbs
Garlic chopped	1 Tbs
Green chilies chopped	1 tsp
Water	2 cups
Onions chopped	1 cup
Bay leaves	4–6
Turmeric powder	1 tsp
Red pepper	1 tsp
Coriander powder	1 Tbs
Fenugreek leaves dry	1½ Tbs
Salt	1 tsp
Tomato sauce	1 cup
Yogurt	1½ cup
Fresh green coriander leaves chopped	2 Tbs
Garam Masala	½ tsp

The potato is a nutritional powerhouse in terms of the four major micronutrients, but more importantly, it is probably the most universally-loved food; people are passionate about potatoes. When a cook looks for a vegetable side dish with that magic mix of value, versatility and nutritional appeal, they see potatoes. They're the perfect, universally loved canvas for tapping into today's hottest culinary trend. Potato is a source of subsistence for millions and millions of people around the world. Potato is the "second bread" and has saved many populations from starvations especially in Europe.

Potatoes cooked whole in a creamy sauce of yogurt, ground poppy seeds, coconut, almonds, onions, ginger, garlic, green chilies and spices, are delightfully tasty because they are completely smeared with the sauce.

Method

1. In a medium size thick-bottom saucepan fry the potatoes in ¼ cup oil or *ghee* and sprinkle ½ tsp of salt while frying. Remove them from the cooking pan with a slotted spoon and set them aside.

2. In a skillet roast the cumin seeds, poppy seeds, almonds, black pepper, cloves, brown cardamom seeds and coconut powder and grind them in the blender with ginger, garlic, green chilies, in ¼ cup of water to make a fine paste and set aside.

136 INCREDIBLE TASTE OF INDIAN VEGETARIAN CUISINE

3. In the same saucepan, used for frying the potatoes, fry the onions, in the remaining *ghee* until the onions turn golden brown.
4. Lower the heat and add the bay leaves, turmeric powder, red pepper, coriander powder, fenugreek leaves, salt and the ground paste and stir. Add the tomato sauce and mix well. Cook for 2 minutes and lower the heat and add 1 cup of yogurt and stir-fry for 5 minutes, or until the sauce separates from the oil.
5. Add the fried potatoes and stir to coat them with the sauce. Cook on slow heat for 5 minutes and add the remaining yogurt and the remaining water and let it simmer until the potatoes are tender (about 20–30 minutes).
6. Sprinkle with *garam masala* and mix well. Cook for another minute. Sprinkle with green coriander leaves.
7. Serve with *poori, nan* or *chappati*.

Note: Cut the potatoes in half, if they are more than 1 inch in diameter.

EXOTIC VEGETABLES

Methi Aloo ki Subzi

Fenugreek Leaves and Potatoes Stir-Fry

Serves: 4-6
Cooking Time: 15 Minutes

Ingredients

Vegetable oil	as needed
Onion chopped	½ cup
Green chilies	1 tsp
Garlic chopped	½ tsp
Ginger chopped	1 tsp
Cumin seeds	1 tsp
Red dry pepper (whole)	2
Potatoes peeled and chopped in ½ inch cubes	1 cup
Salt	½ tsp
Coriander powder	1 tsp
Red pepper	½ tsp
Turmeric powder	1 tsp
Fenugreek leaves washed and chopped	3 cups
Water	2 Tbs
Garam masala	½ tsp
Coriander leaves chopped	2 Tbs

Stir-fry chopped fenugreek leaves and potatoes make a very healthy vegetable accompaniment to any meal. Fenugreek leaves have numerous health benefits and are cooked in several ways. I find this the easiest.

Fenugreek is a herb that has long been used in cooking and in traditional Asian medicine to stabilize blood sugar and fight diabetes. Native to India and southern Europe, the Mediterranean and North Africa, fenugreek is used in the herbal medicinal tradition of the Middle East, India, Egypt, and later in China and Europe is known as *methi* in India. It was used by ancient Egyptians to combat fever and chronic cough. It is very easy to grow from seeds and has a very unique flavour but a slightly bitter taste. It is used in practically all cuisines in every part of India and has great therapeutic benefits and acts as a great digestive aid. It relieves congestion, reduces inflammation and fights infection, and stimulates the production of mucosal fluids to remove allergens and oxidants from the respiratory tract.

Method

1. Heat the oil in a deep 1 quart saucepan and sauté the onions and garlic, ginger and green chilies.
2. As soon the onions are light brown add the cumin seeds. As they start to pop, add the whole red peppers.
3. Add the potatoes and stir the mixture and stir-fry them until light brown.
4. Add the salt, coriander powder, red pepper, turmeric powder and mix well. Add the chopped fenugreek leaves and stir again. Lower the heat. Add 2 Tbs of water.

5. Cover the pan with a tight lid and let it cook for 10 minutes stirring a couple of times to prevent any sticking. Add more water, if needed to soften the potatoes, if the stir-fry is too dry.

6. Remove the lid and let it simmer until most of the water evaporates and potatoes are tender. Mix in the *garam masala* and the chopped coriander leaves and stir to mix. Serve it with *chappatis*, *dal* and *raita*.

Sarson ka Saag

Mustard Greens Curried

Serves: 8-10
Cooking Time: 40 Minutes

Ingredients

Mustard greens*	2 lbs
Spinach leaves washed and chopped	½ lb
Broccoli washed and chopped	½ lb
Fenugreek leaves**	1 cup
Water	4 cups
Salt	2 tsp
Green chilies chopped	2 Tbs
Garlic chopped	1 Tbs
Ginger chopped	2 Tbs
Corn meal	3–4 Tbs
Vegetable oil or *ghee*	4 Tbs
Onions chopped	1 cup
Cumin seeds	1 tsp
Turmeric powder (optional)	½ tsp
Coriander powder	1½ Tbs
Garam masala	1 tsp
Cumin powder	½ tsp
Whole dry red peppers broken (if green chilie not available)	2–3
Red pepper (if desired)	1 tsp

Note: Addition of Spinach, broccoli and fenugreek add a lot of nutritive value to this preparation.

Mustard greens is a speciality from the state of Punjab. It can be made in advance and freezes very well. One can add to the mustard greens, spinach, broccoli, and sometimes small amounts of fenugreek leaves. It is invariably served with buttered corn bread.

In the winter the plains of Punjab are adorned with beautiful mustard plants with their green leaves and yellow flowers. It is then that Sarson ka Saag is prepared with fervour. Mustard greens originated in the Himalayan region of India and have been grown and prepared for more than 5,000 years. Mustard greens are a notable vegetable in many different cuisines, ranging from China to South America. Cancer prevention appears to be a standout area for mustard greens when summarizing health benefits. As an excellent source of vitamin K, mustard greens provide us with great amounts of a hallmark anti-inflammatory nutrient. Use of green chilies is at your discretion, depending on how hot you want this curry to be. It is served with hot corn bread with a dollop of butter and jaggery. It makes a complete meal in itself, full of nutrition, vitamins and extremly healthy. This preparation is a favourite with vegetarians all over northern India in particular.

Method

1. Wash thoroughly all the greens in several changes of water. Drain the greens and chop them.
2. In a large thick-bottom saucepan or a bean pot add the mustard greens, broccoli, fenugreek with the water, salt, green chilies, garlic, ginger, and cook on low heat until very tender (takes about 1 hour) or pressure-cook them for 30 minutes.
3. Remove the pressure and mash the greens with a potatoes masher or cool them and

blend them in a blender. Transfer them again into the saucepan and lower the heat.

4. Add the corn meal and mix vigorously until well blended. Cook and simmer while stirring for 10 minutes.

5. Heat 4 Tbs of the *ghee* in small saucepan and brown the onions. Add the cumin seeds and when they start popping add the turmeric powder, coriander powder, 1 tsp *garam masala*, cumin powder and whole red peppers. Mix the sautéed onions and spice mixture into the greens. Simmer and cook. If it starts to get thick add ½–1 cup of hot water and keep stirring. Remove from heat and add the remaining *garam masala* and mix. Top it with a dash of butter and serve it with buttered hot corn bread.

Note: It is mixed in the flour to make breads like parantha and poori. When chopped fine it can be mixed in fritter batter to make appetizers like pakoras. It is also used to make vegetable stir-fries.

EXOTIC VEGETABLES

Gajar aur Aloo ki Subzi

Carrots and Potatoes Stir-Fried

Serves: 8
Cooking Time: 15 Minutes

Ingredients

Onions chopped	1 cup
Oil	as needed
Ginger chopped	1 Tbs
Garlic chopped	1 Tbs
Green chilies chopped	1 tsp
Cumin seeds	1 tsp
Whole red dry pepper (broken)	2–3
Potatoes* chopped	1 cup
Carrots peeled and chopped	3 cups
Turmeric powder	1 tsp
Red pepper	1 tsp
Coriander powder	1 Tbs
Salt	1 tsp
Fresh fenugreek leaves chopped	1 cup
Or	
Fenugreek leaves dry	2 Tbs
Water	¼ cup
Garam masala	½ tsp
Chopped coriander leaves	1 Tbs

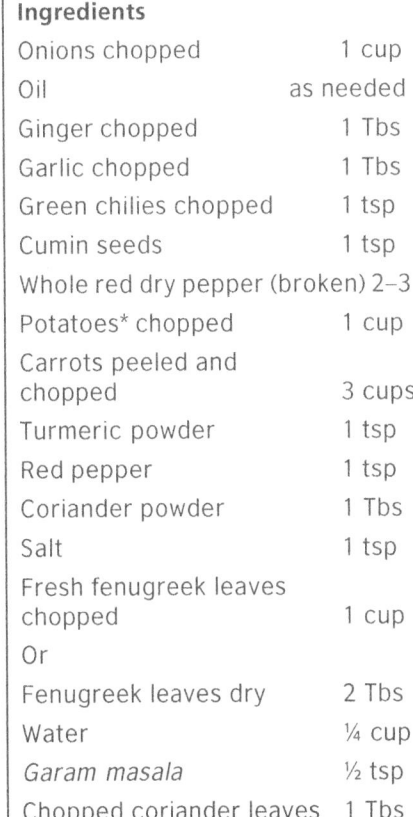

Note: Potatoes are sometimes replaced by 1 cup of fresh or frozen peas. It is your choice, and you can use ½ cup of each of them.

Chopped carrots and potatoes stir-fry is one of the quick fixing (and my favourite) vegetables. It is very healthy and delicious. Serve it with *chappati* and your favourite curry.

Cultivated carrots originated in the Afghanistan region and were yellow and purple. These delicious root vegetables are the source not only of beta-carotene, but also of a wide variety of antioxidants and other health-supporting nutrients. The areas of antioxidant benefits, cardiovascular benefits, and anti-cancer benefits are the best-researched areas of health research with respect to dietary intake of carrots. Today we know that carrots have great nutritional value being low in calories. Carrots are an excellent source of anti oxidant beta carotene, which the body converts into Vitamin A. It is this particular vitamin that really helps with vision, which is why the carrot is an important vegetable to add to your diet.

Method

1. Fry the onions in oil in a deep thick-bottom skillet and add the ginger, garlic and green chilies. Cook until the onions turn light brown.
2. Add the cumin seeds and wait till they pop. Add the whole red peppers and wait till they turn colour.
3. Add the chopped vegetables and stir. Lower the heat and add the turmeric powder, red pepper, salt, coriander powder, and coat the vegetables with the spices. Cover the carrots with a tight fitting lid and add fenugreek leaves and ¼ cup of water. Stir and cook until the potatoes are tender. About 15 minutes. Keep stirring in between to avoid any sticking. Add more water, if needed. Sprinkle with *garam masala* and chopped green coriander leaves. Transfer to a serving dish and serve with *chappati*, *poori* or *nan* along with your favourite curry.

Palak aur Aloo ki Subzi

Spinach with Potatoes Curried

Serves: 4-6
Cooking Time: 15 Minutes

Chopped spinach flavoured with mustard seeds and *garam masala*. Adding a few potatoes really makes these greens far more appetizing and tasty. Even a fussy eater who dislikes spinach in your family may start liking it.

Levels of chlorophyll and health promoting carotenoids (beta carotene, lutein and zeaxanthin). These phyto chemicals have anti-inflammatory and anti-cancerous properties and are especially important for healthy eye-sight, helping to prevent macular degeneration and cataracts.

Ingredients

Vegetable oil or *ghee*	as needed
Cumin seeds	1 tsp
Mustard seeds	1 tsp
Urad dal	2 Tbs
Whole red dry pepper broken in two	2
Onions chopped	½ cup
Ginger and garlic chopped	1 Tbs
Green chilies chopped (not hot)	1 Tbs
Garlic	1 Tbs
Asafoetida	a pinch
Turmeric powder	½ tsp
Red pepper (optional)	1 tsp
Salt	1 tsp
Coriander powder	1 Tbs
Potatoes chopped (medium)	1 cup
Spinach chopped fresh or frozen	1 lb
Rice flour (optional)	2 Tbs
Water*	2–4 Tbs
Chopped coriander leaves	1 Tbs

*2 Tbs of yogurt can be added instead of water to give a creamier gravy to the dish.

Method

1. Heat the oil in a medium size thick-bottom wok or a cooking pan. Add the cumin seeds, mustard seeds, *urad dal* and whole dry red pepper. Wait till they start to pop. Add the onions, ginger and green chilies and stir to cook for 2–3 minutes. Add the garlic and cook till the onions start turning brown.

2. Add asafoetida, turmeric powder, salt, red pepper, coriander powder and mix well. Add the chopped potatoes and stir to mix. Fry them for 5 minutes. Add the spinach. Stir and cover the vegetable mixture with a tight lid and let it simmer on low heat for 15–20 minutes or until the potatoes are tender. Add water (¼ cup), if needed. Stir in between to prevent sticking.

3. Cook for 2–3 minutes and add the rice flour (blended already in 2 Tbs of water). Mix and cook for another 5 minutes. Remove from heat, sprinkle the *garam masala* and chopped coriander leaves and serve.

Palak Paneer

Spinach and Cheese Cubes Curried

Serves: 8-10
Cooking Time: 15-20 Minutes

Ingredients

Frozen chopped baby spinach	15 oz
Or	
Spinach freshly chopped	1 lb
Salt	1 tsp
Ginger chopped	1 Tbs
Garlic chopped	1 Tbs
Green chilies (mild)	1 Tbs
Water	1½ cup
*Paneer or well drained ricotta cheese cut in 1½ inch pieces	1 lb
Oil for frying the cheese cups	3–4
Onions chopped	2 cups
Vegetable oil	¼ cup
Red chilies (whole) broken	3
Cumin seeds	1 tsp
Fresh tomatoes chopped	2 cups
Red pepper	1 tsp
Coriander powder	1 Tbs
Turmeric powder	1 tsp
Cumin powder	1 tsp
Water	¾ cup
Garam masala	1 tsp
Heavy cream	1–2 Tbs
Coriander leaves chopped	2 Tbs

A nutritious dish of spinach with deep fried cubes of homemade cheese or ricotta cheese makes a very popular north Indian curry. It is served in restaurants also as *saag paneer*. *Paneer* is popularly used in Indian cooking as a good source of digestible protein. This is a favourite vegetable accompaniment to curry, vegetarian or non vegetarian. Spinach has high nutritional value.

Spinach is believed to be of Persian origin. By the 12th century, it spread across Europe and became a desirable leafy green known for good health; It is well known for its nutritional qualities and has always been regarded as a plant with remarkable abilities to restore energy, increase vitality and improve the quality of the blood. Primarily it is rich in iron. Iron plays a central role in the function of red blood cells which help in transporting oxygen around the body, in energy production and DNA synthesis. Spinach is also an excellent source of vitamin K, vitamin A, vitamin C and folic acid as well as being a good source of manganese, magnesium, iron and vitamin B2. Vitamin K is important for maintaining bone health and it is difficult to find vegetables richer in vitamin K than spinach. Others include kale, broccoli and green cabbage.

Method

1. Transfer freshly chopped spinach or frozen spinach with 1 cup of water, into a pressure cooker and add 1 tsp of salt, 1 Tbs of ginger and garlic each and 1 Tbs of green chilies, and pressure cook for at least 15–20 minutes. Cool and blend the spinach mixture in the blender to a smooth mixture with the help of ½ cup of water and set it aside.

2. Fry the cheese pieces in the oil, at 350–375°F until slightly brown (5 minutes). Transfer

with a slotted spoon onto a paper towel and drain the oil. Set it aside.

3. In a large saucepan, cook onions in oil over medium heat until tender and light brown.
4. Add the red whole chilies (optional) and cumin seeds and wait till the seeds start popping.
5. Add the tomatoes, red pepper, coriander powder, turmeric powder, cumin powder and mix. Cook until the tomatoes are softened and the mixture looks like a thick sauce and the oil separates from the sauce. Add ¼ cup of water and bring the sauce to a boil.
6. Now add the pressure cooked spinach and remaining ½ cup of water and cook on low heat for about 10 more minutes.
7. Add the fried pieces of *paneer* or ricotta cheese and cook for another 10 minutes or until the *paneer* pieces get soft. Add more water, if needed, depending on the thickness of curry you want. Add more salt, if needed.
8. Add the heavy cream, *garam masala* and chopped coriander leaves and simmer for about 2 more minutes. Serve with *chappatis* or *nan*.

EXOTIC VEGETABLES

Matar Paneer

Peas and Cheese Cubes Curried

Serves: 4-6
Cooking Time: 20 Minutes

Ingredients

Onions chopped	1 cup
Ginger chopped	1 Tbs
Garlic chopped	1 Tbs
Green chilies chopped	1 Tbs
Vegetable oil	as needed
Cumin seeds	1 tsp
Turmeric powder	1 tsp
Red pepper	1 tsp
Coriander powder	2 tsp
Salt	to taste
Cumin powder	½ tsp
Tomatoes chopped	2 cups
Tomato sauce	1 cup
Frozen peas or fresh peas	1 cup
Water or more	1 cup
*Fried cubes of *paneer* (see Introduction) (If the *paneer* is made at home, add ½ tsp of saffron to the milk that is being used to make the *paneer*.)	2 cups
Cream	2 Tbs
Saffron	½ tsp
Garam masala	1 tsp
Coriander leaves chopped	2 Tbs

Completely drained ricotta cheese (see Introduction) can be substituted for *paneer*.

Green peas are cooked with fried pieces of ricotta cheese in creamy sauce of tomatoes, cream and onions. It makes a great dish to be served with *nan*, *chappati* or *paranthas*, particularly for a formal occasion. A very delightful savoury vegetable dish from the state of Punjab.

Matar paneer, matar pulao, green peas sandwich and peas cutlet –what is common here are the nutritively rich peas. They are not only yummy but full of health benefits. Peas are a fruit but used as a vegetable universally. They are ideal food for weight loss, good for your heart, prevent constipation and they improve your bone health. They are a perfect food for children because they are full of proteins. Peas are antioxidants and antiflamatory and reduce your risk of cancer. They also are a great source of Viamin C. Packed with iron, they can help prevent anaemia and fatigue. They are excellent as pea soup and are used in a lot of stuffings. When dry they are used in *dal* and when fried are used as a snack. Peas are cooked extensively in every cuisine of the world.

Method

1. Fry the onions, ginger, green chilies and garlic in 2 Tbs of oil till the onions are light brown in a heavy-bottom cooking pan on medium-low heat.
2. Add the cumin seeds and when they start popping add the turmeric powder, red pepper, coriander powder, salt, cumin powder and stir well.
3. Add the chopped tomatoes, tomato sauce and salt. Mix well. Fry for 5 minutes.
4. Add the peas and stir to mix. Cook the peas in the sauce for 5 minutes.

Note: Sometimes boiling the fried *paneer* pieces prior to adding them into the curry makes the pieces softer.

146 INCREDIBLE TASTE OF INDIAN VEGETARIAN CUISINE

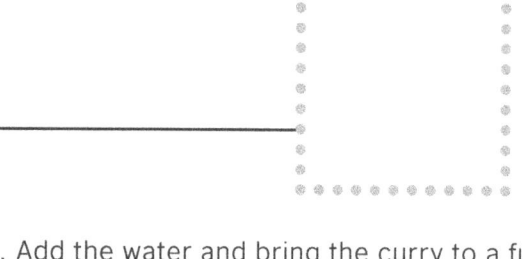

5. Add the water and bring the curry to a full boil. Simmer for 5 minutes.
6. Add the fried ricotta cheese cubes and stir them in gently. Cover with a lid and let it simmer for at least 10 more minutes.
7. Add more water, if the sauce is looking too thick.
8. Add the cream, mix and let it simmer for 5 more minutes. Sprinkle with saffron, chopped coriander leaves and *garam masala* and bring the curry to a boil and serve with *nan, roti, pulav* or plain rice.

EXOTIC VEGETABLES

Sukhi Arbi

Yam Stir-Fried

Serves: 6-8
Cooking Time: 15 Minutes

Ingredients

Yams washed, boiled, peeled and chopped	2 cups
Oil for frying	4 cups
Vegetable oil or *ghee*	as needed
Carom seeds	1 tsp
Cumin seeds	1 tsp
Onions chopped	1 cup
Ginger chopped	1 Tbs
Garlic chopped	1 Tbs
Green chilies chopped	1 Tbs
Coriander powder	1 Tbs
Turmeric	½ tsp
Red pepper	1 tsp
Salt	1 tsp
Amchoor	1 Tbs
Water	¼ cup
Coriander leaves chopped	2 Tbs
Garam masala	1 tsp
Lemon juice	1–2 Tbs

Note: It is a food staple in African, Oceanic and South Indian cultures and is believed to have been one of the earliest cultivated plants. originated perhaps in eastern India and Bangladesh.From here it spread eastward into Southeast Asia, eastern Asia, and the Pacific islands; westward to Egypt and the eastern Mediterranean; and then southward and westward from there into East Africa and West Africa. Whence it spread to the Caribbean and Americas. It is known by many local names and often referred to as "elephant ears" when grown as an ornamental plant. In Tamilnadu and other states the leaves are also used in cookinf fritters and roll ups.

Another great preparation of yams. The curry is drier than the wet curry and the pieces of yam are first deep-fried and then curried. It has its own unique and rich taste. It goes very well as a side dish with meats and other vegetable curries.

Method

1. Peel and chop yams about ½ inch pieces. Heat the oil in a deep wok or a thick-bottom saucepan between 300°F–340°F and fry the chopped up yam pieces until they are golden brown (about 5 minutes) or pan fry them in ½ cup of oil, gently turning them until slightly brown. Remove them from the oil with a slotted spoon on to a paper towel lined bowl and set them aside.

2. Heat the *ghee* or oil as needed in a heavy thick-bottom saucepan or a wok and add the carom seeds, cumin seeds, and wait till the cumin seeds start to pop. Add the onions, ginger, garlic and green chilies. Fry them until the onions are light brown. Lower the heat and add the fried pieces of yam. Add the coriander powder, turmeric, red pepper, salt and *amchoor*.

3. Stir to mix. Add ¼ cups of water and mix well. Cover the pan with a lid and cook on very low heat for 5–10 minutes. Remove from fire, stir well and serve sprinkled with chopped coriander leaves, *garam masala* and the lemon juice.

Palak aur Khumb ki Curry

Mushrooms in Spinach Sauce

Serves: 4-6
Cooking Time: 15 Minutes

Ingredients

Clarified butter (*ghee*) or vegetable oil	3-4 Tbs
Onions chopped	1 cup
Ginger chopped	1 Tbs
Garlic chopped	1 Tbs
Green chilies chopped (mild)	2 Tbs
Cumin seeds	1 tsp
Fenugreek leaves (dry)	2 Tbs
Red pepper (whole dry) broken	2
Tomatoes chopped (medium)	3
Turmeric powder	1 tsp
Coriander powder	2 Tbs
Red pepper (optional)	1 tsp
Salt	to taste
Water	1 cup
Spinach frozen	16 oz
Gram flour	2-3 Tbs
Cashew nuts or almonds ground	¼ cup
Mushrooms (large) sliced in ¼ inch thickness	½ lb
Heavy cream	1-2 Tbs
Garam masala	1 tsp
Fresh coriander leaves chopped	2 Tbs

This is a special recipe which I really like to make to entertain friends. Tender mushrooms in a creamy spinach sauce consisting of fresh tomatoes, gram flour and cream.

Method

1. Start to heat the oil or *ghee* on low heat in a thick-bottom 4 quart cooking pan and add the onions, ginger, garlic and green chilies and keep frying until the onions start to turn light brown. Add the cumin seeds and wait till they start to pop. Add the dry red pepper, dry fenugreek leaves and the tomatoes. Stir to mix. Add turmeric, coriander powder, red pepper and salt. Mix it well and cover the pan with lid for 2 minutes to soften the tomatoes.

2. Remove the lid and add the spinach. Stir to mix and cover it with the lid again and let it simmer for at least 10 minutes. Stir in between, and if it is getting dry, add ½ cup of water. Remove from heat and cool it. Transfer the spinach mixture into a blender and blend it for 2–3 minutes with water (if it is too thick) to a smooth mixture. Transfer it back to the cooking pan and add the gram flour (pre-mixed smoothly in a cup of spinach purée) and ground cashew nuts. Keep the heat low and keep stirring. Add the sliced mushrooms. Mix them in and cover the pan with a lid and let it simmer for at least 10 minutes stirring in between to prevent sticking. Add the cream, *garam masala* and chopped coriander leaves.

3. Stir to mix. Remove from heat and serve as a vegetable accompaniment to any meal.

Kathael ki Subzi

Jackfruit Stir-Fried

Serves: 4-6
Cooking Time: 35 Minutes

Ingredients

Jackfruit peeled and cut in pieces	2 lbs

Marinade:

Lemon juice	2 tsp
Oil	1 Tbs
Salt	1 tsp
Chili powder	1 tsp
Oil to fry jackfruit (*kathael*)	2 cups

Gravy:

Vegetable oil or *ghee* for cooking	3 Tbs
Onions chopped	1 cup
Ginger and garlic chopped (each)	1 Tbs
Green chilies chopped	1 Tbs
Cumin seeds	1 tsp
Curry leaves	4–5
Cardamom powder	½ tsp
Yogurt	½ cup
Turmeric powder	1 tsp
Coriander powder	1 Tbs
Red pepper	1 tsp
Salt to taste	
Vegetable stock	2 cups
Tomato sauce	½ cup
Potatoes chopped	½ cup
Garam masala	1 tsp
Coriander leaves chopped	2 Tbs

A tropical plant native to India, Myanmar, Sri Lanka and southern China. It is believed to be indigenous to the rainforests of the Western Ghats of India, dating back to 3000 to 6000 years ago. Historians relate that Indian Emperor, Ashoka encouraged the cultivation of jackfruit. Jackfruit has powerful anti-cancer, anti-aging, anti-ulcerative, and anti-hypersensitivity properties that are valuable in the treatment of a number of diseases. Chinese medicine uses jackfruit as a treatment for fighting the effects of alcohol in the body. The tree bearing Jackfruit is tall and stately and the fruit can weigh upto 60 lbs or more. The interior of the fruit consists of large bulbs of banana flavoured flesh with a core that can be cooked in the form of curries, *koftas* and with meats to make delicious gourmet preparations. It has large edible seeds that are not used in cooking. *Kathael* is a popular food ranking next to the mango and banana in southern India.

Method

1. If using fresh jackfruit (*kathael*), oil your hands and then peel it. Cut it in quarters and chop the core into cubes. Marinade it in oil, lemon juice, salt and chilli pepper for at least 2 hours and deep fry the pieces in hot oil (2 cups) for frying till light brown. Set it aside.

2. For the Gravy: Heat the *ghee* for cooking on medium-low heat in a heavy-bottom large cooking pan and fry the chopped onions, ginger, garlic and green chilies till the onions are light pink. Add the cumin seeds and wait till they start popping. Add the curry leaves, cardamom powder and stir them well into the onion mixture. Set aside.

3. Beat together yogurt with turmeric powder, coriander powder, red pepper, salt and vegetable stock in a bowl and add to the fried onions and garlic mixture. Stir well and add the tomato sauce. Cook the gravy till the *ghee* separates from the gravy. Add the potatoes and stir to mix.

4. Add the fried jackfruit (*kathael*) to the sauce and cook on slow heat till it is tender and cooked. Add stock, if needed. Sprinkle *garam masala* and chopped coriander leaves and serve. Serves well with rice *pulav.*

Note: Jackfruit is a part of some of the most exotic and lip-smacking delicacies across the world. Eaten raw, blended into a fruit salad or as a dessert topping, jackfruits do not lose their nutritional content. Botanically known as *Artocarpus heterorphyllus*, only a few people are aware of the wholesome benefits that it offers to the body. Jackfruit meal is delicious and nutritious.

Khatte Meethey Baingan

Eggplant in Sweet and Sour Sauce

Serves: 8-10
Cooking Time: 15 Minutes

Ingredients

Eggplants small or a large one chopped into 2 inch pieces	2 lbs
Oil (for frying)	4 cups
Oil (for cooking)	3 Tbs
Onions chopped	2 cups
Ginger finely chopped	1 Tbs
Green chilies finely chopped	1 Tbs
Garlic finely chopped	1 Tbs
Cumin seeds	1 tsp
Fenugreek seeds	½ tsp
Fennel seeds	1 tsp
Tomatoes chopped	2 cups
Turmeric powder	1 tsp
Ground coriander powder	1 Tbs
Red pepper	1 tsp
Salt	to taste
Potatoes cut into 2 inch pieces	1 cup
Water	3 cups
Tamarind pulp dissolved in 2 Tbs of water	1 Tbs
Brown sugar or more to taste	1 Tbs
Garam masala	1 tsp
Coriander leaves chopped	2–5 Tbs

This classic preparation of a versatile vegetable is mainly enjoyed in Andhra and the eastern part of India. The tamarind gives it a tarty taste and the brown sugar or jaggery makes it sweet. The sweet and sour taste is delicious. The delicately sweet and sour Tamarind is rich in the anti-oxidant agent tartric acid and also improves your overall health. Eggplants are deep-fried and then cooked in tamarind sauce flavoured with brown sugar and chilies. The curry is tangy, delicious and hot to the palate. It makes an excellent vegetable side dish to serve with any main meal.

The incredibly versatile eggplant works in everything from Italian to Asian recipes and it makes a tasty substitute for meat. the perfect example is a famour Italian vegetarian dish Egg plant parmigaina that is loved the world over. Eggplant's lovely purple skin adds a colorful punch to many healthy eggplant recipes. And its satisfying texture is very versatile—eggplant slices are sturdy enough to stand up to the fire of a grill to serve as the basis for a hearty vegetarian sandwich, and chunks of eggplant can be roasted and pureed into a silky, smooth dip.

Method

1. Make a crosswise slit in the eggplants and leave it attached at the top. If using large eggplant, chop it into 2 inch pieces and set them aside.

2. Heat the oil for frying in a wok and fry the eggplants light brown and drain them on to a plate lined with a paper towel.

3. In a medium saucepan heat the oil for cooking and fry the onions, ginger and green chilies on medium low heat until the onions are light brown. Add the chopped garlic, cumin seeds, fenugreek seeds and the fennel seeds and wait until they start to pop.

152 INCREDIBLE TASTE OF INDIAN VEGETARIAN CUISINE

4. Add the chopped tomatoes and stir to mix.
5. Add the turmeric powder, coriander powder, red pepper and salt, and stir-fry for a few minutes.
6. Add the potatoes and stir to fry for few more minutes. Add 2 cups of water and let the potatoes cook for about 8 minutes.
7. Transfer the eggplants into the pan and stir to mix. Add the dissolved tamarind and the brown sugar and stir well.
8. Add remaining cup of water and boil the curry for 5 more minutes. Make sure the potatoes are done.
9. Serve sprinkled with *garam masala* and chopped coriander leaves.

Baingan Dum

Fried Eggplant Curried

Serves: 4-6
Cooking Time: 25 Minutes

Eggplant pieces are first fried and then curried in a typical Mughlai style of cooking. It is a little time consuming but is elegant and exceptionally delicious.

Ingredients

Small eggplants or couple of large ones sliced	2 lbs
Vegetable oil	¼ cup
Onions chopped	½ cup
Garlic chopped	1 Tbs
Ginger chopped	1 Tbs
Green chilies chopped	1 Tbs
Cumin seeds	1 tsp
Turmeric powder	1 tsp
Salt	to taste
Coriander powder	1 tsp
Red pepper	1 tsp
Garam masala	1 tsp
Dry fenugreek leaves (from your local Indian grocer)	1 Tbs
Yogurt	1 cup
Tomatoes chopped	1 cup
Cilantro leaves freshly chopped	2 Tbs

Method

1. Chop the eggplants into ½ inch thick and 4 inches long slices. Heat ¼ cup + 2 Tbs oil in a saucepan and fry the eggplant pieces golden brown and set them aside on a plate lined with paper towel. If small egg plants are used then just cut them twice crosswise starting from the bottom and leave them attached at the top end.
2. In a thick-bottom saucepan, heat the rest of the oil and add the onions, ginger, garlic and green chilies, and cook until light brown.
3. Add the cumin seeds and wait till they pop. Add the turmeric powder, salt, coriander powder, red pepper, *garam masala*, fenugreek leaves and stir to mix.
4. Turn the heat low and add the whisked yogurt and stir well to blend the spices into it. Let it simmer for a minute and add the fried eggplant pieces. Fold them gently into the yogurt sauce.
5. Lower the heat and cover the pan partially with a lid and let it cook until the eggplant pieces are tender (about 5 minutes). Cook 5 minutes open without a lid until most of the moisture is gone.
6. Add the chopped tomatoes and stir them in. Cover the pan with the lid and let it cook for another 5–10 minutes. Add 2 Tbs of coriander leaves and stir them in.
7. Serve topped with rest of the chopped coriander leaves.

Beans Nariyal ke Saath

Beans Stir-Fried with Coconut

Serves: 8
Cooking Time: 10 Minutes

Ingredients

String beans fresh	1½ lbs
Or	
Frozen French cut beans	15 oz
Vegetable oil	3 Tbs
Mustard seeds	1 tsp
Garlic chopped	1 Tbs
Ginger chopped	1 Tbs
Green chilies chopped	1 Tbs
Curry leaves	5–7
Podi powder	2 Tbs
Water as needed	
Salt to taste or	1 tsp
Turmeric powder	¾ tsp
Coconut powder dry	2–3 Tbs
Or	
Grated fresh coconut	1 cup
Lime juice	2 Tbs
Coriander leaves chopped	¼ cup
Garam masala	½ tsp

Beans lightly flavoured with *podi* powder. The grated coconut gives it that crunchy crispy taste which is quite different from the other beans preparations.

Method

1. Wash and dry the beans and chop them into 1 inch long pieces and set them aside.
2. Heat the oil in a skillet and add the mustard seeds and wait till they pop and then add the garlic, ginger, green chilies curry leaves and cook for 2 minutes and then add the chopped beans. Add 2 Tbs of *Podi* powder and stir well to completely coat the beans. (If using fresh beans add a little water and cook longer).
3. Add salt and turmeric powder. Lower the heat and cover the pan.
4. Let it cook while stirring occasionally to prevent the sticking until the beans are tender. It will take about 8–10 minutes.
5. Sprinkle the coconut over the beans and stir well.
6. Turn off the heat and sprinkle with the lime juice, chopped coriander leaves and *garam masala* and serve.

Note: If *podi* powder is not available, add in step 2 right after adding mustard seeds, ½ tsp each of *urad dal*, *channa dal* and cumin seeds. When they start to sizzle and the *dal* turns light brown, add a pinch of asafoetida, and 1 Tbs of coconut powder. Immediately add the 1 tsp of sesame seeds and red pepper. Stir to mix in the beans. If using fresh beans, add extra cooking time.

Legumes

Lentils (*dal*) are one of the staple foods in the everyday meal of an Indian household. For thousands of years Indians have practised Hinduism and meat was generally taboo in a land that propagates a vegetarian diet. Over a period of time, we have developed a very delicious vegetarian cuisine and relied heavily on legumes as a source of protein in our daily diet.

Legumes are prepared in many different ways. These are enjoyed by the rich and poor alike and are an integral part of every formal and informal meal. The traditional method to prepare them used to be in a slow cooker or in a fairly large heavy-bottom pan and then season them. It used to take hours to cook them but now, pressure cooking has made things a lot easier.

Among the well-known lentil preparations from north India are Chick-peas in Tamarind Sauce (*Chholey*), *Dal Makhni*, *Dal Panchratan* and *Rajmah*. In every part of the country, the preparation varies a little. *Gujarati Dal,* a little sweet and sour *Dal Vadodra* and *Dal Dhokli, Oriya Dal Dalma,* made with small pieces of eggplant, plantain and flavoured with coconut, the southern delicious *Sambhar* and Rajasthani *Dal Bati* are worth mentioning.

Lentil flours are used to make many different kinds of appetizers like *dhokla, khandvi, vadas* and *muthias*. The flour of the lentils is also used to make many different kinds of fritters like *palak pakoras, planktain pakoras, papads, dahi vadas* and *vada*s. Bean sprouts are used in breakfast and as an ingredient of *chaat*. In southern India, at breakfast time or as snacks, lentil prepaprations like *idli, dosa* with *sambhar* are very common. In the north of India lentil preparations are served for lunch and dinner as a *dal* with rice. A very delicious curry called *Besan Curry* is prepared with yogurt and chick-pea flour all over India.

Many desserts are also prepared with lentil flours like *Besan Ladoos, Pinnis* and lentil fudge as *Besan ki Burfi*. The flour is also used as a binding agent to make many different kinds of *koftas* (croquettes), cutlets and *kebabs*.

Legumes are a great source of proteins needed by the human body without the fat. They are also richer in complex carbohydrates and provide plenty of fibre.

Ayurveda, popularly thought of as the repository of traditional Indian medical knowledge, is composed of two Sanskrit words AYUR "life" and VEDA "knowledge". Its meaning is therefore Science of Life. This 5000-year-old system of health care from India recommends a vegetarian diet. The nutritive contribution of dals in our diets is not just in terms of protein but also in terms of energy, Vitamins B1 and B2, folic acid and fibre. For the vegetarians, pulses are an important source of iron as well. Pulses also have a reasonable content of fatty acids which are essential for the human body.

According to ayurveda, legumes are astringent in taste. They help build all the seven types of *dhatus* or body tissue, especially muscle tissue, which makes them especially important for individuals on a vegetarian diet.Not only are legumes highly nutritious, they are very versatile, lending themselves to all kinds of dishes and combining marvelously with grains, vegetables and spices, and they taste delicious, with a buttery texture and subtly nutty flavour.

The protein in legumes is a very different protein from that which is found in meat products, cheese, eggs, and fish. Vegetarian protein from legumes requires some effort to digest and individuals new to legumes will find it very helpful to use spices that help digestion such as asafoetida, cumin seeds, fresh ginger, and black pepper. Adding these spices to legume dishes will help to reduce any side effect such as bloating or gas that beans are often associated with.

Soaking legume for at least an hour before cooking, then throwing out the water, reduces intestinal gas which are caused by the increased *vata* of peas and beans. If this does not work, then cook the legumes first in water for five to ten minutes and throw out the water. In India lentils and peas are usually split. Splitting exposes more surface during cooking and gets rid of the indigestible outer coat. It is best to cook split pulses into a soup and eat with grains. The best legumes to eat are mung beans, chickpeas, tofu, red lentils and black lentils. Black lentils give strength, but are hard to digest. They should be cooked with extra asafoetida.

Channa Dal

Gram Dal

Serves: 8-10
Cooking Time: 35 Minutes

Ingredients

Split Gram (*Channa dal*) washed and soaked	1 cup
Ginger	1 Tbs
Turmeric powder	1 tsp
Salt	1 tsp
Water	4–5 cups
Zucchini or *ghia* (Indian squash) or *badian* (dried spicy lentil balls)	1 cup
Vegetable oil or *ghee*	3 Tbs
Onions chopped	1 cup
Green chilies	1 tsp
Garlic chopped	1 Tbs
Cumin seeds	1 tsp
Whole dry red pepper broken	2 or 3
Tomatoes chopped	½ cup
Tomato sauce	1 cup
Coriander powder	1½ tsp
Red pepper	1 tsp
Garam masala	1 tsp
Coriander leaves chopped	2 Tbs
Lemon juice	1 tsp

The split and washed *Channa dal* is cooked in several ways. This lentil is highly recommended for people who have diabetes because it does not raise the sugar level of your blood. This Punjabi style preparation is cooked with bottle gourd (*ghia*) or dried spicy ground lentil balls (*badian*) available at Indian grocery stores only. It is quite a different preparation from that of other states of the country where it is enriched with greens, dry fruits, raisins, coconut and brown sugar etc.

Channa dal is rich in B-vitamins which help to energise the body. It is full of fibre which helps diabetics to control their blood sugar levels. Its low glycemic index makes it a practical dal for diabetics. It also has potassium and folic acid. The fibre in it helps lower cholesterol levels, preventing heart problems. It is a favourite in the north of India and in Bengal. Often gourd or squash is added to its preparation. Chick-peas, channa dal, black-eyed and kidney beans should be taken very occasionally and must be thoroughly soaked and well cooked.

Method

1. Transfer the soaked split gram with ginger, turmeric powder and salt into a pressure cooker with 4–6 cups of water. Cook till the grains become soft under pressure

2. Add the chopped bottle gourd or zucchini or dry lentil balls *Badian* into the *dal* after pressure cooking.
3. Cook without pressure for another 10–15 minutes or until the squash or *ghia* or the lentil balls (*badis*) are well softened. Add more water if needed.
4. In a small skillet heat the oil and add the onions and green chilies, and wait till the onions start to get brown. Add the garlic and fry a little.
5. Add the cumin seeds and dry red pepper and wait till the cumin starts to pop. Add the tomatoes, tomato sauce, coriander powder, red pepper and salt. Cook until the tomatoes become mushy and well blended.
6. Add this sauté to the cooked *dal* and mix well. Add water, if needed.
7. Add the *garam masala* and chopped coriander leaves and mix well.
8. Add the lemon juice and wait till the *dal* comes to a boil. Remove from heat and serve with plain rice, *chappati*, stir-fry vegetable and *raita*.

Note: *Badian* (dried spicy lentil balls) can be substituted for the squash. Use them if you want your *dals* really hot and spicy.

Dal Makhani - Page 159

Panchratan Dal - Page 161

Palak aur Mung ki Chilkewali Dal - Page 163

Sukhi Dal - Page 165

Mung Sabut - Page 166

Rajmah - Page 168

Khatte Chole - Page 174

Karhi - Page 176

159 LEGUMES

Dal Makhani

Whole Black Beans with Cream

Serves: 8
Cooking Time: 35-40 Minutes

Ingredients

Urad dal whole	8 oz
Water as needed or cups	4–5
Salt	2–3 tsp
Garlic chopped	2 tsp
Ginger finely chopped	2 tsp
Dried red chilies (optional)	4
Red kidney beans cooked from a can	1 cup
Vegetable oil or *ghee*	3 Tbs
Onions chopped cup	½–1
Green chilies	1 Tbs
Cumin seeds	1 tsp
Coriander powder	1 tsp
*Fenugreek leaves (dry)	2 Tbs
Red pepper	1 tsp
Turmeric powder	1 tsp
Tomatoes chopped	1 cup
Tomato sauce cup	½–1
Heavy cream	2 Tbs
Garam masala	1½ tsp
Coriander leaves	2 Tbs

Legumes are cooked for everyday meals in India and are served with rice or bread. Whole black *urad dal* is very popular in north India. It is sometimes cooked with a handful of kidney beans (*rajmah*) but when cooked alone it is as good. Curried with fresh herbs, spices and cream, it is wholesome and very flavorful.

This is perhaps the most popular dal preparation from the Punjab, now a favourite all over India.

It is most used by South Indians to make *dosa*, *idlis*, etc alongwith rice, making it a complete source of protein. Urad dal is rich in iron, folate, fibre and potassium. It is also a good source of calcium which is important for vegetarians and elderly people who require high amounts for maintaining bone health. It also boosts one's energy and keeps one active.

Urad dal is unique in the plant kingdom, because it is only one of a handful of seeds to contain *Essential Fatty Acids* or EFA.

Method

1. Wash the urad dal and add them to 4-5 cups of boiling water. Add salt, 1 tsp each of garlic, ginger and dry red chilies. Simmer until the *dal* is soft or pressure cook (25–30 minutes) until the *dal* is cooked and then let the pressure drop. Make sure the beans are still holding their shape but are soft and mushy.

2. Drain and wash the cooked red kidney beans and add 1 cup to the cooked *urad dal.*

3. Heat the oil in a deep saucepan. Add chopped onion, 1 tsp each of garlic and ginger, and add the green chilies and fry till the onions turn golden brown

4. Cook on low heat for a few minutes. Move the onion mixture to one side and add the cumin seeds until they pop. Now, add the coriander powder, dry fenugreek leaves,

red pepper, turmeric powder and salt. Add the fresh tomatoes. Cook a little and add the tomato sauce. Stir well. Cook till the sauce separates from the oil.

5. Add the cooked *dal* to the onions and tomatoes mixture and mix well. Add ½ cup or more of water, if the *dal* is too thick. Add 2 Tbs of heavy cream and mix.

6. Cook for 5–10 minutes on low heat. Stir and bring to a boil. Add *garam masala* and chopped coriander leaves. Mix well and serve with rice, *chappati* and vegetables of your choice.

Dal Panchratan

Five Lentils Curried

Serves: 8
Cooking Time: 30 Minutes

Ingredients

Toor dal (*Arhar dal*)	1/3 cup
Urad dal split washed	1/3 cup
Split gram (*Channa dal*)	1/3 cup
Green *mung dal* split	1/3 cup
Masoor dal	1/3 cup
Ginger chopped	2 Tbs
Garlic chopped	2 Tbs
Green chilies chopped	1 Tbs
Vegetable oil or *ghee*	¼ cup
Onions chopped	1 cup
Salt	2 tsp
Cumin seeds	1½ tsp
Mustard seeds	¾ tsp
Red pepper (dry)	2–3
Turmeric powder	1½ tsp
Coriander powder	2 Tbs
Water	6 cups
Red pepper powder	1 tsp
Lemon juice	2 Tbs
Or	
Tomato sauce	1½ cup
Garam masala	1 tsp
Green coriander leaves chopped	2 Tbs

Lentils are the nerves of a daily meal in a common household of India because they are the source of proteins in the mainly vegetarian diet of an Indian. It is usually served with a vegetable curry, yogurt and freshly made bread to complete a meal. To a hungry north Indian '*Dal Roti*' (*chappati and dal*) sounds as familiar and homely as probably 'meat and potatoes' to an American or a European. This *dal* is made by mixing five different kinds of lentils and is unlike any other lentil preparation. It is very easy to make the famous Rajasthani *Dal Baati* from this recipe.

Method

1. Pick and wash the *dals* and soak them in 6 cups of water.
2. Transfer them to a Dutch oven or a slow cooker, add one tsp each of ginger, green chilies, garlic and salt, and cook until the lentils are tender or pressure cook them (for 15–20 minutes). Let the pressure down. Set aside.
3. Heat 3 Tbs of oil or *ghee* and fry the rest of onions, ginger, garlic and the green chilies. When they are golden brown add the cumin seeds, mustard seeds and wait till they start to pop and then add the whole red pepper.

Fry for half a minute and add the turmeric powder, salt, coriander powder and red pepper.

4. Add the tomato sauce and a cup of water. Turn the heat low. Cook and simmer this mixture for 5 minutes.
5. Add this tempering to the cooked lentils. Mix the tempering well into the cooked *dal*, bring it to a boil and simmer for 2 more minutes.
6. Add the *garam masala* and lemon juice (if tomato sauce is not used) and the chopped coriander.
7. Cook a minute longer and remove from heat and serve with just rice or bread and vegetables as a daily meal.

Note: Make *baatis* as follows:

Wheat flour	1 cup	Milk	½ cup
Rawa or *suji*	½ cup	*Ghee* or oil	¼ cup
Gram flour	2 Tbs	Salt to taste	

Mix together flour, *rawa*, gram flour, oil and salt. Knead it into a tight dough with the help of milk. Make lemon size balls and bake in the electric oven for 15–20 minutes, and roast them or brown them in a skillet. Pour and smear them with oil/*ghee* and serve with the *panchratan dal*.

Palak aur Mung ki Chilkewali Dal

Spinach and Split Green Lentils

Serves: 8-10
Cooking Time: 20 Minutes

A very healthy legume and spinach preparation from Uttar Pradesh. It is a nutritious main course as it meets the requirements of proteins and vegetables in one preparation.

According to modern nutritionists, mung beans offer 14 gms of protein per cooked cup. They also contain vitamins A, C and E, folacin, thiamin, calcium, iron, magnesium, phosphorus, potassium and copper. This dal is praised in ayurvedic texts for its nutritional value and ease of digestion.

Mung beans are one of the most cherished foods in ayurveda. They are *tri-doshic*, especially when cooked with spices appropriate for each dosha.

Ingredients

Mung dal spilt washed and soaked	1 cup
Water	6 cups
Fresh spinach chopped	2 cups
Or	
Frozen (10 ozs)	½-1 pkg
Curry leaves	4
Onions chopped	1 cup
Ginger	1 Tbs
Garlic	1 Tbs
Tomatoes chopped	1 cup
Green chilies	1 Tbs
Vegetable oil or *ghee*	3 Tbs
Red whole chilies broken	2
Cumin seeds	1 tsp
Mustard seeds	1 tsp
Salt	1 tsp
Turmeric powder	1 tsp
Fenugreek leaves (dry)	1 Tbs
Red pepper	1 tsp
Coriander powder	2 tsp
Cumin powder	½ tsp
Tomato sauce (8 oz can)	1
Garam masala	1 tsp
Coriander leaves chopped	2 Tbs

Method

1. Drain the water from the soaked dal and transfer it into a deep saucepan with 6 cups of water and frozen spinach and let it cook on medium to low heat. Add water as needed.
2. After 20 minutes add the ginger, garlic, tomatoes, green chilies, and the curry leaves while it is cooking.
3. Cook until it is smooth but grainy and has the consistency of a thick soup or pressure cook the *dal* with water for 10 minutes and set it aside.
4. In a small skillet cook onions in 3 Tbs of oil until they are light brown and add the cumin seeds, mustard seeds and the red whole chilies. Fry till the cumin seeds and mustard seeds are popping.

Note: The amount of water in cooking the *dal* will increase if unsoaked *dal* is used.

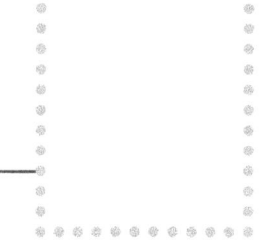

5. Add the turmeric powder, dry fenugreek leaves, red pepper, coriander powder, cumin powder, salt and stir well. Add the tomato sauce. Stir to mix and cook for another 3–5 minutes.

6. Pour this sauté over the *dal* mixture and mix well. Add more water, if *dal* is too thick.

7. Add the *garam masala* and the chopped green coriander leaves. Stir well and serve. It can be served with just plain rice to make a quick meal or as an accompaniment with other main courses.

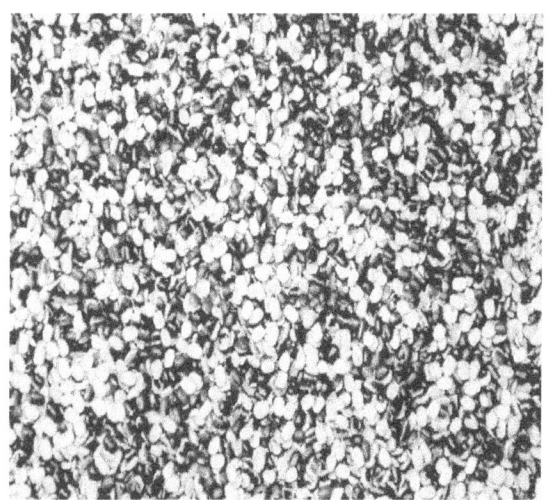

Sukhi Dal

Dry Lentils Curried

Serves: 4-6
Cooking Time: 20 Minutes

Ingredients

Urad or *mung dal* split without skin (washed and soaked in water for ten minutes)	2 cups
Water	3 cups
Turmeric powder	1 tsp
Salt	to taste
Onions chopped	1 cup
Ginger chopped	1 Tbs
Garlic chopped	1 Tbs
Green chillies chopped	1 tsp
Vegetable oil or *ghee*	¼ cup
Red pepper broken (whole)	2–3
Cumin seeds	1½ tsp
Tomatoes chopped	1 cup
Coriander powder	1 Tbs
Red pepper	1 tsp
Bottle gourd or zucchini chopped	1 cup
Garam masala	1 tsp
Coriander leaves chopped	¼ cup
Lemon juice	1 Tbs

Lentils are always cooked to a consistency of a thick soup but in north India it is sometimes cooked dry (without any sauce) garnished similarly with fresh onions, ginger, garlic, green chilies and dry spices. Serve it topped with fresh coriander leaves and *garam masala* with another wet curry and *chappati* or *nan*.

Method

1. Transfer the *urad dal* from the soaked water into a heavy-bottom large cooking pan with (3–3½ cups) of water. Add turmeric powder and salt and cook on the fire, until the grains are soft but not mushy and water is completely absorbed or pressure cook for 5–10 minutes. Set aside.
2. Cook the onions, ginger, garlic and green chilies in oil and fry till light brown. Add the whole red pepper, cumin seeds, and wait for them to start popping.
3. Add the tomatoes, and stir well.
4. Lower the heat and add the coriander powder, red pepper, and add the chopped pumpkin or bottle gourd. Cover the pan and cook for 10 minutes or until the pumpkin pieces get soft. Add the cooked *dal*. Stir well and cook for 2–3 minutes making sure the grains do not get mushy.
5. Add the *garam masala*, chopped coriander leaves and the lemon juice. Mix the *dal* gently but thoroughly.
6. Serve with meat or vegetable wet curry, rice or any kind of bread.

Note: *Mung dal* will take less water (2 2½ cups) and less time to cook (5 minutes) in the pressure cooker. If *dal* has been soaking overnight then it will require even lesser amount of water to cook.

Sabut Mung ki Dal

Whole Mung Beans

Serves: 6-8
Cooking Time: 30-60 Minutes

Ingredients

Whole *Mung* beans or *dal*	2 cups
Water	6 cups
Salt	to taste
Turmeric powder	1 tsp
Kokum pieces	4-5
Onions chopped	1 cup
Ginger chopped	1 Tbs
Garlic chopped	1 Tbs
Green chilies chopped	1 Tbs
Vegetable oil or *ghee*	¼ cup
Cumin seeds	1 tsp
Red pepper whole (dry) broken	2
Coriander powder	2 tsp
Cumin powder	1 tsp
Red pepper	1 tsp
Fenugreek leaves (dry)	1 Tbs
Garam masala	1 tsp
Green coriander leaves chopped	2 Tbs
Cream (optional)	2 Tbs

Whole *mung* is very popular in northern India and is very delicious and nutritious when cooked well. Mostly flavored with onions, cumin and fresh coriander leaves and served with rice and *chappati*. One of the easy lentils to cook and easy to digest, it has a very pleasing taste. Ayurvedic healers value the mung bean most highly, because it is very nutritious and delivers sustenance while being easier on digestion than other beans. When cooked in little butter, mung beans can be digested even by the ill, the very old and the very young, and individuals with a weak digestive fire. Mung beans offer the astringent and sweet tastes, are cooling for the body, and light and soft. When combined with enhancing herbs and spices, mung beans are suitable for everybody.

Method

1. Wash and soak the beans in 2 cups of water.
2. Boil 6–8 cups of water in a large saucepan and transfer the washed and drained beans into the pan.
3. Add the salt, turmeric powder and *kokum*, and let the beans cook on the medium heat until the beans are completely soft and the *dal* has a smooth but grainy look to it (one hour or more) and add more water, if needed. Preferably pressure cook the *dal* in 4–6 cups of water until soft. Let the pressure down and set it aside. Time of pressure cooking may vary from one place to another.
4. Cook the onions, ginger, garlic, and green chilies in 2 Tbs of oil and fry the onions till they are brown.

Note: *Dry mung dal* is also very delicious. Add enough to cook in step 3; see that the beans are soft and then follow the rest of the steps except that no more water is added.

5. Add the cumin seeds and pieces of dry pepper and wait till the cumin starts to pop and then add coriander powder, cumin powder, red pepper, dry fenugreek leaves, salt, and transfer the sauté to the *dal*. Add more (1–2 cups) boiling water as needed and mix well. Let it simmer for 5 more minutes.

6. Add the *garam masala*, chopped coriander leaves and the cream and let it simmer for another 2 minutes. Serve with rice, vegetable curry of your choice and any bread.

Rajmah

Curried Red Kidney Beans

Serves: 8-10
Cooking Time: 35 Minutes

Ingredients

Vegetable oil	¼ cup
Red kidney beans uncooked	2 cups
Red kidney beans cooked 16 ozs cans	2
Cinnamon stick one inch	1
Cardamoms dark brown	2
Cloves	½ tsp
Black pepper corns	½ tsp
Red whole chilies (dry) broken	2
Onions chopped	1 cup
Ginger chopped	1 Tbs
Garlic chopped	1 Tbs
Green chilies chopped	1 tsp
Cumin seeds	1 tsp
Tomatoes chopped	1 cup
Turmeric powder	1 tsp
Coriander powder	1 Tbs
Red pepper	1 tsp
Cumin powder	1 tsp
Tomato sauce	8 oz
Salt	1 tsp
Potatoes chopped	½ cup
Water	2–3 cups
Garam masala	1 tsp
Coriander leaves chopped	2 Tbs
Heavy cream (optional)	1 Tbs

This red kidney bean preparation is very popular in the state of Punjab. It is a wholesome and a complete meal when served with rice. Kidney beans are full of potassium, magnesium, iron and protein. Hence, this is a good meat substitute for vegetarians. Kidney beans also have several disease fighting anti-oxidants that promote a healthy and strong immunity. It is the healthiest legume in vegetarian diet.

Method

1. Drain the liquid from the cans of cooked kidney beans in a colander and wash the beans in tap water and set them aside. If using uncooked beans wash the beans and transfer them into a pressure cooker with 6 cups of water, cinnamon sticks, cloves, black pepper corns, cardamoms, and the whole red chilies. Pressure cook them until tender. Let the pressure down and set them aside.

2. Cook the onions in oil in a deep heavy-bottom saucepan and add the onions, ginger, garlic, and the green chilies till the onions become light brown.

3. Add the cumin seeds and fry till they pop (if cooking with the canned beans then add the whole spices now to the onion mixture like the cinnamon sticks, cardamoms, cloves,

and red whole chilies. Wait till chilies are turning colour) and then add the tomatoes, turmeric powder, coriander powder, red pepper, cumin powder, tomato sauce and the salt and cook until the tomatoes are mushy and the *ghee* separates from the sauce.

4. Add the potatoes and stir-fry them in the sauce. Add the water and cook the potatoes for about 10 minutes. Add the kidney beans. Stir them in the sauce well and cook for 15–20 more minutes or until the sauce is thick and kidney beans are pretty soft. Add more or less water as the consistency requires.

5. Add the *garam masala* and coriander leaves, heavy cream and simmer for 2 more minutes and serve with rice or as side dish to any main course meal.

Note: Whole spices like cinnamon, cloves, black pepper corns, and cardamoms can be enclosed in a small piece of muslin cloth. Tie the ends together with a piece of thread and then add this little bag (*garni*) to the curry. After cooking this bag can be discarded. These spices are added only to flavour the beans. Sometimes fried pieces of tofu or *paneer* can be added alongwith kidney beans and that would make the curry more wholesome.

Sambhar

Lentils Curried with Vegetables in Tamarind Sauce

Serves: 6-8
Cooking Time: 35 Minutes

Ingredients

Toor dal	1 cup
Water	8 cup
Curry leaves	4–6
Turmeric powder	1 tsp
Salt	1 tsp
Red pepper as needed	1 tsp
*Zucchini peeled and chopped	2 cups
Or	
Mixed vegetables	2 cups
Tomatoes chopped (large)	2
Onions chopped (medium)	2
Green chilies chopped	1 Tbs
Ginger chopped	1 Tbs
Garlic chopped	1 Tbs
Fenugreek leaves (dry)	2 Tbs
Tomato sauce	1 cup
Tamarind sauce	1 tsp
Vegetable oil	3 Tbs
Mustard seeds	1 tsp
Cumin seeds (whole)	1 tsp
Coriander seeds	2 Tbs
Red chilies (whole)	4
Urad dal	1 tsp
Asafoetida powder	¼ tsp
Coconut powder dry unsweetened (available at the Indian grocery store)	1 Tbs
Garam masala	1 tsp
Coriander leaves chopped	2 Tbs

A spicy *toor dal* preparation from southern India with fresh chopped vegetables and is garnished with fresh curry leaves, tamarind paste and mustard seeds. This lentil preparation goes best with *idli*, *dosa* and rice preparations.

A very popular and favoured dal, it is light and yummy. Apart from the protein and fibre, it contains folic acid which helps prevent anemia, and is also important for pregnant women as it is essential for fetal development and can help neural tube birth defects such as spina bifida. It is low in calories and good for people who are on weight loss diets. It also helps control blood sugar levels.

Method

1. Wash and soak the *toor* (*arhar*) *dal* in 6 cups of water and transfer it into a deep thick-bottom pan. Cook for 15 minutes with curry leaves, turmeric, salt and red pepper or pressure cook for 5 minutes and then let the pressure down.

2. Add the zucchini, (or mixed vegetables) chopped tomatoes, onions, green chilies, chopped ginger, chopped garlic, fenugreek leaves and cook till the vegetables are tender and are well blended (15–20 minutes).

3. Add the tomato sauce and tamarind paste dissolved in a tablespoon of water. Add more water if needed. Cook and simmer for 5 more minutes or longer, until the *dal* has a uniform consistency. Set it aside.

4. Heat the oil in small skillet and add mustard seeds, cumin seeds, coriander seeds, whole red pepper and the *urad dal*. Wait until the mustard seeds, coriander seeds, and cumin seeds stop splattering and *urad dal* turns light brown. Add the coconut powder, fry till it is light brown (1 minute). Now add the asafoetida powder and wait till it changes color. Grind the mixture in a little coffee grinder and transfer it to the cooked *dal* mixture. Stir well.

5. Add 1 tsp of *garam masala* and coriander leaves, mix it well. Cook the *sambhar* for another 2 minutes. It is ready to be served with rice, *idli* or *dosa*.

Note: Sambar is a vegetable stew or chowder based on a broth made with tamarind and pigeon peas, or toor dal. Sambar is one of the most loved dishes in South Indian cuisine. It accompanies most meals. In South India, there are variations to the vegetables used in sambar. Lentils here are cooked in a tamarind and coconut sauce, tempered with Indian spices and is served hot with rice. Try them with other vegetables. Instead of chopped zucchini, you can also use eggplants, potatoes with bell pepper, white radish with carrots, okra or simply mixed vegetables. It can also be prepared with lima beans or blackeyed beans. Frozen vegetables can be used but if fresh vegetables are used they should be chopped into medium size pieces.

Chole Curry

Garbanzo (Chickpeas) Curried

Serves: 8
Cooking Time: 20 Minutes

Ingredients

Vegetable oil or *ghee*	3 Tbs
Onions medium chopped	1 cup
Ginger chopped	2 Tbs
Garlic	2 Tbs
Green chilies chopped	1 Tbs
Cinnamon sticks very small	2
Cloves whole	½ tsp
Bay or curry leaves	4–6
Cumin seeds	1 tsp
Red pepper whole	2–4
Tomato sauce	1 cup
Turmeric powder	1 tsp
Red pepper	1 tsp
Salt	1 tsp
Coriander powder	2 tsp
Potatoes peeled and chopped	½ cup
Chick-peas drained and washed (15 oz cans)	2
Tamarind pulp (dissolved in ¼ cup of water)	1 tsp
Water	3 cups
Garam masala	1 tsp
Coriander leaves chopped	2 Tbs

A spicy chick-peas preparation. It is proteinaceous and makes a very good meal when served with just plain rice and *raita*. It is also served as a side dish for a formal dinner. Chickpeas are a remarkable food in terms of their antioxidant composition. Not only are they full of antioxidant nutrients such as vitamin C, vitamin E and beta-carotene, they contain concentrated supplies of phytonutrients, plant material necessary for good health. There are copious ways they are used in Indian cuisines, and in vegetarian regions they serve as one of the major sources of protein.

Method

1. In a deep 4 quart saucepan, heat the oil and transfer onions, ginger, garlic, green chilies, and cook till light brown.
2. Add the cinnamon sticks, cloves, bay leaves, cumin seeds, and whole red pepper, and wait till the cumin seeds start popping.
3. Add the tomato sauce, turmeric powder, red pepper, salt, coriander powder, and stir for another 2 minutes. Add the potatoes and stir-fry for five minutes.

4. Now add the drained, cooked chick-peas and stir for 2 minutes.

5. Add water and let them simmer for 20–25 minutes so that the flavor of the spices penetrate the chick-peas and potatoes are tender. Add the tamarind dissolved in ¼ cup of water and stir to mix. Add more water, if the curry is too thick, and cook for another 5 minutes.

6. Serve sprinkled with *garam masala*, and top it with chopped coriander leaves. It makes a great dish to be served with rice only but enhances its appeal when served with vegetable curry, *chappati, poori,* or *nan*.

Note: The whole spices are usually put together in a small porous container (*garni*), and dropped in the beginning into the pot while cooking chickpeas, so that the flavour of the spices penetrates the chickpeas. A Punjabi speciality introduced to India by Afghan traders, chickpeas are also one of the major staple foods in Mediterranean countries as Humus. Humus is ground chickpea paste flavored with sumac, lemon and spices. Chickpeas are packed with proteins and nutrients. Indians love to eat the fresh chickpeas sold by the vendors roasted or grilled with spices. They make a perfect snack and they are delicious. If using uncooked chickpeas, see notes of recipe "*Chickpeas in Tamarind Sauce*".

In Myanmar, Chickpeas are used to make "Burmese tofu", in Sicily, it coats meats or vegetables which are deep fried into chickpea fritters; throughout the Mediterranean region, it is made into flatbread, and in many other areas of the world, including northern Italy, southern France, Gibraltar, Argentina, Uruguay, Algeria and India, it is used to make thin pancakes.

Khatte Chole

Chickpeas in Tamarind Sauce

Serves: 6-8
Cooking Time: 30 Minutes

Ingredients

Vegetable oil or *ghee*	4 Tbs
Onions chopped	2 cups
Ginger chopped	2 Tbs
Garlic chopped	2 Tbs
Green chilies chopped	2 Tbs
Cumin seeds	1 tsp
Cinnamon sticks (very small)	2
Cloves whole	1 tsp
Cardamoms whole (large)	2
Bay leaves	4–6
Black pepper corns	1 tsp
Red pepper (whole)	4
Red pepper powder	1 tsp
Salt to taste Or	1–2 tsp
Coriander powder	2 Tbs
Chick-peas (15 oz cans) drained and washed Or	4 cans
Dry chick-peas	2½ cups
Water	4–5 cups

A spicy chick-peas preparation, which is simply delicious with *bhaturas* (a kind of fried bread). The combination of these two specialities makes one of the most popular and favourite meals in Punjab, a stunning presentation with the wonderful aroma of spices.

Chickpeas were first cultivated about 3000 BC and were popular among the ancient Romans, Greeks and Egyptians. Today, chickpeas are used in the cuisines of South Asia, the Middle East, and the Mediterranean. more so in North Africa, Spain and India, where the chickpea is a staple for India's largely vegetarian population.

Method

1. In a deep 4–quart sauce pan heat the oil and transfer onions, ginger, garlic, green chilies, and cook till light brown. Add the cumin seeds and wait till they pop.

*2. Add the cinnamon sticks, cloves, cardamoms and bay leaves, black pepper corns and whole red pepper. Fry them for 2 minutes. You can also use spice bag or *garni* (see Note).

Pomegranate seeds ground Or *Amchoor*	1 Tbs
Cumin seeds ground roasted	2 Tsp
Garam masala	1 tsp
Tamarind paste dissolved in 2 Tbs of water	1½ tsp
To garnish:	
Coriander leaves chopped	2 Tbs
Tomatoes (sliced)	2
Onions fresh (sliced)	1
Small boiled potatoes chopped	2
Green chilies (small)	a few

3. Add the ground red pepper, salt, coriander powder, and stir-fry for a few minutes.
4. Add the drained chick-peas (*channa*) and 4–5 cups of water and let them simmer for half an hour or so till the flavor of the spices penetrate the chick-peas and they get blend completely with the sauce. Add more water, if needed.
5. Now, add the ground roasted pomegranate seeds (*anaardana*) or *amchoor*, 1 Tbs of ground roasted cumin seeds, *garam masala* and the tamarind paste. Stir well to mix the ingredients. Simmer for another half an hour adding water, if it gets too thick.
6. Serve sprinkled with remaining dry, ground, roasted cumin seeds, *garam masala*, and top it with wedges of tomatoes and slices of onions, pieces of chopped boiled potatoes and chopped coriander leaves.
7. Best served with *bhaturas* and *raita* but can also be served with *pooris* and *nans*, if desired.

Note: If using dry chick-peas, wash them and pressure cook them in 5 cups of water in a pressure cooker with small pieces of ginger, garlic and green chilies. *Put the whole spices like whole red pepper, cinnamon stick, cardamoms, cloves, black pepper in a little porous bag (*garni*) and add this bag with the chick-peas in the pressure cooker. Add ¼ tsp of baking soda. Pressure cook the chick-peas for 45 minutes. Follow the recipe from 1–7 but omit step 2. Discard the bag of spices after pressure cooking is done. Chickpea flour, also known as *besan*, gram flour, channa flour, harina de garbanzo is a popular legume in many Old World cuisines. Its flour is used to make the batter for Indian pakoras. In Mideastern countries ground chickpeas are used as the most famous dip, Humus. The French of Provence make a popular bread called *socca*. Persian Jews mix it with ground chicken to form *qundi* dumplings. Chickpea flour can also be a great substitute flour in the diet of diabetics and for those who want to go gluten-fee!

Karhi

Gram Flour Curry

Serves: 6-8
Cooking Time: 20-25 Minutes

A curry made of a mixture of curd and gram flour is made in all parts of India. The aroma of this dish fills the kitchen when you are cooking it. It takes some time to prepare, but is worth the effort. It is a complete meal when served with plain rice but can also be served as a side dish or with other vegetables and bread. High in protein content, this gluten free flour is extensively used in Indian cuisine.

Ingredients

Gram flour	½ cup
Yogurt beaten smooth	2 cups
Salt	to taste
Red pepper	1 tsp
Turmeric powder	1 tsp
Water	6-8 cups
Onions chopped in ¼ inch rounds	1
Ginger chopped	1 Tbs
Garlic chopped	1 Tbs
Fenugreek leaves dried	1 Tbs
Green coriander leaves chopped	2 Tbs
Garam masala	1 tsp
Vegetable oil	4 Tbs
Cumin seeds	1 tsp
Mustard seeds	1 tsp
Red chilies (whole)	2
Asafoetida	a pinch

For the dumplings:

Gram flour	1 cup
Salt	to taste
Baking soda	a pinch
Carom seeds	1 tsp
Green chilies chopped	1 tsp
Yogurt	½ cup
Water enough to make a thick batter	
Oil (for frying)	4 cups

Method

1. Beat yogurt, salt, red pepper, gram flour, turmeric powder and water together and cook on low heat and bring to boil stirring consistently in a large heavy-bottom cooking pan.
2. Add the onions, ginger and garlic.
3. Cook until the mixture thickens (10 minutes) on medium-low heat stirring occasionally to make sure the mixture does not stick to the bottom. Set aside.
4. Make the dumplings.
5. Mix all the ingredients for the dumplings, gram flour, salt, soda, carom seeds, green chilies and yogurt, and beat to make a smooth but thick batter using water as needed.

6. Heat the oil to 325–350°F for frying.
7. Drop the dough by spoonfuls into the hot oil and fry to golden brown.
8. Remove and set aside in a pan lined with paper towel to drain excess oil.
9. Add these dumplings and fenugreek leaves to the curry and cook the curry for another 20 minutes on low heat.
10. Add the coriander leaves and the *garam masala* and mix.
11. Transfer this mixture to serving bowl and set aside.
12. In a deep small skillet heat the 4 Tbs of oil and add the cumin and mustard seeds, and sauté till they crackle. Then add the whole red chilies and the asafoetida. Remove from fire and pour this tempering over the cooked curry.
13. Mix well and serve with plain rice.

Note: Gram flour (besan) is an excellent ingredient to deep cleanse and exfoliate your skin. It is traditionally used in India for beauty care. It has been used in Indian weddings for thousands of years. Gram flour paste made by mixing it with turmeric, oil, and rose water is used by the bride and the groom for deep cleansing and disinfecting their skin as a ritual prior to getting married.

Accompaniments

The soups in Indian cooking are very distinctive with their special touch of fresh herbs, and delicate spices like cumin and black pepper. Their distinctive aroma has a special appeal in the western world. Soups were not an integral part of a regular Indian meal till recent times, and therefore, earlier Indian cookbooks did not even mention them. Soups in India were never served as first course like in the western countries but were served with a slice of bread as a light meal. It is amazing how fast they have gained an appropriate place in Indian cuisine and are now served for lunch with a salad and bread and are also served as the first course of a meal in restaurants too. Soups and salads are a delightful addition to Indian cuisine and have enhanced its charm tremendously.

There are several kinds of soups in Indian cooking. Some are creamy and smooth like Cauliflower Soup, Bottle Gourd Soup and Cream of Corn Soup. Then there are tangy sweet and sour soups like *Rasam*, Mulligatawny Soup and Tomato Soup. Some wholesome ones are potato leek soup, Mixed Vegetable Soup, Lentil Soup and Spinach Soup.

Hope you will like the soups offered to you in the following pages. Use seasonings at the end of each preparation according to your taste. When preparing a soup as a starter for a meal, select a soup that would complement your dinner and balance it.

In particular, vegetable-based soups are a great option nutritionally because when you consume a low-calorie vegetable based soup before your main meal, you consume up to 20% less calories at a meal because soup fills you up and we eat less. Nutritionally also svegetable soups are rich in Vitamins, fibres and a range of minerals.Ingeneral soups are good because they keep the water balance in your body and that in turn keeps our blood pressure under control.

A hot bowl of soup is not only easy-to-make, but also a great soothing tonic for comfort when we need it the most. Warm hearty vegetable soups are perfect on a cold winter day! Whether you pair it with a salad, a sandwich, or simply a hunk of good bread, a warm bowl of healthy soup on a cold day is one of the most satisfying sensation of winter.

Roasted Potato Leek Soup

SOUPS

Gobhi ka Shorba - Page 183

Milijuli Sabjion ka Shorba - Page 186

Bhune hue Aloo aur Leek ka Shorba - Page 187

Tamatar ka Shorba - Page 188

Kosambari Salad - Page 193

Pyaz, Chukandar aur Tamatar ka Salad - Page 195

Milijuli Sabjion ka Salad - Page 196

Mooli ya Gajar ka Salad - Page 197

Gobhi ka Shorba
Cauliflower Soup

Serves: 4-6
Cooking Time: 25 Minutes

Ingredients	
Vegetable oil	2–4 Tbs
Onion chopped medium	1
Ginger chopped	1 Tbs
Garlic chopped	1 Tbs
Green chilies (mild) chopped	1 Tbs
Potatoes small peeled and chopped	2
Cauliflower florets or ¼ of a large head	2 cups
Salt	to taste
Cumin powder	1 tsp
Coriander powder	1 tsp
Turmeric powder (optional)	1 tsp
Cayenne powder	½–1 tsp
water	8 cups
Heavy cream	½ cup
Garam masala to sprinkle	
Green onions chopped	1 Tbs
Coriander leaves finely chopped	1 Tbs

An elegant soup, that is almost a meal. A great first course for a dinner. Excellent to serve as a lunch accompaniment.

Method

1. Heat oil in a medium size saucepan and cook the onions, ginger, garlic and green chilies until light brown.
2. Add the potatoes and cauliflower. Add 1 tsp salt, cumin powder, coriander powder, turmeric and cayenne pepper and stir to mix. Add the water and bring to a boil. Cover and cook until the vegetables are tender.
3. Put soup in a blender and blend until smooth.
4. Strain well to push all the pulp through. Use ½ Cup of boiling water if needed.
5. Add the cream and gently boil once.
6. Serve garnished with a gentle sprinkle of *garam masala*, chopped green onions and coriander leaves and a dab of heavy cream.
7. Season to taste.

Note: Cauliflower is a super vegetable with **Vitamin C** a powerful antioxidant and anti-inflamatory agent. It also has **folate, Vitamin B** that your body needs to make healthy new cells, **Vitamin K** which your body needs to make healthy bones, **Fiber** which keeps your digestive tract happy and healthy keeping your blood sugar and energy levels steady. **It basically has all cancer preventing compounds** often found in the cruciferous family. These compounds called sulfur-containing phytochemicals have been shown to disrupt the growth of cancer cells, detox carcinogens and break down excess estradiol which is associated with breast cancer.

Makki ka Shorba

Cream of Corn Soup

Serves: 4-6
Cooking Time: 15-20 Minutes

Ingredients

Corn frozen or freshly husked	2½ cups
White potatoes peeled and chopped	1 cup
Onions white or yellow, chopped	½ cup
Fresh ginger and garlic peeled and chopped each	1 tsp
Water	6 cups
Black pepper	½ tsp
Salt	1 tsp
Milk	1½ cups
Sesame oil	1 Tbs
Mustard seeds	½ tsp
Green onions chopped and cilantro	1 Tbs

Note: Corn is a good source of phenolic flavonoid antioxidant, ferulic acid. Several research studies suggest that ferulic acid plays vital role in preventing cancers, aging, and inflammation in humans. It also contains good levels of some of the valuable B-complex group of vitamins such as thiamin, niacin, pantothenic acid, folates, riboflavin, and pyridoxine.

It is one of those simple heart-warming soups with fresh vegetables in a creamy, savory broth. Corn and potatoes soup flavored with fresh ginger, garlic, cilantro and red pepper is different, but delicious. Serve it with crackers and some French bread and it is a complete meal. Corn soup is also a very popular soup in American cuisine. It is creamy less spicy with pieces of celery and carrots. No need to add corn starch as thickening agent because corn itself makes a creamy sauce. Good example of Indo-American fusion cooking here.

Method

1. Boil 2 cups of corn with potatoes, onions, ginger, garlic, in deep, medium size saucepan in 6 cups of water and add salt and black pepper. Boil till the potatoes are tender and soft. Add more water if needed.
2. Cool a little and pour the contents into a blender and purée them.
3. In the saucepan transfer the puréed soup and add the milk and remaining corn and gently bring it to boil.
4. In a small skillet heat the sesame oil and add the mustard seeds till they pop. Pour the oil in a small bowl and set it aside.
5. Serve the soup garnished with a sprinkle of chopped green onions, chopped green cilantro and the flavored oil.
6. Serve this soup with any bread of your choice to make a light lunch or a first course of a dinner.

Kaddu ka Shorba
Cream of Pumpkin Soup

Serves: 6-8
Cooking Time: 30 Minutes

Ingredients

Onions chopped	½ cup
Vegetable oil or *ghee*	2 Tbs
Ginger chopped	1 Tbs
Garlic chopped	1 Tbs
Green chilies chopped	1 Tbs
Mustard seeds	1 tsp
Pumpkin peeled and chopped	4 cups
Turmeric powder	½ tsp
Salt	to taste
Coriander powder	1 tsp
Red pepper	to taste
Water	6 cups
Milk	2 cups
Sugar	2 Tbs
Garam masala	½ tsp
Lemon juice	2 Tbs
sliced	2 tsp
Cream	¼ cup
Pistachio or almonds thinly sliced	
Coriander leaves chopped	1 Tbs

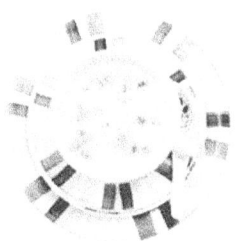

Note: Seasoning of *garam masala* or red pepper can be done according to taste. If you like your soup to be a little more sweet and sour, add more sugar.

Even a humble unconventional and a modest vegetable like the Pumpkin can give you a surprisingly delicious soup. The early Americans used pumpkin in their cooking extensively because it was a staple food of native indians in America and therefore the early settlers cooked and made different dishes of Pumpkin. Pumpkin Soup has been in their cuisine from a long time. This soup is a blend of Indian and American styles of cooking. This is a colorful creamy soup. All you have to do is to flavor it with onions, lemon and some spices and you have one of a kind soup.

Method

1. Cook the onions in 2 Tbs of oil in a thick bottom large saucepan until light brown. Add the ginger, garlic and green chilies, and cook another 2 minutes.
2. Add the mustard seeds and when they start to pop add the pumpkin and stir-fry them with the onion mixture. Lower the heat.
3. Add the turmeric powder, salt, coriander powder, red pepper, and coat the pumpkin pieces well with all the spices.
4. Add the water and let it cook on medium-low heat until the pumpkin is soft.
5. Take the pan off the heat, cool it, and pour the pumpkin mixture into the blender to blend it smooth.
6. Transfer the soup back into the saucepan and add the milk and the sugar. Cook on medium heat for 3–5 minutes. Add the *garam masala* and lemon juice, and stir the soup well. Add more water, if needed.
7. Remove from heat and serve each helping topped with a tsp of cream, shredded almonds or pistachio and green chopped coriander.

Milijuli Sabjion ka Shorba

Mixed Vegetable Soup

Serves: 6-8
Cooking Time: 30 Minutes

Ingredients

Toor dal	½ cup
Water	8-10 cups
Oil or Butter	2 Tbs
Onions chopped	2 Tbs
Ginger chopped	1 Tbs
Garlic chopped	1 Tbs
Green chilies chopped (mild)	1 Tbs
Tomatoes (large) chopped	2
Cumin powder	1 tsp
Turmeric powder	¾ tsp
Salt	2–3 tsp
Coriander powder	1 Tbs
Black pepper	1 tsp
Red pepper (to taste)	½–1 tsp
Potatoes chopped medium	1
Cauliflower florets	1 cup
Carrots chopped	½ cup
Peas fresh or frozen	½ cup
Boiling water	2 cups
Lemon juice	2 Tbs
Green coriander chopped	1 Tbs
Garam masala	½ tsp
Heavy cream	¼ cup

Different vegetables can be substituted for the ones used in this recipe. This is one of the healthiest of soups that is typically cooked with indian spices. Substitute water for 1 cup of coconut milk to make it creamier and a little sweeter. This soup is hearty and appropriately makes a good lunch with any bread. Also makes an elegant first course for a dinner. Enjoy!

Method

1. Cook the *toor dal* to a creamy consistency in 4 cups of water in a three-quart saucepan and set it aside.

2. Chop the vegetables and set them aside.

3. Heat the oil and add onion, ginger, garlic, green chilies and cook in a deep saucepan until the onions are light brown.

4. Add chopped tomatoes, cumin powder, turmeric powder, salt, coriander powder, black pepper and red pepper. Mix well and fry. Cook until the oil separates from the sauce. Add the vegetables and stir them well. Add an other 4 cups of water and cook on low heat until well blended and the vegetables are tender.

5. Transfer the cooked vegetables mixture into the saucepan with cooked *toor dal*. Simmer until the vegetables are well blended into the soup. If the soup is too thick add ½–1 cup of water.

6. When cool pour it into the blender and blend it smooth. Strain the blended soup through the soup strainer. Push the pulp through and discard residue, if there is any. Add 2 cups of boiled water to facilitate filtering.

7. Add the lemon juice. Serve topped with chopped green coriander and *garam masala* and a tsp of heavy cream.

ACCOMPANIMENTS

Bhune hue Aloo aur Leek ka Shorba

Roasted Potato and Leek Soup

Serves: 4-6
Cooking Time: 20-25 Minutes

Ingredients

Potatoes peeled and chopped	2 cups
Water	6 cups
Leeks white and green parts washed and sliced into 1/4 inch slices	2 cups
Green onions chopped	2 Tbs
Ginger finely chopped	1 tsp
Garlic	1 tsp
Green chilies	1 tsp
Salt	to taste
Curry leaves	3–4
Red pepper	½–1 tsp
Heavy cream	2 Tbs
Lemon juice	1 Tbs
Vegetable oil	2 Tbs
Cumin seeds	1 tsp
Mustard seeds	½ tsp
Red pepper dry whole broken (optional)	1
Garam masala	1 tsp
Green coriander leaves finely chopped	1 Tbs

Note: Low fat comfort soup without the guilt of rich cream based soups. Leeks are an excellent source of vitamin C as well as iron and fibre. Even the Roman King Nero believed that it was a superior vegetable and that could improve his singing voice and he favoured it so much that he was called 'The leek eater'.

Potato soup is made by mixing mashed potatoes, cream and garnishing it with green onions, cumin, mustard seeds and green coriander leaves. It is really delicious and makes an excellent first course soup. Leeks provide the same benefits as onions and garlic but are lot sweeter and milder.

Method

1. Boil the potatoes, chopped leeks in 3 cups of water with onions, ginger, garlic, green chilies, salt, curry leaves and red pepper in a saucepan until they are soft and purée the mixture into soup in a blender. Transfer it to a cooking pan and add 3 more cups of water and boil till it is smooth. Add more water if needed to get desired consistency.

2. Add the cream and lemon juice and set it aside.

3. Heat the oil in a skillet and add the cumin and mustard seeds, and wait till they start popping. Add the whole red pepper, and when it starts sizzling, transfer the seasoning into the soup, holding the whole peppers back with the spoon. Stir well.

4. Before serving garnish very sparingly with *garam masala* and coriander leaves, if desired. Season according to taste.

Tamatar ka Shorba

Tomato Soup

Serves: 6-8
Cooking Time: 25 Minutes

Ingredients

Tomatoes (medium) peeled and chopped	6–8
Vegetable oil	3 Tbs
Onions medium chopped	1
Ginger chopped	1 tsp
Garlic chopped	1 tsp
Green chilies chopped (very mild)	1 tsp
Coriander grounded	1 Tbs
Cumin grounded	1 tsp
Red pepper	½ tsp
Turmeric powder	½ tsp
Black pepper	½ tsp
Salt	1 tsp
Water	6 cups
Heavy cream	½ cup
Sugar	2 Tbs
Green coriander chopped	1 Tbs
Garam masala	1 tsp
Heavy cream to garnish	2 Tbs
Bread croutons	2 Tbsp (Optional)

Note: Tomato is a highly nutritious vegetable that contains large amounts of vitamins, minerals, antioxidant and phytochemicals. Eating tomato soup can be beneficial for several health conditions. Tomato contains Lycopene (the red pigment). This pigment is a powerful antioxidant that helps fight cancer. Tomato is a natural antiseptic, therefore protects against various infections. Nicotinic acid in tomatoes helps reduce cholesterol. It has high levels of Vitamin C. Eating cooked tomatoes are far healthier than uncooked.

A hearty and delicious soup. It can be served as an appetizing first course for a dinner or at a lunch with a hearty sandwich.

Method

1. Soak the tomatoes in warm water and peel them. Chop them finely and set them aside.
2. Heat the oil in a large saucepan and transfer onions, ginger, garlic, green chilies. Cook until light brown and then add the ground coriander, ground cumin, red pepper, turmeric powder, black pepper and salt. Mix well.
3. Add the tomatoes. Stir and add 6 cups of water. Cook over low heat until the tomatoes are completely soft and cooked.
4. Put the soup into a blender and blend thoroughly.
5. Strain it and add the heavy cream and 2 Tbs of sugar to the strained soup. Add more water, if needed.
6. Bring it slowly to a boil and serve it garnished with green coriander, a tablespoon of heavy cream and *garam masala*. Adjust the seasoning according to the taste.

Nariyal ka Shorba

Coconut Soup

Serves: 4
Cooking Time: 20-25 Minutes

Ingredients

Coconut milk 16 ozs can	1
All purpose flour	2 Tbs
Olive oil or *ghee*	2-3 Tbs
Cumin seeds	½ tsp
Green chilies finely chopped	½ tsp
Lemon grass	1 stalk chopped
Ginger Chopped	1 tsp
Water	1 cup
Salt	to taste
Black pepper	½ tsp
Chopped potatoes	½ cup
Shredded carrots	½ cup
Frozen Peas	½ cup
Roasted peanuts finely crushed	1 Tbs
Tomatoes fresh, finely chopped	½ cup
Coriander leaves fresh finely chopped	1 tsp
Cucumbers fresh, finely chopped	2 Tbs
Garam masala a sprinkle	
Lemon juice	as needed

Light and fragrant this soup is creamy and delicious with crushed peanuts, freshly chopped tomatoes and cucumbers. Coconut is high in healthy saturated fat, with decent amounts of protein and a low glycemic index. A cup of shredded, raw coconut meat contains 27 grams of fat, mostly saturated; 3 grams of protein; and 12 grams of carbohydrates, Coconut tree is called a tree of life and its health benefits are very significant.

Method

1. Mix the all purpose flour in coconut milk and set it aside.
2. Heat the oil in a two-quart thick-bottom pan on medium-low heat and add the cumin seeds. When they start popping add the chopped green chilli. Lower the heat. Add the lemon grass and ginger.
3. Add the water, salt and black pepper to it and stir, keeping the heat very low.
4. When it starts to boil, add the chopped potatoes, carrots, peas and cook till they are soft adding more water if needed and then add the crushed, peanuts and tomatoes. Mix them in. Cook and let it come to a boil. Add the coconut milk with flour in it and cook for 2–5 minutes.
5. Remove from heat garnish with chopped coriander and add cucumber if you wish and serve hot.
6. Garnish with seasonings as you wish.

Note: Coconut soup offers many health benefits from its ingredients. Ginger for example, is often used to calm nausea, relieve cold and flu symptoms, and increase blood circulation in homeopathic medicine. Lemongrass is known to have calming properties that help reduce stress and anxiety. Lemongrass also has antifungal, antibacterial and antiseptic properties.

Salads

Simple salads are a regular part of an Indian meal. They are a welcome accompaniment at the table as they not only lessen the fiery taste of hot spices but are nutritive and add colour and a refreshing look to the meal. The fresh vegetable and fruit salads provide three out of the six important tastes important to an Indian meal. These three tastes are sour, salty and astringent – all found in salads and relishes. For centuries cooks have kept the focus on the main course and were keen on making the creamy and rich curries. They had forgotten to give importance to the healthy side dishes of a complete meal. Finely sliced salad (*Kachumber*) is the most common side dish in a North Indian meal. It is made by mixing finely chopped fresh vegetables sprinkled with lemon juice, salt and pepper. It is popular all over the country.

    The southern parts of the country have some gorgeous salads. For example, the *Kosambari Salad* of chopped vegetables and boiled lentils goes very well with all vegetarian meals. Kosambari being a low fat, less cholesterol, high protein and high fibre diet, is one of the best dishes for all those who want to lose loads of weight and stay fit. Mung bean also contains rich quantities of Vitamin A, B, C and E. They are also known to be an excellent source of many minerals, such as calcium, iron and potassium. It's hard to believe that something we cannot digest easily can be so good for us! Eating a high-fibre diet can help lower cholesterol levels, and prevents constipation. Salads composed from even a few ingredients make a nutrient-rich meal. The greens alone have calcium, iron, potassium and B vitamins. Many salad basics, including tomatoes, sweet peppers and the greens, are chock-full of antioxidants. Add high fibre and low calories into the mix and you cannot go wrong including a salad in your daily diet. According to Ayurveda, serve salads at the noontime meal, when the digestive fire is most powerful, with spices and seasonings that help digestion. Black pepper, ginger, and cumin are *Agni*-kindling spices, and lemon/lime juice both kindles *Agni* and helps to cut *ama*. From western states comes the Onion Salad, Beetroot Salad, Tomato Salad, Mango Salad and Mango Salsa. Living raw foods or fresh vegetables have the highest biophoton energy. The greater your store of light energy from healthy raw foods, the greater the power of your overall electromagnetic field, and consequently the more energy is available to you for healing and maintenance of your optimal health. Raw vegetables also provide you with omega-3 fats and B vitamins, proven to help reduce anxiety and depression. The vitamin K in veggies helps reduce inflammation in your body, which stress can aggravate. Green leafy vegetables,such as kale, spinach, and Swiss chard, are loaded with magnesium, which helps balance your cortisol,one of your "stress hormones". Low magnesium levels have been linked with anxiety disorders and migraine, both of which are typically aggravated by stress. Magnesium and potassium also relax blood vessels, helping keep your blood pressure low. Magnesium also plays an important role in calcium absorption, helping you maintain good muscle and nerve functions and a healthy immune system.

Around the world, today fancy salads have crep-t up on tables along with Indian food. Green leaf salad is being offered with dressings, nuts, and croutons just like in the western world and this has now acquired an elegant and appropriate place in modern Indian cooking.

Kosambari Salad/Mung ki Dal ka Salad

Carrots, Radishes and Beans Salad

Serves: 8-10
Preparation Time: 10 Minutes

Ingredients

Mung dal soaked in boiling water (split without skin)	½ cup
Radishes white or small red washed and grated	½ cup
Carrots washed peeled and grated	½ cup
Garbanzo beans boiled and cooked and drained	½ cup
Tomatoes finely chopped in small cubes	½ cup
Bell pepper green, grated	$1/3$ cup
Cilantro leaves fresh, chopped	½ cup
Chopped raw mango	½ cup
Coconut fresh, grated	½ cup
Or dry powdered coconut	2 Tbs
Vegetable oil	1 tsp
Mustard seeds	1 tsp
Urad dal	1 Tbs
Dry red chilies or pepper crushed (optional)	2
Salt	1 tsp
Red pepper powder	1 tsp
Black pepper powder	1 tsp
Lemon juice	3 Tbs

Note: It is a popular salad in the state of Karnataka prepared especially at festive times. It is also quite well liked in other southern states too. It is usually prepared with soaked split green mung dal or Bengal Gram (channa dal). Any kind of fresh vegetables can be added to it. Sometimes coconut and raw mango are also added and it is always seasoned with tempering of mustard seeds. It is a colorful dish that is pleasing to the eye.

Carrots, radishes and partially cooked *dal* salad. This crunchy salad, a speciality from south India, is refreshing and can be prepared in many different combinations. The boiled lentils along with grated coconut and other grated vegetables make it rather unique and very appetizing. Ayurveda recommends warm, cooked salads, as the richest source of vegetable protein. Salad, and beans will keep insulin levels in your body low, causing you to feel full for hours and preventing you from overeating later in the day.

Method

1. Soak the *Mung dal* in 8 cups of boiling water for 3 hours and then drain the water. Cool it and set it aside.
2. Mix grated radishes, carrots, cooked garbanzo beans (or from a can), tomatoes and bell pepper in a salad bowl and add to it the cilantro leaves, chopped raw mango, coconut and drained *dal*. Toss them well.
3. Heat the oil in a small saucepan and add the mustard seeds, urad dal. Wait till they pop and add the dry red pepper and cook for half a minute.
4. Remove the saucepan from the fire. Cool and garnish the salad by pouring the oil over it. Hold the peppers back.
5. Add the salt, red pepper, black pepper powder and lemon juice and stir with salad spoon to mix it well.
6. Serve with any meal. It goes very well with barbecued meat dishes.

Channa aur Rajmah ka Salad

Cooked Beans Salad

Serves: 6-8
Preparation Time: 8 Minutes

A refreshing bean salad of cooked chick-peas, red kidney beans and black-eyed beans garnished with lemon juice, freshly ground roasted cumin powder and other spices. It makes a very appetizing salad for a lunch buffet and also with any meal. Consuming beans adds significant amounts of fibre and soluble fibre to a diet, with one cup of cooked beans providing between nine to thirteen grams of fibre. Soluble fibre can help lower blood cholesterol. Beans are also high in protein, complex carbohydrates and iron.

Ingredients

Chick-peas (cooked)	1 cup
Kidney beans (cooked)	1 cup
Black-eyed beans (cooked)	1 cup
Shallots	½ cup
Or	
Onions fresh green chopped	½ cup
Red bell pepper finely chopped	¼ cup
Ginger finely chopped	½ tsp
Green chilies chopped (mild)	1 Tbs
Salt	to taste
Black pepper ground	1 tsp
Cilantro leaves finely chopped	½ cup
Olive oil	2 Tbs
Garlic cloves	2
Cumin powder ground, roasted	1 Tbs
Red pepper	1 tsp
Coconut fresh grated	1 cup
Or	
Dry coconut powder	2 Tbs
Garam masala	1 tsp
Lemon juice	2 Tbs

Method

1. Transfer the cooked beans from the cans into a colander and wash them under running water. If the beans are boiled, then drain the water.

2. Combine the chick-peas, red kidney beans, and black-eyed beans in a large salad bowl. Add the chopped shallot or green onions, bell pepper, chopped ginger, hot green pepper, salt, black pepper and cilantro leaves, and mix them together.

3. Heat the olive oil in a small skillet and add the chopped garlic. Cook the garlic in the oil until it turns light brown. Cool it.

4. Add the oil to the salad holding the garlic pieces back in the skillet.

5. Add the ground roasted cumin powder, red pepper, fresh coconut or dry coconut powder, *garam masala* and lemon juice, and mix the salad well. Mix the beans and the vegetables well with salad fork and spoon and chill it in the refrigerator before serving. Taste and adjust the seasoning according to your liking.

6. A great accompaniment to any meal.

*All beans can either be boiled and cooked fresh or you can buy ready to use cans.

Pyaz, Chukandar aur Tamatar ka Salad

Onion, Beetroot And Tomato Salad

Serves: 8-10
Preparation Time: 10 Minutes

Beetroots make a very good salad with onions and tomatoes. Beetroot is colorful and nutritious and therefore makes a very welcome accompaniment to any meal.

Ingredients

Onions chopped in thin circles	2 cups
Beet root chopped in long 2x1 inch strips	½ cup
Tomatoes chopped in cubes	½ cup
Carrot (long) chopped in thin long strips	1
Olive oil	2 Tbs
Mustard seeds	1 tsp
Cumin seeds	1 tsp
Salt	1 tsp
Red pepper powder	½ tsp
Green chilies finely chopped	1 Tbs
Ginger chopped in thin long strips	2 Tbs
Lemon juice	2-3 Tbs
Coriander chopped	½ cup
Garam masala (optional)	½ tsp

Method

1. Slice onions in thin circles, chop beetroot in long 2 inch by 1 inch wide strips and the tomatoes in small cubes. Chop 1 long-tender carrot into 2-inch long thin match sticks.
2. Transfer them to a salad bowl and set aside.
3. In a small skillet heat the olive oil and add the mustard seeds, cumin seeds, and let them pop.
4. Add the seasoning to the salad and add salt, red pepper, green chilies and ginger.
5. Stir to mix and add the lemon juice. Toss the salad well and refrigerate before serving.
6. Top it all with chopped coriander and a sprinkle of *garam masala.* Serve with your favorite barbecue or a meal preferably with a meat curry.

Note: Beet roots, tomatoes and onions make a great combination of healthy vegetables especially beet root. Just one cup of raw beets is quite high in carbohydrates but low in fat. It also contains phosphorus, sodium, magnesium, calcium, **iron**, and potassium, as well as fiber, vitamins A and C, niacin, and biotin.

Note: Beetroot can be boiled for 10 minutes, before use in order to soften it a little.

Milijuli Sabjion ka Salad

Mixed Vegetable Salad

Serves: 8-10
Preparation Time: 5 Minutes

Ingredients

Cucumber green, peeled and chopped	1
Tomatoes chopped	2
Radish red small Or	
Radish white chopped	10
Bell pepper finely chopped	½
Onions medium chopped	1
Baby carrots, tender, little	1 cup
Green chilies chopped	4
Lemon juice	2 Tbs
Salt	1 tsp
Black pepper	1 tsp
Red pepper	½ tsp
Garam masala (optional)	1 tsp
Cumin powder ground, roasted	1 tsp
Apple green, firm, chopped*	½
Pear firm, chopped*	½
Plum firm, chopped*	1

Note: Sprinkle 2 Tbs of roasted sesame seeds on top of this salad before serving. It will add extra crunch to the salad. Modern science emphasizes that people who eat at least one salad a day have a higher level of nutrients responsible for a healthy heart and better immunity.

A typical salad of Indian cuisine. It has chopped green vegetables tossed in lemon juice, salt, black pepper or red pepper. It is either arranged on a platter or it is tossed in a salad bowl. According to Ayurveda raw vegetables are best to eat during lunch, when the digestive *agni* is at its peak. The ginger-lemon juice salad, of course is an enhancer of digestive *agni*, therefore can be had with dinner too. Onion-lemon juice salad is great for the Indian summer. It protects one from the heat. The *kuchummar* salad is great for Kapha body types.

Method

1. Mix all the chopped vegetables in a salad bowl and arrange in a fancy colourful pattern on a platter.
2. Add fresh or bottled lemon juice, salt and pepper into the salad bowl. With a mixing spoon, mix and coat the salad with the lemon juice and spices. However, if the salad is arranged on a platter, just sprinkle the lemon juice and the spices on top of the salad.
3. Add small pieces of green apples, pears and plums to the salad. The sweet and sour taste of fruits encourages young children into the habit of eating salad.
4. Serve it with meals or with lunch or with a soup and bread.

*For presentation, layer the salad platter – first arrange large salad leaves, then large size vegetable pieces on top of salad leaves and then smaller pieces along with fruits at the top layer.

SALADS

Mooli ya Gajar ka Salad

Radish or Carrot Salad

Serves: 8-10
Preparation Time: 7-8 Minutes

Ingredients

Small red radish chopped cross wise and grated	2 cups
Or	
White daikon radish peeled and grated	2 cups
Ginger grated	1 Tbs
Green chilies finely chopped	1 Tbs
Lemon juice	2 Tbs
Salt	¼ tsp
Red pepper	¼ tsp
Black pepper	¼ tsp
Vegetable oil	1 Tbs
Mustard seeds	½ tsp
Turmeric powder	¼ tsp
Asafoetida a pinch	
Peanuts roasted crushed	2 Tbs
Coriander green, finely chopped	1 Tbs

Note: A similar salad of radish is prepared in Punjab without any peanuts and It is called "Mooli ka Lacha". Radishes contain glucosinolates, a beneficial sulfur-containing compound only found in members of the cruciferous vegetable family. This compound protects you from cancer, and very beneficial for the functioning of Liver and gall bladder.

A very easy way to serve fresh radishes with crushed roasted peanuts, chopped green chilies and lemon juice. A crunchy salad that can be served with any meal. Radishes provides vitamin C, which helps maintain your cardiovascular health by controlling blood cholesterol levels. Vitamin C also helps your body produce collagen, a protein that strengthens blood vessel walls.

Method

1. Grate radishes in a salad bowl and add grated ginger and the green chilies to it. Set it aside.
2. Add the lemon juice, salt, peppers and mix the salad well with salad fork and spoon.
3. Heat the vegetable oil in a small skillet and add the mustard seeds and let them pop.
4. Add the turmeric powder and the asafoetida. Remove from heat and add the seasonings to the salad.
5. Stir the seasonings well into the salad and add the roasted and crushed peanuts. Mix them well. Sprinkle chopped coriander leaves.
6. Cover and refrigerate before serving.

Raitas, Chutneys and Achaars

There are six tastes described in Ayurveda. The term *taste* not only applies to the perception of taste buds located on the ongue, but to the final reaction of food in the acid medium of the stomach. These tastes are sweet, sour, salty, astringent, bitter and pungent. *Vata dosha* is balanced by the sweet, sour, and salty. *Pitta dosha* is balanced by the bitter, astringent and sweet, and *Kapha dosha* is balanced by the pungent, bitter, and astringent. All the six tastes are combinations of the five building blocks of nature and these are Air, Water, Earth, Fire and Space. A balanced diet does not revolve around calories, vitamins, carbohydrates and proteins only. These nutrients are known to us intellectually but the tastes are a direct experience and give enormous and useful information directly to the tissues in the body. Ayurveda exphasizes a balanced diet naturally guided by our own instincts, without turning nutrition into a complicated intellectual exercise.

It is best to include all six tastes in each meal, but include more of the tastes that balance your individual physiology and follow the rhythms of the seasons and a lesser amount of the tastes that create imbalance in your body and mind.

Raitas are nothing but smoothly beaten yogurt flavoured with freshly chopped vegetables or fruits garnished by ground roasted cumin, salt, red and black pepper. Sometimes a little sugar is also added. The *Raitas* are known as *pachadi* in south India.

There are fresh vegetables *Raitas* like *Spinach Raita, Eggplant Raita, Cucumber Raita, Banana-Raisins Raita*, and *Mint Raita*. You will come across many more kind of *Raitas* in this book and they are as delicious as the ones mentioned above and are equally complimentary and interesting. It is not unusual to see both the side accompaniments, *Raita* and salad, in a meal depending on how spicy the food is.

A dab of *chutney* or achaar (pickle) makes the food go down in the most delightful way. These condiments are not only full of zest and taste but are also a powerhouse of health benefits. They provide a full spectrum of all six tastes which form a complete Indian meal according to the ancient *Vedas*. They provide digestive ingredients to reduce high blood pressure and have antibacterial properties. Fresh *chutneys* and *achaars* pickles have been a part of the Indian meal from ancient times. They are a powerhouse of antioxidants. Some *chutneys* preserve very well and can be bottled and enjoyed over a period of time.

Whenever we complained of food being dull and drab in our childhood days, our mother would tell us to take a little *chutney* or *achaars* pickle which made all the difference to taste and the palate.

Chutneys are usually served with snacks. *Coconut Chutney*, *Eggplant Chutney*, *Channa Dal Chutney* and *Peanut Chutney* are very popular in south India. They are served with snacks like *Dosa*, *Idli* and *Vada*. Fresh herbal and fruit *chutneys* like *Mint Chutney, Coriander Chutney, Tamarind Chutney, Zucchini Chutney* and *Red Pepper Chutney* are from north India and are served with regular meals as well as snacks like *Pakoras*, *Samosas*, *Dahi Vada* and *Chaat* etc. Fruit *chutneys* like *Mango Chutney, Pineapple Chutney, Cranberry Chutney, Apple* and *Ripe Mango Chutney* are famous all over the world. Mint chutney recommended with each meal in North Indian cuisine is a good appetizer and provides roughage and therefore it is good for intestines and people suffering from constipation.

Use of *chutneys* and *achaars* pickles is rather essential in the tropical weather because in the hot summer months the body tends to get sluggish in producing digestive juices and physical activity slows down. Pickles and *chutneys* stimulate the appetite and enhance digestion.

Achaars are also similar to *chutneys* except that these are made in a more sterilized manner and are prepared with pungent mustard oil so as to give them a longer shelf life. The contents are very well heated and all the moisture is removed so that the pickle can stay fresh in a bottle even without an airtight cap at room temperature. These are used as accompaniment to a meal that can do with little extra spicing.

Achaars also act as digestives (*Lemon Pickle*) and balance different tastes of the food. Pickles go very well with *Paranthas*, *Khichadi*, *Rava Dosa* and *Gram Flour Pancakes*. Carrot and radish pickles are made fresh to go with daily meals. These do not stay fresh for more than a couple of days.

Our cuisine is unique for its emphasis on making sure that each dish is cooked and spiced to achieve maximum digestibility and avoid the formation of toxins (AMA), the result of improperly digested food.

According to the ancient healing tradition of Ayurveda, the combination of foods that you eat and how they are digested (or not) actually shapes your health and well-being. Ayurveda defines us as unique beings, and thus our dietary needs are unique as well. Ayurveda also gives us great insight about which foods will suit and balance every individual according to his or her age, constitution, the season, the environment, and needs, at any given time.

Pickles and chutneys are the specialty of Indian food. They generally accompany the staple diet and have their own importance.

Aam ka Achaar

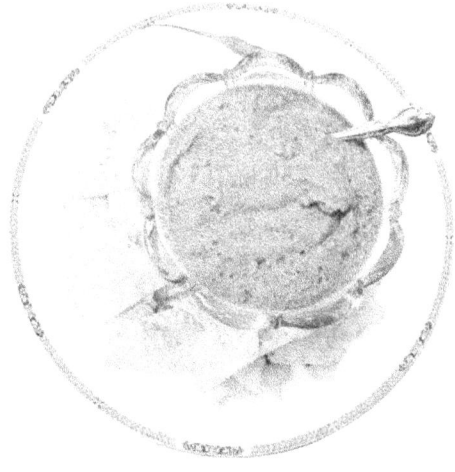

Dhania ki Chutney

Boondi Raita

Fried Gram Flour Balls in Yogurt

Serves: 6-8
Preparation Time: 5 Minutes

Ingredients

Boondi	½ cup
Hot water	3 cups
Yogurt	2 cups
Salt	1 tsp
Red pepper	½–1 tsp
Cumin ground, roasted	1 tsp
Black pepper	½ tsp
Garam masala	½–1 tsp
Coriander leaves chopped	1 Tbs

Note: Raita is gaining popularity. In the western world very fast. Boondi is the most common item to make Raita in a Indian meal. But there are many vegetables and herbs that can be added to make the Raita. 1 cup of grated Carrots or Zuccini or Broccoli or 2 cups of grated Cabbage (all parboiled) and drained or pulp of I medium size roasted Baingan can be added to 2 cups of smooth yogurt with all the spices above to make very delicious Raita. A small beetroot grated and parboiled with ½ cup of fresh coconut + all the spices above in 2 cups of beaten Yogurt also makes a delicious Raita.

Yogurt dish made with the tiny fried gram flour balls called *Boondi*. Boondi is made by pressing a rather thick gram flour batter through a fine sieve into the hot oil or ready to use *boondi* can be bought from your local Indian grocers. Add *boondi* to the plain smooth yogurt and sprinkle with spices. This is one of the very popular yogurt condiments in a North Indian meal.

Method

1. Soak the *boondi* in medium size bowl in medium hot water and set aside for 10 minutes.
2. Whip the yogurt with a whisk and set it aside.
3. Add cold water to the bowl with soaked *boondi* and squeeze out the water. Transfer the *boondi* into the whipped yogurt. Mix the yogurt gently and add the salt, red pepper, ground roasted cumin, black pepper and *garam masala*.
4. Mix well. Serve sprinkled with chopped coriander leaves.
5. If the *raita* looks too thick add a couple of tablespoons of milk or buttermilk and stir it well. Makes a delicious accompaniment to any meal.
6. Serve with any curry, *pulav* and bread of your choice.

Note: Homemade *boondi* can be added directly to the whipped yogurt (keep it little thin in consistency). Stir and garnish it as usual and serve.

Kheere ka Raita

Cucumber Raita

Serves: 8-10
Preparation Time: 5 Minutes

Ingredients

Yogurt	2 cups
Cucumber grated	1
Salt	½ tsp
Red pepper	½ tsp
Cumin seeds ground, roasted	¼ tsp
Black pepper	¼ tsp
Garam masala	¼ tsp
Coriander leaves chopped	1 Tbs

Note: Another very well liked Raita in India as well as in European countries. It is really very complimentary when served with barbecued meats and vegetables. ½ cup of finely chopped tomatoes (seeds removed) and ¼ of finely chopped onions can also be added to make this Raita more wholesome.

Yogurt with grated cucumber and sprinkled with spices makes a very cool and refreshing accompaniment to any meal and is very easy to prepare.

Cucumber is a native plant of India and other tropical regions; it is used as a popular fresh vegetable in a variety of salads and sandwiches and is a mainstay of many of today's lunches. Cucumber is an important health food. It provides a very healthy juice beneficial for increasing the flow of urine. For rheumatic conditions, it complements the effects of celery and carrot juice. Its juice is soothing to the skin and is the best skin lotion. The peel, like lemon peel, is good to be used on the hands most especially after it's been in a strong detergent or in a very hot water. It has become part of daily beauty products into face packs, facials, juice and many other things which can affect your skin. Due to its cooling effect it can be termed as a magic wand for all your skin problems.

Method

1. Beat two cups of yogurt with an eggbeater until smooth in a deep serving dish.
2. Grate the cucumber and squeeze its juices. Save the squeezed juice and set it aside. Add the squeezed cucumber to the yogurt and stir to mix. Use the squeezed juice to thin the *raita* to desired consistency and mix well.
3. Serve sprinkled with salt, red pepper, roasted ground cumin powder, black pepper and *garam masala* and garnish with chopped coriander leaves. Serve.

Pudina ke Raita
Mint Condiment

Serves: 8-10
Preparation Time: 5-10 Minutes

Ingredients

Mint leaves fresh washed	2 Tbs
Coriander leaves green	2 Tbs
Green chillies chopped (mild)	1 Tbs
Yogurt	2 cups
Freshly boiled chopped potatoes (optional)	1 cup
Salt	1 tsp
Black pepper	½ tsp

To garnish:

Green onions chopped to garnish	1 Tbs
Red pepper	½ tsp
Cumin seeds ground, roasted	1 tsp
Garam masala	½ tsp

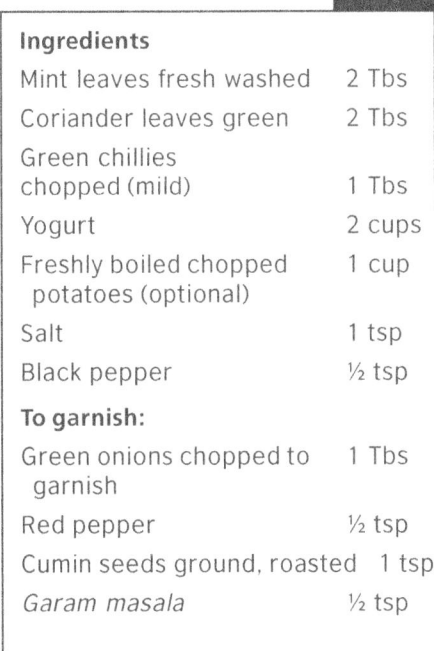

Yogurt mixed with ground mint and the spices makes a refreshing accompaniment to any meal.

Mint is a powerhouse of health benefits. Use it as much in your food as possible. You can also add fresh mint leaves to your regular cup of tea. This in fact reduces the caffeine in regular tea and makes it more palatable.

Add chopped mint to soufflés, soups, omelets, salads and fresh fruit for a refreshing change. Just make sure you add the mint at the end of the cooking process as overcooking can cause mint to turn bitter. Mint leaves are great additions to sauces - both savoury and sweet as well as roasted vegetables and rice dishes. The latest research indicates that mint might be useful in treating certain cancers due to the presence of certain enzymes.

Method

1. Grind or blend in the blender, mint, cilantro, green chilies and whipped yogurt, and transfer to a serving bowl.
2. Add boiled chopped potatoes*, salt and black pepper to this and mix well.
3. Garnish with finely chopped onions, red pepper, ground roasted cumin seeds and *garam masala*. Serve.

*Freshly chopped potato can be substituted by one finely chopped yellow or white onion.

Subjion ka Raita

Fresh Vegetable Raita

Serves: 8
Preparation Time: 5-7 Minutes

Ingredients

Yogurt	2 cups
Cucumbers peeled and chopped in small cubes	½ cup
Radish fresh finely chopped	½ cup
Tomatoes fresh finely chopped	½ cup
Carrots grated	2 Tbs
Green onions chopped	¼ cup
Green hot peppers chopped	1 Tbs
Bell peppers finely chopped	2 Tbs
Salt	to taste
Black pepper	½ tsp
Cumin powder roasted ground	1 tsp
Red pepper	1 tsp
Garam masala	1 tsp
Green coriander leaves chopped	1 Tbs

This refreshing yogurt preparation with chopped up salad vegetables and topped with ground roasted cumin powder, salt, red pepper, *garam masala* and chopped coriander leaves is very well liked with any curry. Try it.

Method

1. Whip the yogurt smooth with a whisk and add all the chopped vegetables. Mix well and refrigerate.
2. Just before serving, top it with salt, black pepper, ground roasted cumin powder, red pepper, *garam masala*, and the chopped green coriander leaves. Makes a very appetizing and elegant presentation.

Note: Instead of serving salad and yogurt separately, mix the chopped up salad in the yogurt to make a Raita and it is also a good way to have the kids eat their vegetables easily. Fresh vegetable *raita* soothes the palate while taking spicy food and also provides a salad to complete a meal.

Kheere ka Raita - Page 204

Nariyal ki Chutney - Page 211

Mungphali ki Chutney - Page 215

Lal Mirch ki Chutney - Page 216

Tamatar ki Chutney - Page 220

Khatta Meetha Achaar - Page 221

Nimbu ka Achaar - Page 224

Different kinds of Pepper

Aam ka Raita

Mango Raita

Serves: 6-8
Preparation Time: 5 Minutes

Ingredients

Yogurt	2 cups
Salt	¾ tsp
Red pepper	1 tsp
Black pepper	1 tsp
Cumin seeds ground, roasted	1 tsp
Garam masala	1 tsp
Lemon juice	1 tsp
Karhi leaves chopped	½ tsp
Mangoes (ripe and non-fibrous kind) chopped	1½ cup

Note: This slightly sweet and sour Raita is especially good with hot and spicy food. The "king of fruits" has been around for at least 6,000 years. Native to India and Burma, this sweet fruit was described in the ancient Sanskrit literature, for example in Valmiki's Ramayana. The mango was also the fruit of the kings in ancient India, where princes used to pride themselves on the possession of large mango gardens. Persian traders took the fruit into the Middle East while the Portuguese brought it to Europe and the New World. Mango cultivation arrived in Florida in the 1830s and in California in the 1880s, and now it is also grown in Hawaii, Mexico and South America.

This mango condiment is the most delicious of all the *raitas* especially if right ingredients are used. It is important that we use fibreless and firm ripe mangoes. Flavoured with ground roasted cumin, lemon juice and curry leaves, this *raita* is appetizing with any meal. Mango is one of the very ancient fruits of India and is greatly revered. Mango leaves are also used to decorate the canopy under which weddings and other auspicious events take place.

Ever since the Vedic period, mangoes have been highly appreciated in ayurvedic healing and cooking. All parts of the tree are used for different purposes. The leaf plays an important role in Hindu festivals and ceremonies. The bark, leaf, flowers, fruit and seed offer a variety of medicinal purposes.

Method

1. Whip the yogurt and add the salt, red pepper, black pepper, ground roasted cumin seeds, *garam masala*, lemon juice and chopped *karhi* leaves and stir and mix the ingredients well.
2. Add the chopped mangoes and gently mix and coat them well with the spiced yogurt.
3. Chill a little and serve with any meal.

Kela aur Kishmish ka Raita

Bananas and Raisins Raita

Serves: 6-8
Preparation Time: 5 Minutes

This Banana condiment has a special significance and is usually made on an auspicious or a religious occasion and has a sweet taste. It also makes a great accompaniment to a hot and spicy meal. Banana is one of the oldest and ancient fruits of India and is held in great reverence by the Indian people.

Ingredients

Yogurt	2 cups
Salt to taste or	½ tsp
Red pepper	1 tsp
Black pepper	½ tsp
Sugar to taste or	1–2 Tbs
Bananas cut into ½ inch pieces (depending on the size)	1–2
Raisins washed and soaked and drained	2 Tbs
Walnuts finely chopped (optional)	2 Tbs
Or	
Coconut fresh grated	2 Tbs
Or	
Dried dates soaked and grated	2 Tbs
Cumin seeds roasted and ground	1 tsp
Garam masala	½ tsp

Method

1. Whip the yogurt and add salt, red pepper and black pepper. Mix well.
2. Add the sugar and stir to mix.
3. Add the chopped bananas, raisins and chopped walnuts. Stir well to mix.
4. Serve topped with ground roasted cumin seeds and *garam masala*.
5. Makes a great side dish with a hot and spicy meal. Adjust the seasonings if you wish.

Note: Omit the spices and add a little sugar to the yogurt. You can serve banana and nuts flavoured yogurt as a breakfast item.

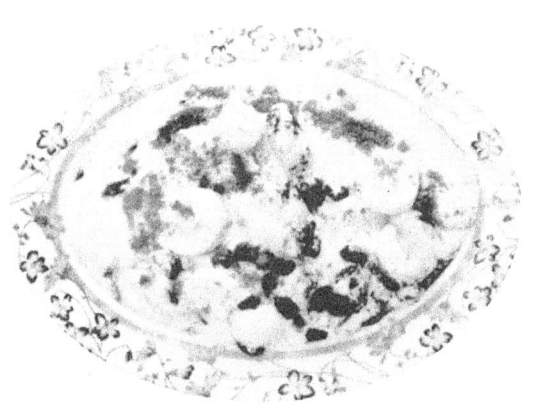

Seb ki Chutney

Apple Dip

Serves: 15-20
Preparation Time: 15 Minutes

Ingredients

Vinegar	¼ cup
Brown sugar	1½ cup
Cumin powder roasted ground	1½ tsp
Fennel seeds crushed	1 tsp
Fresh ginger finely chopped	1 Tbs
Mustard powder	1 tsp
Red chilies dry broken	2
Garam masala	½ tsp
Black pepper freshly grated	1 tsp
Salt	1 tsp
Lemon juice	¼ cup
Apples washed, peeled and chopped	2 cups
Plums washed, peeled and chopped	2 cups
Walnuts chopped	½ cup
Raisins	¼ cup

Note: This chutney is pefect accompaniment for all kinds of sandwiches. It isn't an authentically Indian condiment—after all, apples are not native to India. Fruit chutneys came as of result of cultural exchange after colonization of south Asia by Great Britain and it falls between jam and pickle. Despite its origins, apple chutney is delicious. Unlike apple sauce, which slides down the throat without leaving much of an impression, apple chutney hits the tongue in all the right places. It's sweet, sour, and spicy, all at once, and—when done right—It's hard to stop eating once you've started.

Apples are delicious, when fresh, but in the Indian Himalayan states where apples grow in abundance they are cooked with sugar, spices, lemon, raisins and nuts to make very delectable *chutney*. This can be served with regular meals but goes especially well with *tandoori nan* and a meat curry.

Method

1. In a saucepan combine the vinegar with brown sugar and cook on low heat until the syrup is thick and sticks to the side of the pan (about 8–10 minutes). Remove from heat.
2. Add the ground roasted cumin powder, crushed fennel seeds, chopped ginger, dry mustard powder, dry red chilies broken, *garam masala* and freshly ground black pepper, salt and lemon juice. Mix the spices well into the syrup.
3. Add the chopped apples and plums, and continue cooking until the fruits are soft (about 15 minutes).
4. Remove from heat and stir in the walnuts and raisins.
5. Cook for 2 more minutes and cool the *chutney* to serve.

Channa Dal Chutney

Gram Legume Dip

Serves: 15-20
Preparation Time: 10 Minutes

Ingredients

Channa dal washed and soaked in 2 cups of water overnight	1 cup
Oil	¼ cup
Onions	1 cup
Green chilies	1 Tbs
Whole red peppers	2–3
Ginger	1 Tbs
Grated coconut	½ cup
Yogurt	1 cup
Red pepper	1 tsp
Salt	1 tsp
Cumin seeds	1 tsp
Water as needed	1 cup
Mustard seeds	1 tsp
Urad dal	1 tsp
Curry leaves	4–5
Asafoetida powder	¼ tsp
Garam masala	½ tsp
Coriander leaves chopped	2 Tbs

Note: They are rich in protein, high in fiber, zinc, folate, calcium and most of all low in poly unsaturated fat. It is extremely delicious and is used very extensively in Indian cooking.

A typically South Indian chutney/ Pachadi can be served not only with Dosa and Idli but with Pongal (khichadi),Upama or with any kind of bread or even sandwiches.

Chana dal is a good source of fiber, calcium, zinc and protein. Chana dal is made from black chickpeas, also known as "kala chana." The outer layer is removed and then the kernel is split into half. The kala chana has no gluten and highly recommended for diabetic patients because the carbs found in channa dal do not increase the sugar level in blood though give you full nutrition needed for your body.

Method

1. Drain the water from the soaked gram legume.
2. Heat the oil in a skillet and fry the *dal* until dry and light brown. Remove the *dal* with a slotted spoon into a bowl lined with paper towel, and set aside.
3. In the same oil fry the onions, green chilies, whole red peppers and ginger, until the onions are brown. Transfer the contents to an electric blender and grind the fried *dal*, onions, green chilies, ginger, grated coconut whole dry red peppers with yogurt, red pepper powder and salt to a rather coarsely smooth paste by adding a cup of water slowly. Add more water, if needed. Set it aside in a serving bowl.
4. Heat the same oil in the skillet and add the cumin seeds, mustard seeds and wait until they pop and add the *urad dal*. As soon as it turns brown add the curry leaves and asafoetida powder and garam masala. Stir for half a minute and add this seasoning to the ground *chutney* in the bowl and mix. Add the chopped coriander to the *chutney*. Stir well and serve.

Nariyal ki Chutney
Coconut Dip

Serves: 15-20
Preparation Time: 10 Minutes

Coconut Chutney makes wonderful accompaniment for *dosa, idli* and various appetizers. It is mostly served in the south-western parts of India.

Since the ancient times, the coconut holds a unique place among the millions of inhabitants living in South-East Asia, and Pacific islands. It is one of the most sought-after ingredients in the kitchen as it has found its place in almost each and every diet prepared in these parts of the world. Coconut water is packed with simple sugar, electrolytes, minerals, and bioactive compounds such as cytokinin, and enzymes such as acid phosphatase, catalase, dehydrogenase, peroxidase, polymerases, etc. Coconut kernel is an excellent source of minerals such as copper, calcium, iron, manganese, magnesium, and zinc. It is also a very good source of B-complex vitamins such as folates, riboflavin, niacin, thiamin, and pyridox.

Ingredients

Vegetable oil	4 Tbs
Split Gram (*Channa dal*) pan roasted	¼ cup
Coconut flesh fresh cut in small pieces	1
Or	
Dry unsweetened coconut	½ cup
Ginger chopped	2 tsp
Green chilies chopped	3 Tbs
Onion chopped	½ cup
Green coriander leaves	1 cup
Yogurt	¼ cup
Tamarind paste	½ tsp
Or	
Lemon juice	1 Tbs
Water as needed	
Salt	2–3 tsp
Mustard seeds	1 tsp
Red peppers dry, whole to taste or	3–4
Curry leaves	¼ cup
Urad dal	1 tsp
Asafoetida powder	½ tsp

Method

1. Heat 2 Tbs of oil in a skillet and fry the split gram until light brown. Remove from oil and set aside.
2. Remove the flesh of a fresh coconut *(see introduction)* and chop the pieces coarsely. Transfer them to blender and add ginger,

green chilies, onions, coriander leaves, roasted split gram, yogurt, lemon juice or tamarind paste and grind them into a paste by adding as much cold water as needed to make a smooth and thick paste as a regular vegetable dip.

3. Add the salt to taste and set aside.
4. Heat the same oil in the skillet used for frying the split gram and add the mustard seeds, dry whole red peppers, curry leaves, *urad dal*, and asafoetida powder.
5. Cook until the mustard seeds start to pop and *urad dal* is light brown.
6. Add the ground coconut mixture to this skillet and stir the mixture for 10–20 seconds on the heat.
7. Remove from heat and transfer the *chutney* to a serving bowl.
8. Ready to be served with appetizers, *dosas* or *idlis*.

Coconut Vendor

RAITAS, CHUTNEYS AND ACHAARS

Dhaniye ki Chutney

Coriander Dip

Serves: 20-25
Preparation Time: 5 Minutes

Ingredients

Coriander leaves green	2 cups
Green chilies (mild) chopped	½ cup
Onions chopped	¾ cup
Salt to taste	
Red pepper (optional)	1 tsp
Ginger chopped	1 Tbs
Lime juice or green mango Or	2 Tbs
Tamarind paste	½ tsp
Water as needed or	1½ cup

Note: Dhaniye Chutney is typically North indian and is refreshing and full of flavour. if you plan on serving a spicy curry this chutney will complement it perfectly. As well as being pleasing to the palette, coriander chutney is full of great health benefits. Coriander supplies a rich source of dietary fibre and nutrients, such as iron, magnesium, and potassium as well as antioxidants and is also known to lower cholesterol. In south of india roasted grated coconut,sesame seeds, Gram dal along with yogurt are added to it to give it more substance. Coriander chutney is an easy-to-make classic Indian condiment that should be a 'must' in your fridge. Serve it for breakfast on the side with idli and dosa, or use it to marinate paneer or chicken before grilling. You'll never grow tired of its fresh flavour.

Coriander Chutney is a staple of homes both in North India and South India. Its creamy smooth texture and flavourful taste makes it a versatile condiment used in many ways. Added to cream cheese or served just as is, it makes a delicious sandwich spread. Mixed with curd or yogurt, coriander chutney becomes a tangy dipping sauce which can be served with many traditional Indian finger foods. In restaurants it's a common accompaniment for grilled or tandoori vegetarian and non vegetarian Kababs.

This refreshing *chutney* of green coriander leaves, onions, green mango or lime juice and green chilies is very healthy and delicious. It goes very well with *pakoras, samosas, vada,* or *bondas* and can be served with any meal.

Method

1. Put all the ingredients in a blender and blend with the help of little water to a smooth paste.
2. Add salt to taste, store in the refrigerator and serve chilled.

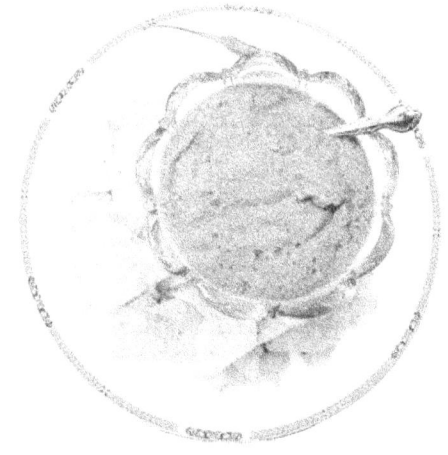

HINT

Grind ½ cup of cooked chick-peas (from a can) and 2 Tbs of chopped coconut with the above ingredients to give it a south Indian touch.

Pudina ki Chutney

Mint Dip

Serves: 10-20
Preparation Time: 5 Minutes

Ingredients

Fresh mint leaves washed	1 cup
Fresh coriander	2 cups
Green chilies chopped	2 Tbs
Lime juice	2 Tbs
Or	
Tamarind paste dissolved in 2 Tbs of water	1 Tbs
Sugar	to taste
Salt	to taste
Red pepper	½ tsp
Ginger chopped	1 Tbs
Green mangoes chopped (if available)	2 Tbs
Onion chopped	1 cup
Water needed to make smooth *chutney*	

Note: Mint *chutney* is served both ways, sweet and sour or only salty and tangy. Sweet and sour is more common.

In south of India freshly grated coconut is also added as one of the ingredients in making this chutney. It is a wonderful accompaniment as a side dish to most main dishes like Biryani, Tandoori chicken, Paneer Tikka.

A refreshing herbaceous accompaniment for *pakoras, samosas* and a real meal. It is one of the most commonly used *chutneys* in Indian cuisine. It has many health benefits. It is packed with antioxidants and acts as an excellent digestant.

Mint has been known for its curative properties for over 2000 years. The ancient Greeks and Romans used it in medicine and in cooking. It aids in digestion, fights headaches and other pains. It is also used in skin care products such as skin creams, toners, body lotions and face masks. Mostly used in North Indian Cuisine.

Method

1. Put all the ingredients in the blender and add as little water as possible to grind to a smooth paste to a consistency of a vegetable dip. Taste and adjust seasoning.
2. Chill till ready to serve.

HINT

*Tamarind turns the *chutney* to a darker shade of green, and that is why lemon or lime juice is preferred. Omit sugar if you want salty and tangy *chutney*.

Mungphali ki Chutney

Peanut Dip

Serves: 10-12
Preparation Time: 10 Minutes

Ingredients

Oil	3 Tbs
Peanuts roasted	1 cup
Onions chopped and fried	1 cup
Green chilies	2
Ginger chopped	1 tsp
Garlic chopped	1 tsp
Red peppers whole, dry, broken	4
Tamarind pulp	1 tsp
Salt to taste	1 tsp
or	
Brown sugar to taste or	1 tsp
Mustard seeds	1 tsp
Cumin seeds	½ tsp
Channa dal	1 tsp
Asafoetida powder	a pinch
Curry leaves	4–6
Red pepper	1 tsp
Coriander leaves chopped	1 Tbs
Water	1 cup

Note: The use of peanuts in Indian cooking is quite extensive. They not only make the food creamier but also add nutrition by adding extra protein to our vegetarian diet.

The delicious *chutney* from south India. Is usually served with *idlis*, and *dosas*.

Peanuts are one of the popular oil seeds known to humankind for centuries. The nuts are enriched with many noteworthy health-benefiting nutrients essential for optimum health and wellness. The kernels are a good source of dietary protein; composed of fine quality amino acids that are essential for human growth and development and vitamin E that helps maintain the integrity of cell membranes. Peanuts are rich source of minerals like copper, manganese, potassium, calcium, iron, magnesium, zinc, and selenium and are packed with important B-complex, pantothenic acid avitamon B-6 and folate. They contribute to your brain health.

Method

1. Heat the oil and add the green chilies, chopped ginger, garlic and the red peppers to the oil and roast them until brown and transfer them to a bowl and add the onions and peanuts. Dissolve tamarind pulp in a cup of water and set it aside.

2. Cool and grind the onions, green chillies, garlic, ginger, red peppers and peanuts in an electric blender to a smooth purée with the help of tamarind water. Set aside the *chutney* in a medium size bowl. Add salt and sugar, and mix it well.

3. Heat the same oil used for frying onions and add the mustard seeds, cumin seeds, and wait till they pop and then add *channa dal* and fry till it turns golden brown. Add the asafoetida and curry leaves and fry for a minute or two.

4. Add the above tempering to the *chutney* in a bowl. Add red pepper, salt and stir to mix it well with a salad spoon and serve sprinkled with coriander leaves. Adjust seasonings.

Lal Mirchi ki Chutney

Red Pepper Dip

Serves: 8-10
Preparation Time: 7-8 Minutes

Ingredients

Oil	¼ cup
Red bell pepper seeded and finely chopped	1 large
Soaked roasted peanuts	¼ cup
Onion chopped	1 large
Ginger chopped	1 tsp
Garlic chopped	1 tsp
Green chilies chopped	1 tsp
Cumin seeds	1 tsp
Asafoetida powder	½ tsp
Whole red dry peppers	3–4
Yogurt	1 tsp
Tomato chopped	1
Tamarind paste	1 tsp
Red hot chili powder	1 tsp
Brown sugar or to taste	1 Tbsp
Salt	1 tsp
Water as needed	
Mustard seeds	1 tsp
Curry leaves	4–6
Urad dal	1 Tbs
Coriander leaves chopped	2 Tbs

Note: Add 2 Tbs of roasted Peanuts and 1 tsp of Jaggery (or Gur) to give it extra creamy and sweet taste.

This chutney of South Indian origin should be prepared with ripenend bell peppers. Research shows that with ripening the activity of the carotenoids and the vitamin C found in bell peppers increases many folds therefore their total antioxidant capacity also increases. Besides bell peppers are also rich in vitaminE and and a very important mineral that is anti cancer and antioxidant manganese. Roasting of the peppers should be done on modest heat as high heat can destroy all the vitamins and minerals in the peppers.

Method

1. Heat 3 Tbs of oil and fry the chopped red bell pepper till they start turning brown, then add the chopped tomato. Cook for few more minutes until they turn brown. Remove them from the oil and set them aside.

2. In the same oil fry onions, ginger, garlic and green chilies, and cook until the onions turn brown. Add the cumin seeds, asafoetida, and wait till the cumin start popping and then add the whole red dry pepper and cook for a few more minutes. Cool and transfer the contents into a blender.

3. Add the browned bell peppers, drained peanuts, yogurt and tomatoes also to the blender along with the tamarind paste, red chili powder, brown sugar, salt and blend it. Add more water, if needed to have the fine consistency of a vegetable dip. Transfer the *chutney* to a mixing bowl and set it aside.

4. Heat the remaining oil in a skillet and add mustard seeds, curry leaves, *urad dal*, and fry until the *dal* is brown and the mustard seeds start popping. Pour the tempering over the *chutney* in the mixing bowl and mix it well.

5. Mix and garnish the *chutney* with chopped coriander leaves and serve with your favourite bread, like *idli, dosa* or *parantha*.

Aam ki Meethi Chutney

Sweet Mango Dip

Serve with meals
Preparation Time: 10 Minutes

Ingredients	
Raw mangoes grated	1 lb
Ginger 2-inch piece grated	1
Water	½ cup
Bay leaves	4
Salt	5 tsp
Vinegar	½ cup
Dates dried grated	¼ cup
Sugar	1 lb
Red pepper	1 Tbs
Black pepper corns crushed	¼ tsp
Cumin roasted powder	1 Tbs
Cinnamon ground	1 tsp
Cloves ground	1 tsp
Nutmeg or mace ground	½ tsp
Cardamoms seeds crushed	½ tsp
Almonds toasted, chopped	¼ cup
Pistachio nuts chopped	1 Tbs
Raisins	¼ cup
Lime juice fresh	1 Tbs

History of Chutney is linked to 500 B.C but there is no exact record of the time of origin of Mango chutney. This chutney is the most favourite chutney of all with an irresistible delicious taste. It is sold in jars in almost every part of the world and is very well liked by everyone. Its sweet, sour and tangy taste is unique and delightful. Tastes best with any regular meal, especially with *paranthas* or *pooris*.

Method

1. Wash and peel the mangoes and ginger and grate them fine.
2. Boil them in ½ cup of water on low heat with bay leaves and salt stirring regularly to avoid sticking. On low heat, cover and simmer until they are tender and soft.
3. Pour the vinegar in a heavy bottom sauce pan or wok and cook the grated dates. As soon as they are cooked remove them from the vinegar with a slotted spoon and set them aside. Mix the sugar with the vinegar in the pan and cook the syrup (a drop should make a string when pulled between two fingers) and add the cooked shredded mangoes and ginger, cooked grated dates, red pepper, black pepper, ground roasted cumin powder, cinnamon, cloves, nutmeg, mace and cardamoms, and cook till the mixture looks like a sauce.
4. Add the sliced almonds, pistachios, raisins, and lime juice.
5. Simmer till the sauce is thick.
6. Remove from heat, cool it and store or can the *chutney* in sterilized containers.

Note: Mango chutney can be remarkably versatile. Spread it on sandwiches, use it as marinate, use with any spicy meal. It makes everything taste better.

Imli ki Chutney
Tamarind Dip

Serves: 15-20
Preparation Time: 15 Minutes

Ingredients

Tamarind de-seeded	1 cup
Tamarind pulp	¼ cup
Water	2 cups
Oil	2 Tbs
Asafoetida	a pinch
Cloves whole	4
Black pepper whole	1 tsp
Cardamoms seeds	½ tsp
Ginger chopped	2 Tbs
Salt to taste or	1½ tsp
Red pepper	1 tsp
Sugar to taste or	¼ cup
Cumin powder roasted	1 Tbs
Garam masala	1 tsp
Raisins or dried dates finely chopped	1 Tbs
Apple sauce	½ cup

Tamarind Dip is also one of the most popular *chutneys* of India and can be served with almost all North Indian snacks. It is commonly served with *golgappa, papri, chaat, samosa, pakora, bhelpuri* and many other snacks. It can easily be compared with ketchup of the west.

In India, tamarind has been used for ages, be it in candy form, in chutneys, in soups, curries or as an Ayurvedic medicine. It is an indispensable ingredient in cuisines of South Indian states. Perhaps due to its strong and unique taste, tamarind found diverse uses across the world. Tamarind has the ability to lower levels of bad cholesterol (LDL) thereby promoting cardiovascular health, this because of the presence of phenols, antioxidants beneficial for levels of HDL. In Ayurvedic medicine, Tamarind is a major ingredient used to treat digestive and gastric problems. Tamarind chutney is used in a number of recipes. Bhel-Puri, a popular and tasty street snack, contains a large portion of sweet tamarind chutney. Tamarind chutneys are served with fried street snacks in India. Tamarind pulp is used in several marinade recipes. Many countries in Asia use tamarind in lentils, sprouts and soups.

Method

1. Mix and stir ¼ cup of ready to use tamarind pulp into 2 cups of water. Cook on slow heat till it gets thick and saucy. Set it aside.

   To make fresh tamarind paste from deseeded tamarind:

2. If you are using solid deseeded dry flesh of tamarind then soak it in 2 cups of water overnight. The pulp will become soft.

3. Push the pulp through the strainer. Add more water to the pulp to have the consistency of a sauce.

RAITAS, CHUTNEYS AND ACHAARS

4. Put it on fire and cook on low heat till it becomes thick like custard. This will take about 10 minutes. Set it aside.
5. Either one of the above tamarind sauces can be used.
6. Heat 2 Tbs oil and add the asafoetida, cloves, black pepper corns and cardamom seed. Wait till they sizzle. Add ginger, salt, red pepper and cook for few minutes until ginger browns. Add prepared tamarind sauce. Stir to mix. Transfer the mixed *chutney* to a blender and blend it smooth. Pour it into a little cooking pan.
7. Add sugar, ground roasted cumin powder, *garam masala*, raisins or dried dates and apple sauce. Stir to mix and cook until the *chutney* is of the consistency of a thick sauce. Add more sugar, if needed.
8. Simmer a little on low heat. Transfer it to a serving bowl. Chill till ready to serve.

Note: Tamarind has this sweet and tart taste that makes it a perfect herb for a chutney. Just spice it up a little and add some sugar and you have a delicious chutney. More over tamarind is very healthy for you.

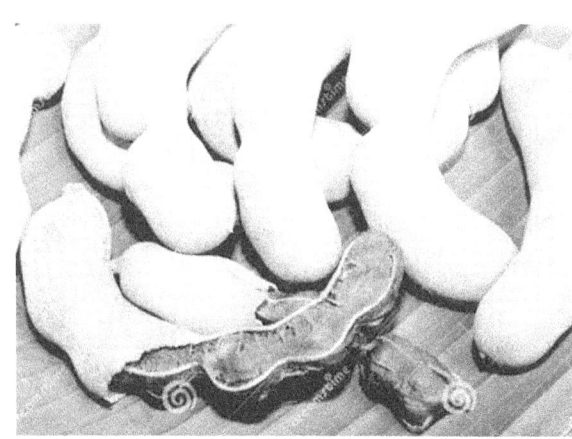

Tamatar ki Chutney

Tomato Dip

Serves: 6-8
Preparation Time: 25-30 Minutes

Ingredients

Vegetable oil	3 Tbs
Cumin seeds	1 tsp
Mustard seeds	1 tsp
Onion chopped	1 cup
Ginger chopped	1 Tbs
Garlic chopped	1 Tbs
Green chilies chopped	2
Tomatoes chopped (ripe)	4 cups
Prunes or dry apricots soaked in ½ cup of warm water, chopped	¼ cup
Raisins	2 Tbs
Salt	to taste
Turmeric powder	¾ tsp
Sugar	to taste
Lemon juice	1 Tbs
Red pepper ground	1 tsp
Garam masala	1 tsp
Cilantro fresh chopped	2 Tbs

Note: Chopped green mangoes can be used instead of apricots or prunes. It will keep the original flavour of the *chutney*. This chutney can be served also with Idlis, Dosas, and Vadas. It can be used as a dip too once you grind it into a smooth paste. The chutney can be used on Breads, Salads, and snacks. Tomatoes release lot more vitamins and minerals when cooked and they are full of Vitamin C and antioxidants. Once prepared this chutney can last you a week in the refrigerator without any harm.

This chutney is a perfect example of preserving the summer freshness of healthy tomatoes. Indian chutneys are usually served fresh to accompany a variety of dishes, but in European countries jam-loving colonial British cooks have made it into more of a preserve, while retaining the all-important spices. It is very much loved in the western countries. Simply delicious everybody falls in love with this easy-to-prepare Chutney. Serve it with Pulaos and Biryanis. It also tastes really good with Stuffed Parathas.

Excellent accompaniment with a meal or an appetizer. Perk up your meals and enjoy the contasting flavours of the red beautiful chutney.

Method

1. Heat the oil. Add cumin seeds and mustard seeds. Wait till they start popping and then add chopped onions, ginger, garlic and green chilies. Fry the onions in oil till they turn light brown and then add the chopped tomatoes, prunes or apricots, raisins, salt and turmeric powder. Cook on low heat for about half an hour or till the oil separates from the mixture and tomatoes are puréed.

2. If you prefer smooth *chutney*, put the mixture in a blender and blend it smoothly, otherwise go to step 3.

3. Add sugar, lemon juice, red pepper and *garam masala* and stir.

4. Cook on low heat till it is of creamy consistency. Top it with fresh coriander and serve with appetizers or with a regular meal.

RAITAS, CHUTNEYS AND ACHAARS

Milijuli Sabjion ka Khatta Meetha Achaar

Classic Sweet & Sour Pickle of Mixed Vegetables

Serve with meals
Preparation Time: 20 Minutes

Makes 12 – 14 One lb Jars

Ingredients

Turnips, carrots, cauliflower, daikon radish washed and chopped	10 lbs
Water	4½ cups
Salt	1 cup
Mustard oil	4 cups
Ginger chopped	½ cup
Garlic chopped	½ cup
Green chilies chopped	¼ cup
Onions chopped	1 cup
Cinnamom large pieces	6 or 7
Cardamoms whole black	¼ cup
Cloves whole	2 tsp
Black pepper corns	2 tsp
Red pepper whole (dry)	½ cup
Dry fenugreek leaves	¼ cup
Mustard ground	1½ cup
Red pepper	2 Tbs
Garam masala	⅔ cup
Vinegar	1 cup
Brown sugar or jaggery (*gur*)	1 lb

Pickling originated in india 4000 years ago using cucumbers native to India. Our cuisine is unique in its emphasis on the proper digestion of each food with proper cooking and spicing because any undigested food produces toxins in the body. Achars were designed to improve digestion. Pickling may also improve the nutritional value of food by introducing B vitamins produced by bacteria. This was also a way to preserve food for out-of-season use and for long journeys, especially by sea. It can be served with any meal.

Method

1. Wash and chop turnips, carrots, cauliflower and daikon radishes.
2. Boil enough water that the vegetables can submerge, in a deep pan with 1/2 cup salt. Add the vegetables boil them for a minute and drain the water
3. Transfer the vegetables to a paper towel lined basket and dry them for at least 6 hours or dry them in the sun.
4. Heat the oil to smoking 320°F and cool it.
5. Heat again 4 cups of oil and fry the ginger, garlic, green chilies and the onions. Add cinnamon, cardamoms, cloves, black pepper and whole red peppers and fry until the peppers sizzle. Lower the heat, add the dry fenugreek leaves, dry mustard, red pepper, *garam masala* and the rest of the salt. Mix well. Add the dry vegetables, stir to coat the vegetables with spices and set them aside.
6. In a separate pan heat the vinegar and add the crude sugar (*Gur*) or brown sugar and stir until it dissolves. Cool it. Transfer the sweetened vinegar to the vegetables mixture. Cook on low heat until the oil separates from the vegetables. Cool the pickle. Transfer the pickle in canning jars. Leave them in sun for few days before serving.

Aam ka Achaar

Mango Pickle

Serve with meals
Preparation Time: 10 Minutes

We try to pickle many vegetables and raw fruits but raw mango is one of our most favourite. It is pickled in many different ways. Sometimes in combination with other vegetables, sometimes with hot green chilies, ginger and spices. Whatever the preparation, it is always delicious and unique, and can be served with any meal of your choice.

Makes few jars

Ingredients

Washed and dried raw mangoes sliced into pieces	1 lb
Ginger fresh sliced	½ cup
Carrots finely chopped	¼ cup
Gooseberries	¼ cup
Drained can of small button onions or fresh onions	¼ cup
Hot green chilies cut in half	¼ cup
Mustard oil	2 cups
Asafoetida	½ tsp
Whole red pepper	1 Tbs
Turmeric powder	2 tsp
Red pepper powder	1 ½ tsp
Fennel seeds crushed	1 Tbs
Nigella seeds crushed	1 Tbs
Fenugreek seeds crushed	1 Tbs
Peppercorns crushed	1 tsp
Brown cardamom seeds crushed	1 tsp
Salt	½ cup

Method

1. Wash and cut the mangoes in small slices. After washing and drying grate the ginger and carrots. Wash and dry the gooseberries, button onions. Chop the green chilies in halves. Set them aside.
2. Heat the oil to 320°F and remove from heat. Cool a little and then add the asafoetida. When it is cooked add the whole red pepper, turmeric, powdered red pepper, crushed fennel seeds, nigella seeds, and the fenugreek seeds.
3. Stir and add the mango slices, grated ginger, gooseberries, button onions, green chillies, grated carrots, and stir to mix.
4. Add the crushed peppercorns, crushed brown cardamom seeds and salt and mix well. Cook through for a few minutes.
5. Pour the pickle into sterilized glass jars with tight lids and store.

Note: Spicy pickles are a very important item in Indian meals. Pickles enhance the taste of the meal and increase the satisfaction after every meal. Pickles are easy to prepare and can be preserved for months. It can increase your appetite, they are low in saturated fat and cholesterol and are a good source of iron, vitamin A and fibres. However, too much intake of pickle is not good for your health as it is high in sodium and acid.

Hari Mirch ka Achaar

Green Chilies Pickle

Serves: 4-6
Preparation Time: 15 Minutes

Makes 2 – 3 jars

Ingredients

Green chilies	1 lb
Ginger grated	2 Tbs
Crushed mustard seeds	¼ cup
Fenugreek seeds crushed	2 Tbs
Anise seeds crushed	1 Tbs
Mustard oil	¼ cup
Asafoetida	a pinch
Red pepper	1 Tbs
Black pepper	1 Tbs
Turmeric powder	1 tsp
Salt	1 Tbs

Note: It is said that eating green chillies is always better than adding red chilli powder to the food. Green chillies have plenty of dietary fibres. Contrary to common conceptions, eating chillies actually help you digest your food faster. Having green chillies has been linked with a lowered risk of having lung cancer. They have anti-bacterial properties. These anti-bacterial properties help to keep infections at bay. This is especially true for skin infections.

Another great spicy pickle to go with a plain and bland meal like *khichadi*, rice and *dal* or a stuffed *parantha*. It can really add a lot of taste and zing to any simple and quick meal. Green chillies are healthy for those who are prone to iron deficiency. Green chillies are a natural source of iron.and are rich sources of antioxidants and this makes them act like janitors of the body. They can protect the body against free radical damage giving you natural immunity to cancer and also slowing down the ageing process.

Method

1. Wash and cut the green chilies in halves and grate the ginger and set it aside.
2. Crush the mustard seeds, fenugreek and anise seeds.
3. Heat the oil and add the asafoetida and let it cook for a minute until it swells up and immediately add the red pepper, black pepper, turmeric, salt, crushed anise seeds, mustard seeds and fenugreek seeds, and stir the mixture.
4. Add the green chilies and grated ginger and coat them well with all the spices and add the salt.
5. Stir well and heat through about 3–5 minutes on low heat. Transfer it to sterilized jars with airtight lids.

Nimbu ka Achaar

Lemon Pickle (Sweet & Sour Lemon, Pickles)

Serve with meals
Preparation Time: 10 Minutes

According to some naturopaths, a tablespoon of lemon pickle a day helps with liver problems, arthritis and skin disorders.

A spicy and digestive accompaniment to snacks and meals. It is a good substitute for *chutney* and a quick folktale remedy for indigestion or stomach ache. Lemon skin is very good for bile stimulation and will thus help with the alkalinity of the small intestines. It is good with greasy food and cleans the palate.

Makes few jars

Ingredients

Fresh lemons cut in quarters	1 lbs
Table salt	¾ cup
Fenugreek seeds roasted, ground	1 Tbs
Mustard oil	1 cup
Mustard seeds ground	1 Tbs
Red dry chilies whole	1 Tbs
Asafoetida powder	1 tsp
Red pepper	2 Tbs
Black pepper	1 Tbs
Fresh ginger sliced	1 cup
Green serrano chilies	2 Tbs
Sugar	½ cup
Lemon juice squeezed from lemons	12

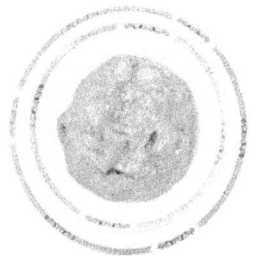

Note: Lemon or lime is consumed throughout the world in sorbets, beverages, refreshing drinks, pickles, jams, jellies, snacks, candies, sugar boiled confectionaries and culinary and the oil extracted from its peel or skin is extensively used in soft drink concentrates, body oils, cosmetics, hair oils, tooth pastes, toilet and beauty soaps, disinfectants, mouth washes, deodorants and innumerable other products.

Method

1. Wash and dry the lemons and cut them in quarters and put them in a bottle or a plastic container.
2. Add salt and let them sit by a sunny window for 2–3 weeks, occasionally shaking them.
3. Roast the fenugreek seeds on a hot skillet but not burn and grind them and set them aside.
4. Heat the mustard oil in a large wok to 320°F. Remove from heat and after 2–3 minutes, add the mustard seeds and the whole red peppers. Wait till the mustard seeds start to pop.
5. Add the asafoetida, wait till it starts to swell up and then add the red pepper, black pepper, and cook but not burn.
6. Add the ginger, green hot chilies, sugar and stored and chopped lemons and stir to mix.
7. Cook till the lemons and ginger are a little soft and tender (about 10 minutes) on low heat
8. Squeeze the lemon juice of 6–8 fresh lemons and add to the pickle and boil through for 2–3 minutes.
9. Cool and store in a sterilized jar with a tight lid.

Desserts

Indian cuisine sweets (*mithai*) are not only enjoyed as dessert but as snacks too. Boxes of sweet are offered as gifts on festivals like *Diwali* (Festival of Lights), *Raksha Bandhan* (a festival when sisters tie a holy-thread round the wrist of their brothers), *Holi* (Festival of Colors) and also during weddings or other family occasions. Not only are desserts part of our staple fare, but they are also offered in our places of worships. Be it the *khada prasad* at Gurudwaras or the *boondi laddoos* served at temples, desserts form an integral part of our sacred offerings. Indian desserts can be divided into two categories. The first category is milk based such as *Kalakand, Rasgulla, Rasmalai, Burfi* etc. The second category of Indian desserts are based on flour such as *Gulab Jamun, Malpuwa, Halwa, Laddoo*, etc.

Most of the sweets are milk based and are prepared mixed with nuts, coconut, *ghee* and sugar. They are often flavoured with cardamom, rose water, *kevra* essence and sometimes decorated with ultra thin gold or silver leaf (*varq*). One of most loved desserts is the milk fudge, *Burfi*. It is prepared with dried milk (*khoa*) and sugar, and flavoured with ground cardamom and saffron. It has several versions and is also made mixed with nuts like cashew nuts, pistachios, coconut and almonds. These variations are respectively called *Cashew Burfi, Pistachio Burfi, Coconut Burfi* and *Almond Burfi*. Sweets are also served at teatime and as snacks during weddings, engagements and birthday parties.

Some Indian sweets are only prepared during specific festivals. *Pongal* in Tamil Nadu would not be complete without the famous *kheer* called *Payasam*. Similarly, *Ganesh Chaturthi* (a festival when Lord Ganesha, the son of Shiva and Parvati, is believed to bestow his presence on earth for all his devotees) in Maharashtra would be incomplete without *Rava Ladoo* (*Modak*). Muslims celebrate *Eid-ul-Fitr* (a festival that marks the end of *Ramzan*, the Islamic holy month of fasting) with *Sevian Kheer*. Sweets are normally distributed among family and friends, to celebrate a happy occasion, like the arrival of a new baby, a wedding, an engagement, on moving into a new house and virtually any celebration. Therefore, some sweets are made specifically for an occasion or a celebration. India has a wide variety of desserts. Many popular Indian sweets, such as Rasgulla, are popular throughout South Asia, while many others are local favourites and are confined to one or the other etnic groups of India.

There are sweets that are *paneer* or cheese based like *Rasgullas, Sandesh, Chumchum, Rasmalai* and *Gulabjaman*. During festival times Indian markets are flooded with vendors selling beautifully decorated and gift-wrapped sweet boxes filled with *Burfi, Gulabjaman, Gajar ka Halwa, Jalebi, Imarti* and many assorted fudges. People buy sweets to perform *Lakshmi Puja* (prayer to Goddess of Wealth) at their house in the company of their dear ones on *Diwali*. The whole city twinkles with lights like a firefly, crackers and fireworks fill the skies at night. Every city in India has dozens of sweet shops managed as family business. The *halwai* (the sweet-meat maker), who crafts these sweets is normally very possessive about his own – often inherited – recipes and there is a lot of scope for innovation or fusion in the making of even more improved varieties of sweets. These shops are conspicuous by their smoke blackened big vats of milk sitting on large open coal stoves. But for a few desserts, normally sweets are not prepared at Indian homes and are bought from the traditional sweet shops found in almost all markets.

Cakes and pastries are also popular in India indicating clearly the merging of western and eastern cuisines. Still, local sweets are preferred by a very large section of society. Nowadays mango and pistachio ice cream, mango mousse and pudding are also very popular in India. A delicious preparation close to the ice cream is the Indian *kulfi* which is now being served by some restaurants in the US too. It is flavoured with cardamom, saffron and grated nuts, and is served with noodles like corn flour vermicelli called *Faluda*.

It would be worth remembering that most Indian sweets aid in digestion and are normally consumed after spicy meals. Coconut is a natural ingredient for a sweet dish. Indian desserts are very often decorated with cardamom, raisins, almonds pistachios, cashew nuts and fruits such as mango, guava, pineapple, melon, cherries orange and banana.

Burfi
Milk Fudge

Serves: 10-12
Preparation Time: 15 Minutes

Ingredients

Ricotta cheese or *paneer* or *khoa*	2 lbs
Clarified butter (*ghee*)	½ cup
Sugar	1½ cup
Water	½ cup
Dry milk powder cups	3–4
Almonds crushed	½ cup
Saffron sprigs dissolved in water	¼ tsp
Green cardamom seds crushed	1 Tbs
Gold or silver leaves (*varq*)	2

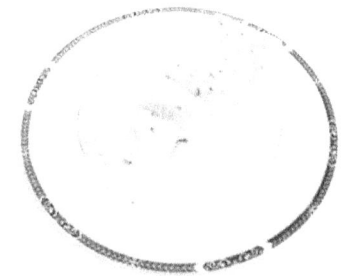

Note: It comes in scores of different varieties and flavours. Easiest way to make Burfi is to place a can of condensed milk in a heavy bottom frying pan with a couple of strands of saffron. Stir fry on low heat until all milk solids come off the edges of frying pan in a big mass. Spread it on a cookie sheet in ½ inch thick layer and decorate it with shredded nuts, powdered cardamoms and Gold or silver leaf. Cut it in diamond shapes and serve. You can make coloured burfi of several colours by adding food colour to condensed milk before frying. Similarly different kinds of burfi can be made by adding those ingredients to the condensed milk before cooking.

Burfi (*barfee, burfee*) is a traditional sweet delicacy consumed in the Indian subcontinent. The word 'burfi' is of Persian origin and means snow, ice. This is due to the white colour it has in its most simple form. It is made of condensed milk (*khoa*) sugar and ghee. It is usually sold, cut in cubes, round or diamond shaped pieces. Burfi is sometimes called the Indian fudge. Barfi is a popular sweet to gift or serve to family and friends during Diwali. There are many varieties available throughout India. The recipe is extremely adaptable and differs from region to region and its apperance can change according to what is added to it.

This *paneer* or ricotta cheese preparation with dry milk powder, *ghee* and sugar is one of the most popular sweets of India. Ricotta cheese here can be (as in this recipe) substituted for the traditional milk solids like *khoa*.

Method

1. In a deep thick-bottom saucepan cook the cheese with ¼ cup of *ghee*, sugar and water. Fry until it starts to leave the sides of the pan or till the water dries up.

2. Remove from heat and add the powdered milk one cup at a time. Stir well and add the remainder of the *ghee* and fry the mixture for a few minutes until you see the fudge is no longer sticking to the sides of the pan.

3. Add the almonds and saffron dissolved in water and mix well. Grease a rectangular cake pan and spread the mixture evenly, 1 inch thick. Sprinkle with ground cardamoms and layer the top with gold or silver leaf.

4. Chill and cut preferably in square or diamond shapes. Serve as a dessert after dinner or as a snack at teatime or a coffee break.

Besan ki Burfi

Gram Flour Fudge

Serves: 6-8
Preparation Time: 20 Minutes

Ingredients

Milk (2% fat)	2 Tbs
Gram flour	2 cups
Clarified butter or *ghee*	$^2/_3$ cup
Almonds crushed	1 Tbs
Pistachio crushed	1 Tbs
Sugar	1½ cups
Water	1½ cups
Dry milk powder (optional)	1 cup
Saffron	¼ tsp
Cardamom powder	½ tsp
Silver or gold leaf (*varq*)	as needed

Note: It is usually made for auspicious occasions and for Lord Krishna. Mohan is another name for Lord Krishna and it is said that Lord Krishna loved this dessert and that is why this Burfi is named after him and is also called Mohan Thal.

Gram flour fudge is enjoyed all over India. It has different names in different parts of the country. It is called *Besan ki Burfi* in northern states whereas in Gujarat it is called *Mohan Thaal*. It is very delicious and is prepared with proteinaceous gram flour.

A half-cup of Besan flour (chick pea flour) is naturally higher in protein than wheat-based flours. It has 10 gm of protein and 3 gm of fat. 70 percent of this fat comes from healthy unsaturated fats that can lower cholesterol. The same portion has 5 gm fibre, and 201 mg of folate. This important vitamin is critical for the production of proteins and genetic material. Folate is important especially during periods of rapid growth. It helps prevent birth defects of the brain and spinal chord. It is a good source of thiamin and vitamin B-6. Thiamin converts food into energy, while B-6 is needed for the synthesis of red blood cells and the neurotransmitter serotonin that regulates appetite and mood. Therefore having Besan flour in your diet in any snape or form is very healthy for you.

Method

1. Mix the milk into the dry *besan* flour in a medium size bowl and rub it through the fine sieve into powder and set it aside.

2. In a large heavy-bottom frying pan fry the *besan* with the clarified butter until light brown and as soon as you smell the aroma add the crushed nuts. Fry a little and remove from fire and set it aside.

3. In a medium size pan transfer the sugar with water and bring it to a boil. Cook till the syrup is stringy (when the syrup is dropped slowly from the spoon it shows a stringy consistency) about 20–30 minutes.

4. Add a cup of dry milk powder to the cooked *besan* flour and stir to mix well (about 3–4 minutes on low heat). Add the cardamom powder and stir to mix.
5. Add the warm syrup to the cooked *besan* flour and stir and mix well for 2 minutes.
6. Pour the mixture into a 8-10 inches baking pan that is about 2 inches deep. Let it cool and spread a gold or silver leaf *(varq)* if you wish (available at your local Indian grocer).
7. Sprinkle the saffron powder, crushed pistachio and almonds on top and cut into 1 inch squares or into diamond shapes.
8. Serve as a snack or as a dessert after dinner.

Jalebi

Fried Spiral Sweet Rings

Serves: 8-10
Preparation Time: 15 Minutes

Ingredients

All purpose flour	2 cups
Baking powder	½ tsp
Rice flour	¼ cup
Yogurt	½ cup
Water	1½ cup
Saffron (dissolved in 1 tsp of water)	½ tsp
Cardamom powder	½ tsp
For Syrup	
Yellow food color	¼ tsp
Sugar	2 cups
Water	1 cup
Oil for frying	4 cups
Kevra essence	2 drops

In a country like India where umpteen varieties of sweets are available, *Jalebi* is a national favourite. Not only on Holi, Diwali or any other festive occasion, *Jalebi* is something which is included in the regular diet of all born with a sweet tooth. In a land of festivals, Jalebi is offered at all festival occasions. These circular safforn coloured rings adorn sweet shops and dessert tables. They are also popular in the Middle East, East Africa and North Africa, especially during the festival of Ramadan

These juicy rings most certainly are a desirable dessert. Almost everybody's favourite. Made with fermented flour, deep-fried and soaked in the sugar syrup these are crunchy and a bit sweet and sour. The name for a similar dish in Iran is *Zulbia* and it is suggested that it was probably brought to medieval India by the Persian or the Mughal invaders.

Method

1. Combine all purpose flour, baking powder, rice flour and yogurt in a bowl, and add 1½ cup water, saffron water, cardamom powder, and yellow food colour. Whisk it well.
3. Cover it with a cloth and set it aside at a warm place for two hours.
4. Add 2 cups of sugar water with 1 cup of water and a drop of yellow food colour in a deep saucepan and boil. Wait until the sugar syrup is starting to make a string when pulled between fingers. Add the *kevra* essence to it and stir to mix.
5. Beat the flour batter again and pour it into a pastry bag.
6. Heat oil in a large wok or a large thick-bottom saucepan to 300°F–340°F. Squeeze the batter into the hot oil from the batter filled pastry bag going round and round making a string

Rasgulla - Page 232

Rasmalai - Page 233

Gulab Jamun - Page 235

Kheer - Page 241

Sevian Kheer - Page 242

Shahi Tukra - Page 244

Mango Pie - Page 246

Nan Khataii - Page 247

of circles starting from outside ending inside. Each disc of string of circles should not be more than 4 inches in diameter. Several such discs of strings can be fried at the same time. Fry until golden brown. Remove from the oil with a slotted spoon or tongs and transfer into the hot sugar syrup.

7. Leave these in the syrup for at least 10–15 minutes and then remove with tongs from the sugar syrup into a serving platter.

8. Serve hot or cold. They are delicious when eaten dipped in hot milk.

Note: You can make the Jalebi by pouring the batter in a sqeezable empty Ketchup bottle and sqeeze in circular motions to make circles in the oil and fry them until golden brown.

Rasgulla

Cheese Balls in a Sweet Syrup

Serves: 6-8
Preparation Time: 15 Minutes

A sweet for all seasons and all occasions that originated in Bengal in the 1830s, but are prepared and consumed all over India. These are spongy cheese balls made of *paneer* or homemade cheese. These white balls, the size of golf balls, are cooked in plain, rose flavoured or cardamom flavoured sugar syrup and are always served chilled.

Ingredients

Homemade *paneer* or well-drained Ricotta cheese	1 lb
Baking powder	a pinch
Cream of wheat and all purpose flour (each)	1 Tbs
Raisins	1 Tbs
Sugar	2 cups
Water	4 cups
Cardamom powder	½ tsp
Rose water	1½ tsp

Method

1. Rub together cheese (see note below) and a pinch of baking powder, all purpose flour and cream of wheat into a smooth and creamy dough. Use blender to blend it for 30 seconds. Divide into 16 equal parts.

2. Insert a raisin in the centre of each one of them and form them into small cherry size smooth round balls.

3. Mix 2 cups of sugar with 6 cups of water in a large deep pan and boil it for 3–5 minutes. Add the cardamom powder.

4. Add the cheese balls one by one into the hot syrup. *Rasgullas* puff up a lot in size, so add a few at a time. Cook for about 5 minutes in the open pan.

5. Lower the heat and cover the pan. Cook for another 10–15 minutes. The *rasgullas* should puff up and become spongy. Keep adding a little water to keep the syrup thin (1 Tbs every 2–3 minutes).

6. In another pan boil the rest of the sugar in two cups of water to make thick syrup. Set it aside. Transfer the cooked *rasgullas* from the thin syrup to this thick syrup and flavour them with rose water before serving.

Note:
1. Washing of *paneer* or *chhenna* (as soon as you make it) with clean water to remove all traces of vinegar or lemon juice is very important for making good *rasgullas*. Draining of water from the *paneer* or *chhenna* is also very important.
2. You can pressure cook them for 6 minutes (or longer if need be) instead of cooking in the syrup.

Rasmalai

Sweet Cheese Patties in Cream

Serves: 12-14
Preparation Time: 8-10 Minutes

Ingredients

Homemade cheese or *paneer* completely drained ricotta cheese	2 lbs
Heavy cream	1 cup
Condensed sweetened milk	2 cups
Sugar	1 cups
Water	4 cups
Almonds slivered chopped	1 Tbs
Pistachio chopped	1 Tbs
Cardamoms crushed	½ tsp
Rose water	1 tsp
Saffron	1 tsp

Ras Malai, is one of the most popular Indian desserts. Originating from the traditional sweet kitchens of West Bengal.

These sweet patties of *paneer* cooked in flavoured heavy cream are a very popular dessert for festive occasions. These are prepared the same way as the *rasgullas* but are served in heavy cream instead of sugar syrup. These sweet delicious patties are everyone's favorite.

Method

1. Rub the (see notes 1 and 2 below) homemade *paneer* or cheese or beat it in a food processor until it is smooth. Divide the cheese into 24 equal parts and roll each into smooth round balls.
2. Flatten the cheese balls into about 2 inch diameter flat patties.
3. Heat the heavy cream and the condensed milk together in a deep fairly large saucepan and add the sugar as needed. Cook for 5–10 minutes. Set it aside.
4. Prepare the syrup by boiling 2 cups of sugar in 10 cups of water in a large heavy-bottom saucepan and add the flat patties of cheese and cook. Keep sprinkling water over the discs until they double in size.
5. Lower the heat and cover the pan and cook for another 5 minutes. As the patties get cooked they should puff up and float on top of the syrup. Keep adding water to keep the syrup watery or they can be pressure cooked until first whistle. Turn off the heat and let them sit in the cooker for few minutes. Cool the cooker and open.
6. Remove the completely cooked and cooled *rasmalai* out of the syrup with a slotted spoon and squeeze out the syrup a little and transfer them into the heavy cream mixture. Let them sit on very low heat for 2 minutes.

7. Cool in the refrigerator and serve in a serving bowl topped with chopped slivered almonds and chopped pistachio and add the rose water and saffron before serving. It is a delicious and refreshing dessert, especially during summer months.

Note 1 : Rasmalai can also be made by mixing together 1 cup of dry milk powder with one egg 1 tsp of ghee and 1/4 tsp of baking powder. Knead and make a dough. Make 12 smooth patties and drop them in a boiling mixture of heavy cream and condensed milk on low heat. As they get cooked they come to the top. Cook for a few more minutes. Cool and add rose water. Serve garnished with shaved nuts and silver leaves. Prepare the homemade cheese or *paneer* as mentioned in the recipe for *rasgullas* and follow the notes 1 and 2 under that recipe.

Gulab Jamun

Golden Cream Cheese Balls in Syrup

Serves: 8
Preparation Time: 10 Minutes

Ingredients

Sugar	2 cups
Water	2 cups
Cardamoms	4 pods
Cinnamon	4 sticks
Dry milk powder	1 cup
Bisquick or pancake mix*	2/3 cup
Baking soda	1/8 tsp
Butter softened	3 Tbs
Whole Milk	1/2 cup
Almonds sliced	1/4 cup
Shortening or oil or as needed for frying	2 cups
Saffron to sprinkle	

*Bisquick is available in western countries at local grocery store. Ready to make *gulabjamun* mixes are available at Indian grocery stores. If Bisquick is not available the *gulabjamun* dough can be made with 2½ cups of *mawa* flour mixed with ½ cup of all purpose flour, ¼ cup of any shortening or crisco and a pinch of soda. Knead this mixture with heavy cream and make a smooth dough. Then follow step 5 onwards. Makes excellent *gulabjamun*.

The word "*Gulab*" means rose and "*Jamun*" is a delicious purple Indian berry which grows during the monsoon season in India. These rose coloured *Jamuns* (favourite of the Mughal queen *Noorjahan*) will really steal your heart. The dessert also became popular in Turkish-speaking areas, spreading to the *Ottoman Empire*. The Gulab Jamun was the child of Jamundas Gulabani, a Sindhi chef. They are popular in every part of the Indian subcontinent and served by each and every Indian restaurant in the world.

Method

1. Combine the sugar and water in a pan. With a sharp knife, make a slit in the ends of each cardamom pod and drop the seeds into the sugar mixture alongwith cinnamon sticks. Also 1 Tbs of lemon juice.
2. Bring to a boil, stirring until sugar is dissolved, and boil until reduced. Turn the heat to low and set it aside to be used later.
3. Combine the dry milk powder, bisquick mix and baking soda, and add the softened butter. Mix until well distributed.
4. Stir in the milk and then turn out on a lightly floured board and knead well for 10–15 minutes or more until the dough is smooth and elastic.
5. Break off pieces of dough, roll into balls about the size of cherries.
6. Roll in a piece of almond inside each, if you wish.
7. Drop the balls, few at a time, into the oil heated to 340–350°F. Slow browning is very important in cooking the *Gulabjamuns*. The oil should not be very hot. It should take 2–3 minutes in browning them.
8. Remove from fat with a slotted spoon and drop them into the hot syrup.

236 INCREDIBLE TASTE OF INDIAN VEGETARIAN CUISINE

9. You can cook the balls ahead of time and let the cooked balls sit in a bowl at room temperature. Add them to the warm syrup for a few minutes before serving. The cooked balls can be refrigerated in a ziplock bag to be used later. Just make fresh syrup and add the frozen balls to the hot syrup and heat them on slow heat until they become plump with sugar syrup, and serve.

Note : Try making Gulabjamun by mixing together 2 cups of dry milk powder, 2 tsp of crisco or any other shortening with 2 tsp of all purpose flour, ½ tsp of Baking powder, 2 tsp of water soaked and squeezed cream of wheat. Knead it into a fluffy dough with the help of a few drops of milk. Make into balls and fry them by slowly browning them on low heat. Drop them in hot syrup (make as in the recipe above and soak at least an hour)

Suji Halwa
Cream of Wheat Pudding

Serves: 10-12
Preparation Time: 10 Minutes

Ingredients

*Cream of wheat (instant) see Note below	2 cups
Clarified butter or *ghee*	½ cup– 1½ cup
Raisins (optional)	2 Tbs
Almonds grated or slivered	2 Tbs
Water	4–5 cups
Sugar	1½ cup
Cardamom seeds crushed	½ tsp
Saffron	a pinch

Note: If *suji* (the uncooked cream of wheat available at an Indian grocery store) is used then frying time will be double and the water used will be almost 3 times as much. Traditionally the quantity of *ghee* and sugar added to the *halwa* is equal to the quantity of cream of wheat used but I have reduced the amount to cut down on calories. The *halwa* is equally delicious with these reduced amounts in the above recipe but if you wish you can make it in the traditional way.

One of the most popular and favourite desserts in India. Think of a celebration and the first item that comes to mind is the *Halwa* (Pudding). Be it *Gajar ka Halwa*, *Moong ki dal ka Halwa* or any other variety, it is always a welcome dessert. Quick and nutritious, it fulfils the need for a dessert very elegantly.

This Halwa of cream of wheat is one of the very quick and easy desserts to fix for any occasion. It is delicious and very nutritious. It is usually served at a religious gathering but is a versatile dessert and can be served anytime. In Egyptian culture, there are 101 variations of this dish. Halwa is also served in various African countries, Balkans, Easten Europe and the Jewish world. There are 2 types of halwa, made from grain flour or semolina based made with clarified butter and sugar. Nut based made from tahini (sesame paste) or sunflower seed based made with butter and sugar.

Method

1. Cook the instant cream of wheat on medium-low heat in the clarified butter or *ghee* for a few minutes until the cream of wheat turns light brown (about 5–7 minutes).
2. Add the raisins or the almonds or both and cook for a few more minutes and then add the water. The amount of water can vary from place to place. Lower the heat.
3. While mixing and stirring, add the sugar. Stir until the water dries up and the butter or *ghee* starts to separate from the *halwa*. It takes about 10 minutes of stirring patiently.
4. Sprinkle with the crushed cardamom seeds, saffron and serve.

Note: Apple *Halwa* can be made similarly. Sprinkle some lemon juice and sugar over 2 cups of peeled, chopped and grated green apples. Set it aside. In a heavy bottom saucepan, heat ¼ cup of *ghee* and fry the grated apples (10 minutes). Add sweetened condensed milk (¼ cup flavored with ½ tsp of saffron, 1 Tbs of slivered almonds and raisins. Pour it over the fried *halwa*. Stir well. Cook until it stops sticking to the pan. Serve garnished with almonds, pistachio and cardamom powder.

HINT

Use any Instant brand of cream of wheat with 1 minute or 5 minute cooking time.

Kulfi Faluda

Indian Ice Cream with Starchy Noodles

Serves: 8-10
Preparation Time: 5-7 Minutes

Ingredients

Milk (whole)	2 cups
Arrow-root powder dissolved in water	2 Tbs
Heavy cream	2 cups
Sugar	¾ cup
Dry milk powder (Pkg to make quart)	1 cup
Almonds shredded	1 Tbs
Pistachio shredded	1 Tbs
Kevra essence drops (optional)	2–3
Mango pieces small (optional)	½ cup
*Faluda** (corn flour vermicelli) as needed	

Indigenous ice cream preparation of India with finely chopped almonds and pistachio with *faluda* (arrowroot flour vermicelli). Till a few years back, it was made by a hand-churning machine. In spite of its being rich, it is still very popular especially when served with the calorie less *faluda*. Traditional small aluminum moulds give it a conical shape and it is a great dessert on a summer night.

Kulfi has lately become very popular in north America and is being served in the most elite restaurants. Highlight the presentation by colouring the faluda in different food colours.

Methods

1. Boil the milk in a thick-bottom saucepan for a few minutes and add it to the dissolved arrow-root flour and stir well to blend it. Cook for 2 minutes. Add the heavy cream and stir to mix.
2. Add the sugar and the dry milk powder. Stir and remove from heat. Cool.
3. Add the shredded almonds, shredded pistachio and the *kevra* essence. Add the mango pieces, if you wish.
4. Blend everything well and pour it into moulds.
5. Tightly close the moulds and lay them all side-by-side in a box and put them in a freezer. Takes about 3–4 hours to set.
6. Serve the *kulfi* with *faluda* or plain.

Note: **Faluda* is available at the local grocery store. Known as traditional ice cream of the Indian subcontinent. Kulfi likely originated during the Mughal era, 16th to 18th centuries. It was prepared in royal kitchens using ice brought in from the Himalayas. This is documented in the *Ain-i-Akbari*, a detailed record of the Mughal emperor Akbar's administration.

Phirni

Ground Rice Pudding

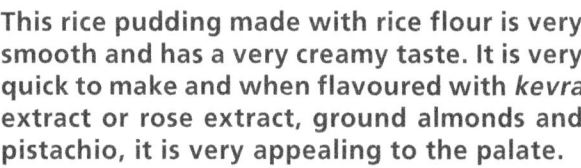

Serves: 6-8
Preparation Time: 15 Minutes

Ingredients

Milk (2% fat)	4 cups
Rice flour	4 Tbs
Sugar to taste or	½ cup
Blanched slivered almonds	1 Tbs
Rose extract drops	1–2
Silver leaves	3–4
Pistachio grated	1 Tbs
Fresh strawberries chopped	½ cup
Or kiwi fruit slices	

This rice pudding made with rice flour is very smooth and has a very creamy taste. It is very quick to make and when flavoured with *kevra* extract or rose extract, ground almonds and pistachio, it is very appealing to the palate.

Phirni is a traditional north Indian dessert with a Kashmiri origin. It probably originated during the Moghul era. To make it delectable and palatable it is usually flavoured with different fruits, essences and nuts. It is smooth and velvety just like its western counterpart pudding and custard but does not have any egg.

Method

1. Heat the milk to a full boil. Lower the heat. Add the sugar and mix.
2. Mix the rice flour into a couple of teaspoons of milk separately and then mix it into the boiled milk.
3. Cook on low heat and keep cooking until the mixture thickens to a consistency of a pudding, about 10-15 minutes.
4. Add ¾ Tbs each of grated pistachio and the rose extract and stir to mix well.
5. Cool and pour in pretty pudding cups or ice cream cups for individual serving or pour in one serving bowl. Refrigerate until set.
6. Serve it topped with remaining almonds and pistachio and silver leaves, or freshly sliced small pieces of strawberry or kiwi fruit.

Note: You can add 1 cup of chopped and pureed or chopped strawberries or mangoes or passion fruit or Guava or apple, or pineapple, right after you add the sugar to the hot milk.

Kheer

Rice Pudding

Serves: 6-8

Preparation Time:*

10 Minutes

Ingredients

Milk 2% fat	2 quart
Basmati rice	3 Tbs
Cardamom pods pods	2–4
Whipping cream	1 cup
Sugar	½ cup
Almonds	1 Tbs
Kevra essence	4 drops
Pistachio	1 Tbs
Raisins	1 Tbs
Powdered coconut	1 Tbs

Note: *The time of preparation of this dessert can be cut by half, using the method below:

Add 6 Tbs of boiled rice to a quart of milk, stir and cook for 10 minutes and add 1 cup of dry milk powder. Cook until thickened (about 10 minutes) and serve with the same garnishing as above.

This is made by boiling rice in milk on slow heat and then sweetening with sugar. It is served flavored with rose or it *kevra* essence, ground cardamoms, almonds, pistachio or coconut. It is one of the most commonly served and very well liked desserts of Indian cuisine. Rice pudding, is an ancient traditional South Asian sweet dish made by boiling rice or broken wheat with milk and sugar, and flavoured with cardamom, raisins, saffron, cashewnuts, pistachios or almonds. It has different names in different parts of India, Payasam in the South, payesh in Bengali. It is prepared during festivals, in temples and on all special occasions.

Method

1. In a Dutch oven (heavy bottom cooking pan) pour the milk, washed and drained rice and cardamoms and cook over low heat until milk is reduced to half (see Note below). Add a cup of whipping cream.
2. Keep stirring diligently because milk tends to stick to the bottom if you stop stirring. Cook until the consistency is somewhat like pudding but bit thinner.
3. Remove from heat. Add the sugar and nuts and mix well.
4. Cook over very low heat for 2–4 minutes until the sugar is well dissolved. Add a few drops of *kevra* essence and stir. Cook for a few more minutes.
5. Leave it to cool. Serve garnished with chopped nuts, raisins and coconut. It can be made couple of days ahead and refrigerated and can be reheated when needed or can be served cold.
6. Serve after a meal.

Sevian Kheer

Sweet Vermicelli Pudding

Serves: 6-8
Preparation Time: 10 Minutes

Ingredients

Vermicelli (*Sevian*)	1 cup
Ghee	2 Tbs
Milk (2% fat)	3 cups
Almonds ground	2 Tbs
Almonds grated	1 Tbs
Pistachio grated	1 Tbs
Kevra extract drops	2–3
Cardamom powder	½ tsp
Sugar	¾ cup
Silver leaves small	6

Note: Significantly made on *Eid* - a festival celebrated by the Muslim community. *Eid-ul-Fitr* is the end of one month long fasting called *Ramadan*. The end of this fasting is celebrated with great religious fervour and bonhomie, with *sevian kheer* or stir-fried sweet sevian.

Moghul emperors greatly influenced Indian cuisine with persian culture and cuisine. This is the Indian name of milk & vermicelli dessert of Iranian origin called "Sheer Khorma" in Persian. It is laced with dry fruits and saffron and is a must at festivals and celebrations. A sweet thin vermicelli pudding with nuts and flavouring. A perfect light dessert after dinner.

Method

1. Fry the *sevian* in *ghee* in heavy-bottom medium size saucepan until light brown.
2. Add the milk and cook on low heat until the milk thickens and the *sevian* are soft.
3. Add the ground nuts and continue cooking until the mixture thickens and is still of even pouring consistency. Add more milk if needed.
4. Add the *kevra* extract and cardamom powder.
5. Stir well and cook for few more minutes on very low heat. While stirring, add the sugar. Stir it.
6. Cool and top it with silver leaves and grated nuts and serve.
7. Another dessert which you can fix for a weekend company in a rush.

HINT
Milk can be substituted with water to make real *sevian* that are made on *Eid-ul-Fitr*

Meethey Chawal

Sweet Rice Pulav

Serves: 4-6
Preparation Time: 15 Minutes

Ingredients	
Ghee	½ cup
Cloves	6
Turmeric powder	½ tsp
Cardamoms green	8
Rice	2 cups
Raisins soaked in sugar water	¼ cup
Milk (2% fat)	2 cups
Sugar	1 ¾ cup
Pistachio nuts	¼ cup
Water	2 cups
Almonds chopped	¼ cup
Saffron (dissolved in a 2 tsp of water)	¼ tsp
Silver leaves	3-4
Extract of *kevra* drops	5-6

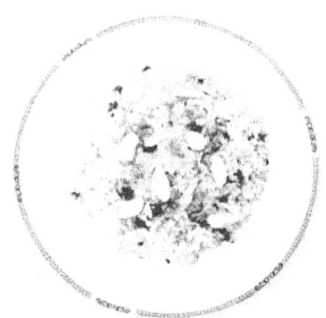

Note: You can use brown sugar or Gur instead of the white sugar too. Saffron has been grown in India since ancient times. It became popular during Mughal times when they started to adorn their sweet dishes for its beautiful aroma and colour. It is an essential ingredient of Spanish paellas, Indian *biryanis*, desserts and *pulavs*.

Sweet rice *pulav* is a welcome sight at almost every auspicious occasion in northern India. Whether it is the birth of a new baby, birthday or a wedding anniversary, Sweet Rice is a part of all celebrations. Its sweet and delicious aroma is enticing. Sweet rice is popular in many cuisines of the world with different names. To name a few there is Filipino Biko sweet rice, then there is Portugese Arroz Doce sweet rice, there is Mexican sweet rice and the Thai sweet rice. Preparations look very similar to Indian sweet rice dish.

Method

1. Wash and drain the rice and set it aside.
2. Heat the *ghee* and add the cloves, turmeric powder, cardamoms, and fry for 5 minutes on slow heat.
3. Add the rice and fry in the *ghee* for 2–3 minutes. Add 2 cups of water. When water dries up add 2 cups of milk with sugar dissolved in it.
4. Add the dissolved saffron, 2 Tbs of almonds, pistachio and all the raisins and stir the rice gently.
5. Cover with a lid and cook for another 10–15 minutes on very low heat until there is no moisture floating on the top. Lower the heat to minimum and cook till rice is tender.
6. Add the *kevra* essence and serve sprinkled with the rest of the almonds, pistachio and decorate with silver leaves.

Shahi Tukra

Rich Bread Pudding with Dry Fruits

Serves: 6-8
Preparation Time: 8-10 Minutes

Ingredients

Full-cream milk	1 litre
Sweetened condensed milk	1 can (400 g)
Cardamom powder	1 tsp
Grated fresh pistachio	1 Tbsp
Saffron threads crushed	1/8 tsp
Slices raisin bread toasted	6-8
Raisins/Sultanas	½ cup
Ghee to deep fry the bread	
Blanched almond slivers to garnish	

Truly a royal dessert, as its name suggests, Shahi Tukra is a rich bread pudding with dry fruits, flavored with cardamom. It is common in all the cuisines starting from Argentina, to Colombia to Belgium, Canada, Cuba, France, Germany, Ireland, Malta, Mexico, the Netherlands, Slovakia, the Philippines, Puerto Rico, India and the United Kingdom, as well as the United States. In the Philippines, banana bread pudding is popular. In Mexico, there is a similar dish eaten during Lent called capirotada. This is a very famous dish from the State of Hyderabad and it is simple to make and a great dessert for times when you're in a hurry. This dreamy dessert fare made by delicious crisp pieces of bread doused in sweet creamy sauce and decorated with nuts is a mesmerizing delicacy that you'll never forget and everyone who will try this dessert must fall in love with it. It is too tasty to resist. It is great for a large dinner party as the recipe can be easily multiplied to make more. It is best served chilled. You can enhance the flavor by adding few drops of Kewra essence to the milk mixture once it has cooled.

Bread pudding is a similar bread based dessert that is popular all over the world. It is made with stale bread and milk or cream, generally containing, a form of fat such as oil, butter or shortening, and depending on whether the pudding is sweet or savory, a variety of other ingredients. Sweet bread puddings may use sugar, syrup, honey, dried fruit, as well as spices such as cinnamon, nutmeg, mace, or vanilla. The bread is soaked in the liquids, mixed with the other ingredients, and baked. Savory puddings may be served as main courses, while sweet puddings are typically eaten as desserts.

The dish has its roots in Pakistani cuisine and Mughlai Cuisine. It is particularly prepared during the festive month of *Ramadan* and on *Eid*.

Method

1. Mix the milk and condensed milk in a thick-bottomed pan and boil till it reduces to half its original volume. Add the cardamom, grated pistachio and Saffron. Stir frequently to prevent from burning the milk. Once thickened mix it well and remove from the heat.
2. Cut the crusts off from the slices of toasted raisin bread and slice them in quarters.
3. Heat the ghee on a medium flame in a medium size deep frying pam. Deep fry the pieces of bread in the hot ghee till they are crisp and golden. Drain on paper towels.
4. In the same ghee, sauté the raisins till they puff up. Remove from the ghee and drain well on paper towels.
5. Put a layer of fried bread pieces at the bottom of a flat serving dish and top with the thickened milk mixture. Keep adding layers of bread and the milk mixture alternating as you go, till all the bread and milk mixture is used up.
6. Garnish the dish with the raisins and almond slivers, chill for an hour and serve.

Mango Pie

Serves: 10-12
Preparation Time: 15 Minutes

Made with mango pulp, sour cream and gelatin, it is a dessert that can be quickly fixed for your guests and still remain very unique and delicious. It is quite refreshing for a summer informal party. Children love it.

Ingredients

Gelatin (unflavoured)	3 pkgs
Boiling water	3 cups
Cream cheese	1 cup
Sugar	1 cup
Sour cream	2 cups
Mango pulp from a can	3 cups
Gram cracker crumbs	¾ cup
Butter	4 Tbs
Mint leaves	2 Tbs
Saffron threads	1 tsp
Fresh mango or nuts to decorate	

Method

1. Dissolve 3 packages of gelatin in 3 cups of boiling water. Cool it and blend in the cream cheese, sugar and the sour cream. Use a hand held mixer if possible.
2. Add the mango pulp and mix. Make it smooth and set it aside.
3. Mix the gram cracker crumbs with butter, knead into a paste and layer evenly on the surface of a 13x9x2 inches pan. Refrigerate for a couple of hours until set.
4. Remove the pan from the refrigerator and pour the mixture of gelatin and mango pulp over the layer of bread crumbs. Cover it and place the pan back into the refrigerator for another 3–4 hours or until the mango pie is set.
5. Cut into squares and serve, sprinkling each square with a mint leaf and couple of saffron threads and some pieces of fresh mango.

Note: A regular Pie can also be made with a pie crust for top and bottom of pie. Combine 2/3 cup brown sugar with 3 Tbs of cornstarch in a large bowl and mix well. Add 4 cups of chopped up mango wedges. Toss to coat. Add mango mixture to prepared pie plate; sprinkle evenly with 1 tablespoon butter. Cover it with top pie crust and brush with a beaten egg yolk. Make steam slits in top crust to allow steam to escape. Brush top of crust with milk Combine ginger and granulated sugar and sprinkle evenly over dought. Place pie plate on a foil-lined baking sheet; bake at 425°F for 20 minutes. Reduce oven temperature to 375°F; bake an additional 30 minutes or until pie is golden brown. Cool completely on a wire rack and serve with ice cream or whipping cream. You can set the pie in small decorative individual dessert dishes also without the gram cracker layer at the bottom.

Nan Khataii

Eggless Crisp Biscuits

Serves: 4-6
Preparation Time: 30 Minutes

Ingredients

All purpose Flour	1 cup
Fine Suji	½ cup
Gram flour	½
Baking powder	½ tsp
Salt	1/8 tsp
Cardamom Powder	¼ tsp
Nutmeg Powder	¼ tsp
A pinch Saffron	
Ghee	1 cup
Yogurt	2 Tbsp
Powdered Sugar	1½ cup
A few drops of lemon extract or ¼-tsp of lemon zest	
Ground Pistachio or Almonds	½ cup

Nan khatai is an egg-less light and crispy biscuit that is perfect to serve with tea or coffee. These shortbread biscuits or Nankhatai as we call them in India are buttery melt-in-mouth cookies. They are very close to 'Pecan Sandies' in United States. There is interesting history behind origin of Nankhatai in India. It is believed that Nankhatai originated in Surat a large port city in Gujarat. Near the end of 16th century, Dutch explorers set up a bakery in Surat to produce bread for their own consumption. They used eggs and Palm Toddy and almonds in their dough. As the locals did not care for egg and palm Toddy they just used three main ingredients flour, butter and sugar with all the three in almost equal proportion. Some used pinch of baking powder (though some did not even use that). Now adays you will find lots of variations to these ingredients.

Here is recipe with Pistachio powder in the cookie dough and a few drops of lemon extract and that gives them a wonderful nutty taste with a delightful citrus flavor.

Method

1. Heat the oven to 300°F
2. In a medium size bowl mix together the dry ingredients, all purpose flour, suji, gram flour, baking powder, salt, cardamom powder nutmeg powder and a pinch of saffron and sift them if possible on to a large piece of clean paper or wax paper. Set it aside. Mix in the saffron.
3. In the same bowl beat together softened butter or ghee with powdered sugar and yogurt until white and fluffy.
4. Add the dry ingredicnts and the finely chopped nuts and knead in to soft dough.

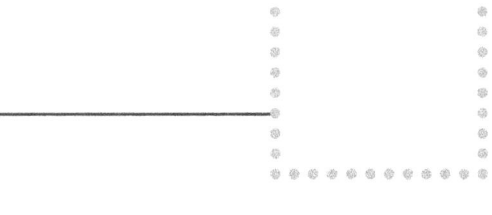

5. Place small slightly flatted balls in a column on a cookie sheet with at least ½ inch of
6. Space between the balls and bake them in the preheated oven for 20-25 minutes until done. Place the tray in the middle of the oven so that they stay light brown when cooked.
7. Enjoy them your favorite beverage or hot drink.

Unniappam

Serves: 4-6
Preparation Time: 8-10 Minutes

Ingredients

Rice Flour	1 cup
All purpose flour	½ cup
Cream of wheat	2 Tbsp
Brown sugar	½ cup
Cardamom powder	½ tsp
Baking powder	¼ tsp
Sesame seeds	2 tsp
Raisins	1 Tbsp
Finely chopped coconut/ 1-Tbsp of Un sweetened coconut powder	2 Tbsp
Ghee	1 Tbsp
Soaked poha	¼ cup
Bananas –mashed well	2-3
Utensil	
Paniyaran pan optional	

Unniappam, one of the best creations from the Kerala kitchen, is a real sweet indulgence in every bite. A popular snack from the traditional days has now popularly become a festive specialty and a common prasadam at many Ganapati temples. These appams get the round ball like shape from the pan it is made in, called the unniapam pan but you can also give them round shape by hand and then deep frying them. In short this Appam is a perfect bite with a crunch on the outside and a soft centre. This is a dessert that's mostly prepared during South Indian festivals but for those with a taste, it's a celebration anytime you make it.

Method

1. Mix together rice flour, all purpose flour, Suji, brown sugar, cardamom powder, baking powder, sesame seeds, raisins and soaked Poha with enough water to make a batter slightly thicker than pancake batter.

2. Fry the coconut in a Tbsp of ghee and add it to the batter and add the mashed bananas. Stir to mix and beat it gently to make it a smooth batter.

3. Heat oil in a wok or fryer and fill a deep spoon with the batter or pour in round balls in to the oil.

4. Pour as many spoons as the pan has space for. However, each ball should almost completely immerse in the oil. Fry till both sides of an Appam turn golden brown/deep brown.

5. To make them absolutely round use a special pan called "Paniyaram Pan" for frying appams. If you are using this pan then add oil/ ghee till ½ of the depth of each hole of the Unniappam pan/Appakaaram pan and heat the pan directly on the heat.

6. Pour spoonfuls of batter into the holes and let them cook on a medium heat. The centre of the appams starts to rise as they cook. At this time, you can turn them around easily with a fork or a pointed stick. Fry until all sides are uniformly brown.
7. Be careful not to burn them up. Take them out and drain off the excess oil.
8. Enjoy them while they are warm. These can be stored for a couple of days.

Note: Uniappam is a traditional temple offering for Gods in Kerala. Made especially at Onam festival. It is made with rice, jaggery and banana, Uniappams are also perfect for a sweet snack. In Malayalam, unni means small and 'appam means rice cake.

Drinks

India, being a tropical country, is one of the largest consumers of soft drinks. Day-to-day common drinks are not a luxury but a necessity. With hot and dry weather in its central states and hot and humid all along the coastal regions, quite a few nourishing and very highly delicious drinks have originated here over time. They replenish the lost electrolytes of the body and are refreshing. Some special Indian drinks are mango coolers like *Aam Panna*, *Zeera Paani* (*Jalzeera*), *Kanji*, *Nariyal Paani*, *Sattu*, *Nimbu Paani* and Kokum Water. These are seasonal drinks and depend on the availability of the fruit. They are inexpensive and a large number of people in India make them at home.

Then, there are nutritious traditional Indian drinks like *Thandaai*, *Mango Lassi* and fruit *Sherbets* and squashes. *Sherbets* are age-old drinks of India but these days they are not as popular. These are made by bottling the extracts of fruit juices, herbs, petals of flowers, barks of trees, nuts with sugar syrup. Essence for flavour and preservatives are added later. For an Indian household these are not just drinks but also remedies for some common ailments. Squashes came to India a few hundred years ago with the British. These are made from extract of fruits like Lemon, Orange, *Phalsa*, Mango, Lichi and Pineapple. At the time of serving, squashes are diluted with water and ice.

Thandaai is an ancient drink made by mixing milk with the paste of ground almonds or cashew nuts, spices and sugar. It is then served cold with ice. It is still very popular in the summers of India. Plain *Lassi* and Mango *Lassi* are very popular drinks and liked all over the world. Most of the Indian restaurants serve this drink. Mango *Lassi* is made by gently stirring mango pulp in fresh yogurt, sugar and ice.

Spiced tea, *Kahva* and south-Indian coffee are very well loved hot drinks of India. Spiced tea called *Masala Chai* is becoming very popular in the US too. South India has coffee plantations all over and it is the most popular hot drink here. In these parts coffee is made by boiling coffee powder with milk, sugar and water which is foamed by pouring it from one glass to another. *Kahva* is Kashmiri green tea that is milder in flavour than the regular Indian tea. It is prepared by simmering the *kahva* leaves in boiling water and flavouring it with nuts and honey and is served without milk.

It is pertinent to mention here that some semi-alcoholic drinks are brewed in villages and mountain valleys across India by the country folk. Some of these are *Chhang* from the mountain regions, *Feni* from Goa, *Mahua* from Orissa, Bihar, Kerala and Gujarat.

Chhang is made by fermenting rice or barley and it tastes like beer. *Feni* is made by fermenting cashew nuts or coconut extract for a couple of days and then distilling it yields the crude extract, which through redistillation yields *Feni* which makes a good base for cocktails and is a popular drink of Goa. *Mahua* is made from the edible flowers of the *Mahua* tree. These flowers are also used to make syrup for medicinal purposes. *Mahua* drink is an essential item in the daily life of the tribals of Bastar, the Santhals and among certain tribes in Maharashtra. From the eastern part of India, Bihar, comes a semi-alcoholic beverage called *Tadi* (palm wine) made from the sap of various palm trees as date palm, coconut palm and Palmyra. This drink is common in various parts of Asia and Africa and goes by various names. It is also consumed in Sri Lanka and Myanmar. Then there is *Bhang*, which is marijuana. It is ground together with nuts, spices and milk and is consumed on the festival of *Shivratri*. It is believed that to please Lord Shiva, one should forget the world by intoxicating oneself with *Bhang* and dancing and chanting his name. With a climate as varied and extreme as India's, the people require myriad options to keep their thirst appropriately quenched according to the weather conditions, be it a steaming hot beverage during the winters or a frosty cold drink in the summers. Different regions in the country serve different drinks made with a eclectic assortment of ingredients including local spices, flowers and herbs.

DRINKS

Masala Chai

Spiced Tea

Serves: 5-6
Preparation Time: 5 Minutes

Ingredients

Water	5 cups
Milk	1 cup
Tea leaves (3 Tea bags)	2 Tbs
Cardamoms	5
Cinnamon ½ inch by ¼ inch	1 stick
Cloves	5
Sugar	to taste

HINT

Omit the spices to make the plain *chai*, if desired. Indian or British blend teas can be purchased at the local Indian grocery stores. **Tea plants** grow wild in the cool and humid climate of the hills. The natives of hilly regions flavoured their tea with ingredients such as saffron, honey, yak butter, *ghee*, herbs and salt. During the British rule rich people started having tea in the manner of the British aristocrats in the luxury of their lawns or estates with cream and sugar which started the large scale cultivation of tea in hill states of Sri Lanka and India.

In India, guests are known as "Emissaries of God," they drop by any time they want without warning. When they come, you almost always serve them Chai. India, is the world's largest consumer of tea and it uses nearly 30 per cent of the global output. India is also the second largest producer of tea and also the largest exporter of black tea. India has been consuming tea for thousand of years. In the practice of ayurveda it is used to cure maladies like common colds and body aches once it is mixed and boiled with traditonal herbs like Basil (Tulsi) Cardamom, Black pepper, Liquorice and Mint. Addition of milk and sugar hides the bitterness of the herbs and spices and makes it delicious and desirable. It is now officially the national drink of India. People drink chai at least twice a day and it is sold by the vendors on the streets all over india. There are few varieties but mainly it is the masala chai that has become the univerasal favourite.

Method

1. Bring the water, cardamoms, cinnamon, and cloves to a full boil.
2. Add the tea leaves or the tea bags.
3. Lower the heat, let it simmer for two minutes.
4. Add the milk and stir well and let it come to a full boil and stir.
5. Using the tea strainer. Strain boiling hot tea in mugs or pour it into a teapot.
6. Keep the teapot hot by using a hot plate or teacozy. A stainless steel teapot can be used that can be heated on the stove to keep warm.
7. Prepared *chai* should be served within half an hour because it loses its full flavour if it is reheated and served again.

Kashmiri Kahva

Kashmiri Tea

Serves: 4-6
Preparation Time: 5 Minutes

Ingredients

Water	4 cups
Honey or sugar	2 Tbs
Fine crushed cashew and almonds	2 Tbs
Cinnamon sticks (small) one inch (crushed)	2
Cloves	½ tsp
Cardamoms brown broken	2
Kahva leaves	2 tsp
Fennel seeds	1 tsp
Saffron (optional)	a pinch

The samovar is a metal container traditionally used to heat and boil water also found in Russia and Persia, is characteristic container for Kashmiri tea. Kashmiris make two or three types of tea in the samovar(samovars were an economical permanent carriers of hot water in older times) and many say that good Kashmiri tea has to be made in a samovar. The kehvi (also call kahva) used to be a Turkish word for hot Coffee.

Kahva leaves are green tea leaves of Kashmir.

Method

1. Transfer 4 cups of water to a medium size saucepan and add cinnamon, cloves, cardamoms and fennel seeds. Heat the water and add the sugar or honey.
2. As soon as the water starts to boil add the *kahva* leaves. Let it simmer on low heat for 2 minutes.
3. Transfer and strain the tea into a heated teapot. Divide the nuts into 4 cups. Add a few sprigs of saffron to each cup and pour *kahva* into these cups and serve immediately. Makes an excellent hot drink in cold winters.

Note: Kashmiris call it "Bombay tea," but in the tea trade it is known as gunpowder, named after the way the more mature tea leaves curl up into pellets when dried. I enjoy the uplifting combination of flavours and make kahva often, especially during the winter months. It makes an excellent post dinner digestive as well.

Kashmiri Kahva - Page 254

Coffee - Page 255

Dahi ki Lassi - Page 256

Gajar ka Doodh - Page 257

Mango Panna - Page 260

Kanji - Page 261

Zeera Pani - Page 262

Falooda Drink - Page 265

South Indian Coffee

Serves: 4
Preparation Time: 5 Minutes

Ingredients

Instant coffee	2 Tbs
Water	2 cups
Milk or as needed	2 cups
Sugar	to taste

South Indian Coffee, also known as Filter Coffee is a sweet milky coffee made from dark roasted *coffee* beans especially popular in the southern states of *Tamil Nadu and Karnataka*.

Traditionally the South Indian coffee is prepared as follows.

The coffee beans have to be roasted and ground. Then the powder is put into a filter set (South Indian coffee filter) and boiling hot water is added and by slow dripping a strong decoction is prepared. This is allowed to set for about 15 minutes. A couple of tablespoons of this decoction is then mixed with milk, more hot water and sugar to taste. The final drink is poured individually from one container to another in rapid succession to make the ideal frothy cup of filter coffee.

Coffee in south India is as popular a drink as *chai* in the north. It can also be made by simply adding well-roasted instant coffee to the boiling water and milk. Add sugar to taste before serving it. See below:

Method to make Instant Coffee:

1. Boil the water and the milk and remove from heat before it boils over.
2. Mix coffee and sugar in a coffee pot or teapot and add the boiled mixture of water and milk and stir vigorously with a tablespoon until the coffee is a little frothy.
3. Serve hot.

Note: Coffee was brought to India by Bata Budan, a traveler who went from Chikmagahur, Karnataka, to Arabia for *Hajj*. He liked the drink so much that he brought some coffee seeds and planted them in his village. To this day, the best coffee comes from this village now called Bata Budan Giri.

Dahi ki Lassi

Yogurt Shake

Serves: 4
Preparation Time: 5 Minutes

Ingredients

Yogurt	4 cups
Sugar	4 Tbs
Water	2–3 cups
Crushed cardamom powder	¼ tsp
Saffron	½ tsp
Mint leaves	a few
Ground nuts	1 tsp
Salt & pepper	to taste
Mango pulp	1 cup
Ice as needed	

A universal drink now available in all the Indian restaurants all over the world. Had its origin in the heated plains of the state of Punjab in india. It is a blend of yogurt, water and spices to make a savoury drink. It can be served with a meal or without a meal. It is salty when flavoured with salt and ground and roasted *cumin*. It is a sweet lassi, however, when flavoured with sugar or fruits and spices like cardamon, nutmeg and shaved nuts. It is also used as a *folk remedy* for *gastroenteritis*.

Lassi is a very popular drink in north India. It is made with plain yogurt, sugar, pieces of ice, cardamom powder blended with some water in a blender. It is a very appealing and invigorating drink in the hot summer months. To make it more delicious, mango pulp is added, which is available abundantly in the summers. Canned mango pulp can be bought at any grocery store.

Method

1. Pour plain yogurt, water, sugar, cardamom powder into the blender except the ice and blend until well blended.
2. This is plain sweet Lassi. Serve in glasses with ice, couple of mint leaves and a sprinkle of saffron.
3. Plain salty *Lassi* (shake) is also very popular and it can be prepared by blending the plain yogurt with salt, pepper and ice. Serve with mint leaves.

Mango Lassi

For making mango *lassi*, blend together yogurt, mango pulp, cardamom powder and water, until smooth. Pour it into a glass and serve sprinkled with saffron, mint leaves fine grated nuts, and ice cubes.

Gajar ka Doodh

Sweetened Carrot Milk

Serves: 2-3
Preparation Time: 10 Minutes

Ingredients

Steamed and puréed carrots	2
Cashew nuts, almonds (blanched). Soak together in some milk for 10-15 minutes.	2 Tbsp
Clove	1
Cinnamon stick	3
Milk	1¼ cup
Sugar (adjust according to your choice)	4 Tbsp
Unsweetened condensed milk	2 Tbsp
Cardamom powder	½ tsp
Few strands saffron (optional)	
Chopped toasted almonds and Pistachio as needed	

It all starts with some fresh carrots, milk, evaporated unsweetened milk, sugar, infused with a hint of cinnamon, clove and a dash of freshly ground cardamom and saffron. It is a recipe from North Indian cuisine. If using sweetened condensed milk then reduce the quantity of sugar. This richly flavoured comforting and nutritious drink makes an ideal summer drink/a perfect party drink and can also be served at a time when unexpected guests arrive. The drink will definitely taste better the next day or the day after it is prepared.

Saffron gives this dish a delicious sweet note, aroma and a lovely enticing beautiful yellow colour.

Method

1. Steam the carrots, cool and purée. Keep aside.
2. Grind the cashews and almonds to a smooth paste. Keep aside.
3. Add the clove and cinnamon stick to the milk and bring to a boil. Reduce heat and boil the milk for at least 10 minutes while stirring it.
4. Add the sugar and stir till it is completely dissolved.
5. Add the carrot paste and condensed milk to the milk mixture, combine well and let it cook for 3-4 minutes.
6. Add the nuts paste, and cardamom, combine well. Turn off heat after 2 minutes and cool completely. (Remove the clove and cinnamon stick from the mixture and discard them).
7. Blend the cooled mixture till you get a smooth consistency.
8. Garnish with saffron strands, toasted almond slivers or pistachio. Serve warm or chilled. It is delicious.

Sambharam

Spicy Yogurt Drink

Serves: 1-2
Preparation Time: 2-4 Minutes

Ingredients

Green chilies small or to taste	2-3
Ginger	½ Inch piece
Stalks -Lemon grass/ couple lemon leaves / lime leaves/cilantro	2 Inch
Yogurt	1½ cup
Water	3 cups
Curry leaves torn into pieces	5-6
A pinch Asafoetida	
Salt to taste	

A classic drink of Kerala and a perfect thirst quencher in its true sense, it is a very refreshing summer drink. It was served even before lemonade and other aerated drinks were served to guests. It used to be and still is the most favoured drink of the working class of India, who spend their entire day under the hot sun, to cool down their body. It is also a traditional way of finishing the feast as it aids in digestion. It has many names in different parts of India like the masala mor (thalicha mor) from Tamil Nadu, spicy lassi from Punjab, chaas (chaach) from Gujarat and Rajasthan etc.

Method

1. Crush the green chilies, ginger and lemon grass /cilantro using a mortar and pestle.
2. Beat the curd nicely using a beater and add the water to it. Mix the curd-water mixture nicely using a hand blender or with a spoon.
3. Add the crushed mixture of herbs, torn curry leaves, a pinch of asafoetida and required salt and mix everything together.
4. Serve on a hot summer day as a refreshing drink or with some plain rice, after dinner or lunch.

Note: In some parts of India a seasoning of mustard seeds, cumin seeds, dry red chilies and some curry leaves is prepared and added to the sambharam. This gives a great flavour to the drink.

Thandai

Milk and Almond Drink

Serves: 4-6
Preparation Time: 10 Minutes

Ingredients

Boiled and cooled Milk	6 cups
Cashew nuts	1 Tbs
Almonds	¼ cup
Poppy seeds	¼ cup
Watermelon and cantaloupe (*kharbuja*) seeds	¼ cup
Sugar	½ cup
Black pepper corns	½ tsp
Cinnamon 1 small piece	
Green cardamom seeds	½ tsp
Rose leaves (dry)	10-15 leaves
Saffron strings soaked in water (optional)	a pinch

The drink is believed to have originated during the mythological times. It was the favourite drink of Lord Shiva. Thandai is one of the traditional drinks of India and mainly prepared on the occassion of Mahashivratri and Holi. People often mix *bhaang* (Marwana) in thandai specially on the occasion of Holi to make an intoxicating drink.

A nutritious and proteinaceous cold drink made with milk, nuts and spices is very popular in the state of Punjab during the summer months. Once you have the right ingredients it does not take too long to prepare it.

Method

1. Mix together almonds, cashew nuts, poppy seeds, watermelon seeds (dehusked), black pepper, cardamoms and rose petals, and soak them in water overnight. Peel the almonds.
2. Grind the above ingredients in a blender to a fine paste with the help of half or one cup milk for few minutes. Add a little water to thin down the mixture and keep grinding if the mixture is still thick.
3. Transfer the mixture into a large bowl. Add the rest of the milk and sugar. Mix well. Strain the mixture through a muslin cloth or cheese cloth and squeeze well to get all the juice out from the mixture. Discard the residue.
4. Transfer the strained liquid to refrigerator or add ice to serve immediately.
5. Flavour the drink with the soaked saffron before serving in drinking glasses.

Note: Ready-to-make mixes of *thandai* are available at your local grocery store. A drink called *bhang* is prepared mixing marijuana paste into *thandai*. This drink is traditionally enjoyed by devotees on *Shivaratri* fesitval.

Panna

Mango Drink

Serves: 4-6
Preparation Time: 15 Minutes

Ingredients

Mangoes slightly unripe and firm	2 large
Green chilies cut in half (mild)	2
Water	6–8 cups
Brown sugar or *gur* (jaggery)	1 cup
Lemon juice	¼ cup
Black salt	sprinkle
Cinnamon powder	sprinkle
Cumin powder ground, roasted	1 tsp
Black pepper	a dash
Mint leaves	a few

The state of Gujarat is famous for its mangoes and some of the best varieties grow there. This appetizing sweet and tangy drink is made by boiling the pulp of slightly unripe mangoes in water and flavouring it with ground roasted cumin, black salt, brown sugar, lemon juice (if the mangoes are too sweet) black pepper and fresh mint. It is very refreshing when served with ice.

Aam (Mango) Panna is an Indian drink renowned for its heat resistant properties. It is a rich source of pectin, and is considered beneficial in the treatment of gastro-intestinal disorders.

Method

1. Peel and chop the mangoes in small pieces and transfer them to a large saucepan along with the pit of the mango. Add the chopped green chilies and water and boil the mixture until the mango pieces are soft and tender (about 20 minutes).

2. Discard the green chilies and the pit of the mango and pour the chopped mangoes and water into a blender. Add brown sugar, lemon juice, a pinch of black salt, cinnamon powder, ground roasted cumin powder, black pepper and blend it smooth. Strain the *panna* and save it in a bottle. Dilute further according to taste before serving, because this is a concentrate of the drink.

3. Pour a couple of teaspoons of *panna* into glasses and add the water and the ice. Stir to mix and serve topped with couple of mint leaves.

Note: Add green chilies, if you want a mildly hot drink.

Kanji

Fermented Carrots Drink

Serves: 4
Preparation Time: 4-5 Days

Ingredients

Carrots washed peeled and cut into 2 inch pieces lengthwise	2 lbs
Water	8 cups
Ground mustard	2 Tbs
Black salt	1 tsp
Salt	2 tsp
Red pepper	1 tsp
Garam masala	1 tsp
Mint leaves	1 Tbs
Small strips of fresh carrots	

This sour tangy drink is very popular in north India. It is made by fermenting carrots in water with ground mustard and salt for 48 hours and flavouring it with red pepper and *garam masala* **before serving. It is very refreshing in the hot summer months and delightfully tasty. It is traditionally made from black carrots.**

Method

1. Boil one quart of water and add the chopped carrots to it. Set it aside and let it cool.
2. Transfer the cooled water with the carrots to a large size pitcher and add the ground mustard, black salt, salt and water to it and let it ferment for 4-5 days in a warm place. Close it tight and shake it at least twice a day.
3. Taste it for tanginess and add the red pepper, *garam masala* and refrigerate.
4. Serve chilled with couple of mint leaves and carrot pieces.
5. It is great drink to have with meals or for a lazy summer afternoon drink.

Note: *Kanji* is a fermented drink mostly made during Holi. It is an excellent drink as it replenishes that lost bacteria that live in our stomach and help us in our digestion. In other words, it comes in a category of drinks that are probiotic in nature. They are good for the stomach and should be included in one's diet. The other examples are dosa, idli, yogurt and sour dough.

Zeera Paani

Cumin Flavoured Drink

Serves: 8-10
Preparation Time: 15 Minutes

Ingredients

Tamarind pulp	2 Tbs
Or	
Amchoor	½ cup
Water	8 cups
Fresh mint ground	1 Tbs
Ginger fresh, ground	1 Tbs
Lemon juice	¼ cup
Cumin ground roasted	1 Tbs
Red pepper	1 tsp
Garam masala	½ tsp
*Black salt	2 tsp
Sugar	2–3 Tbs
Lemon slices	3–4
Sprigs of mint	3–4
Ice to chill	
Salt as needed	

A very ancient tangy, sweet and sour drink made by mixing roasted ground cumin powder, ground fresh mint leaves, black salt (sulphur salt) and other herbs into strained tamarind water. It has digestive properties and it can be served before or with meals at any occasion. But mainly this is a drink that is served with *golgappas*. (See Appetizers section). It is extremely delicious and refreshing during the hot, sweaty, summer months of tropical India.

Method

1. Mix the tamarind pulp well into 8 cups of water.
2. Grind the mint, ginger in a blender with help of lemon juice and add the roasted ground cumin powder, red pepper, *garam masala* and black salt to the ground paste. Pour this mixture into the tamarind water and mix the water well with a hand whisk or a large spoon.
3. Now, add the sugar and taste the tartness.
4. It should be sweet and sour.
5. Adjust the sugar and salt to your taste.
6. Filter it through a fine sieve and chill it with ice to serve immediately or refrigerate with the sprigs of mint and lemon slices.
7. It can be served as a punch (dilute it further) and is served always with the *golgappas* (hollow and translucent puffs of flour). Adjust the seasonings according to taste if need be.

Note: *Black salt (*Kala namak*) is actually a sulphur compound and has great digestive properties. It is used mainly as a sprinkle for *chaats* and is an ingredient of *chaat masala*. To me this salt brings back vivid memories of childhood. It is an integral part of a mix called *churan*. To make *churan*, black salt is mixed with ground dates, raisins and spices. *Zeera paani* is somewhat similar to the *kokum* water of Maharashtra. It is made from *kokum* flower (a souring agent used in the cooking of this state).

Kokum Water

Kokum Drink

Serves: 2-4
Preparation Time: 5 minutes

Ingredients

Lemon (Squeezed)	1
Cranberry Juice	1 Cup
Black salt	½ tsp
Roasted ground Cumin powder	½ tsp
Crushed Green chilies	½ tsp
Kokum Syrup	2 Tbsp
Chilled water or carbonated water	2 Cups
Ice to taste	
Sugar if needed	

Spicy kokum drink, an appetizing coolant made using kokum and delicately flavoured with fresh corriander leaves is best suited for summers. Use Sugar substitute instead of sugar to make this Indian drink low in calories and just perfect for a summer day

Method

1. Squeeze juice of 1 lemon into the cranberry juice and add salt, roasted ground cumin powder, green chilies and 2 Tablespoons of Kokum syrup. Mix it well and set it aside.

2. Add 2 cups of carbonated water in a pitcher and add the cranberry juice and kokum syrup mix. Add ice and stir to mix. Adjust the taste by adding more salt or syrup or sugar.

*See note below how to make Kokumdrink from kokum flowers.

*The Kokum is native to the western coastal regions of India and is rarely seen beyond. Konkani cuisine has a splendid appetizing drink prepared with Kokum and coconut milk. Dissolve 10-12 Kokum dry flowers into a cup of warm water for half an hour or overnight. Add 1 cup of coconut milk to it. Also add ½ tsp each of green chilli and 1 tsp roasted ground cumin seeds. Stir to mix. Add salt and brown sugar to taste and grind it and strain. Mix it well. Its sweet and sour taste will get you hooked on to this amazing drink. Use 2 Tbsp of this sherbet, water and ice to make a cup of the drink. It is delicious.

Kala Khatta

Spiced Indian Blackberry Drink

Serves: 1
Preparation Time: 5 Minutes

Ingredients

Jamuns / Indian blackberry	10
Fresh Lemon juice	1 tsp
Sugar	½ tsp
Black salt	¼ tsp
Cold water or sparkling water	1 Cup
Pinch of ground pepper	

During the soaring summers in India how does one keep cool and get a feel of the Bahama breeze ? Here is one drink that can help.

Indian summer vacations are fun with the juicy mangoes to raw mango juice (Panna, with kokum water to Kala Khatta). It can be either served as a cold drink or used to make cocktails or poured on crushed ice to form a pop sickle. Kala Khatta drink can be made from fresh limejuice spiced by ground pepper and rock salt and jamuns. Jamun, the black berry-like fruit of India, is an incredible coolant for the body; it is digestive and also a natural medicine to control diabetes. Kala Namak is a mineral salt which helps replenish what you lose sweating it out and also improves eyesight. Even the leaves and bark of the Jamun tree are used in India to cure blood pressure and Gingivitis. The seeds are used in Ayurvedic, Unani and Chinese medicine to treat digestive ailments like dysentery. The antioxidants present in this fruit help in preventing several diseases such as cancer, heart disease, diabetes and arthritis. It is not just the fruit but the entire tree is beneficial for our health.

Kala Khatta concentrates are commonly available in a grocery store.

Method

1. Remove the seeds from all the jamuns and grind the fruit to get a coarse paste. Strain the mixture by sifting it through a sieve.
2. Add lemon juice, sugar, black salt and stir well.
3. Pour the mix into a glass and add 8oz of sparkling or chilled water and sprinkle with black pepper. Stir to mix.
4. Or make your own pop-sickles by pouring the drink in the pop-sickle moulds.
5. Makes one glass of Kala Khatta.

Falooda Drink

Sweetened Milk Flavoured with Ice-Cream and Starchy Noodles

Serves: 2-4
Preparation Time: 35 Minutes

Ingredients

Basil Seeds (Tukmaria)	1 tsp
Water	2 Cups
Handfull-Falooda Sev	
Whole Milk	2 Cups
Cardamom powder	1 Pinch
Sugar	1½ Tbsp
Rose Syrup	5 Tbsp
Vanilla Ice Cream	½ Cup
or	
Condensed Milk	½ Cup
or	
Cream	½ Cup
Vanilla Ice Cream for serving	2 scoops
Coarsely ground Pistachios for garnish	1 tsp

Falooda is an adaptation of the non-liquid Persian dessert faloodeh, from which it has adopted its name. It is a yummy drink/dessert made with milk, a hint of refreshing rose flavour and healthy basil seeds... all topped off with a scoop of ice cream. It probably originated in India during the time the Mughals were ruling India.

It is a chilled, tasty drink-dessert that truly is easy to make.

Falooda can be made with or without the milk. Both versions are very popular in India! If you decide to go without the milk just assemble the dessert in a bowl instead of a glass. I've also added nuts (in the milk) that aren't traditionally used in Falooda but that what makes my version – Shahi Faloodah—extra yummy! Please feel free to experiment. This chilled drink-dessert version is the perfect way to cool off in the summer heat. It is a milky rose-flavoured ice cream float that makes a fragrant end to your favourite Indian meal.

Method

1. Soak the Basil Seeds (Tukmaria) in water for a minimum of 30 minutes, longer is better.
2. Meanwhile, heat 2 cups of water in a pan; let it come to a boil.
3. Add Falooda Sev and let it cook for 3 minutes. Take it off the flame.
4. Also, heat the milk and let it come to a boil. Take it off the flame.
5. Strain the Falood Sev and add them to the milk.
6. Add cardamom powder, sugar and rose syrup. mix.

7. Allow the milk-mixture to chill in the refrigerator – approximately 3 hours.
8. Strain the basil seeds and add them to the chilled milk.
9. At this time, also add the 1/2-cup of vanilla ice cream or unsweetened condensed milk or heavy cream and mix it well.
10. In a glass, add 1 scoop of vanilla ice cream and then pour the chilled milk.
11. Garnish with the coarsely ground pistachios and serve immediately.

Note: Tukmaria seeds are also known as falooda seeds (tukh malanga seeds) and sweet basil seeds. Sabja seeds or Tukmaria seeds contains sufficient amount of minerals like iron, calcium, manganese which aid metabolism. These seeds are very popular in Asian desserts and drinks, specially in India, Thailand and Pakistan. These seeds resemble chia seeds and they have cooling properties and therefore very good as summer drinks. Ocimum basilicum or sweet basil is an attractive and ornamental plant that has flowers and purple stem. Rich aroma is also one of basil's characteristics. They are of great medicinal value. They are good for mind, bone growth, urinary system issues and cardiac or heart problems. These seeds help to get benefits of Vitamin K. Tukmaria seeds are beneficial for curing mental fatigue, depression, nervous tension and migraine. These seeds make the mind stronger and healthier. Tukmaria are mostly used in aromatherapy and they increase memory and brain growth.

Note: If you are running short on time, you can use cold milk (without boiling). The flavour is slightly different. To make this dessert fat free—use low fat milk and low fat Ice cream and for thickening the milk use 2-Tbsp of corn flour or 2-Tbsp of ground roasted rice flour instead of condensed milk.

Coconut Water

Coconut water is the clear liquid inside young green coconuts. Coconut water has long been a popular drink in the tropics, especially in India, Brazilian Coast, Southeast Asia, Pacific Islands, Africa, and the Caribbean, where it is available fresh, canned, or bottled. Coconuts for drinking are served fresh, chilled or packaged in many places. They are often sold by street vendors who cut them open with machetes or a sharp knife right in front of the customers. Coconut water can also be found in ordinary cans, tetra paks, or plastic bottles (sometimes with coconut pulp or coconut jelly included). Bottled coconut water has a shelf life of 24 months.

In recent years, coconut water has been marketed as a natural energy or sports drink due to its high potassium and mineral content. Marketers have also promoted coconut water for having low levels of fat, carbohydrates, and calories. However, marketing claims attributing tremendous health benefits to coconut water are largely unfounded.

Unless the coconut has been damaged, it is likely sterile.

The "coconut water" inside the young fruits can be a lifesaving hydrator when hiking in tropical regions. Many are in easy reach!

Open one in a few seconds with a pocketknife, and gulp down the sweetish and nutrient-rich fluid; your body will thank you for it!